Des Griffin

Fourth Reich of the Rich

Revised from

The MISSING DIMENSION In World Affairs

DEDICATION

This book is dedicated to those rare individuals — whoever and wherever they may be — who sincerely want to know and understand WHAT is happening on the national and international scenes — and WHY!

The author trusts that the material in *Fourth Reich of the Rich* may prove to be as exciting and educational to the reader as it was to him when the book was being researched and written.

FOURTH REICH OF THE RICH

#1776, 9205 SE Clackamas Rd., Clackamas OR 97015
Phone/Fax: (503) 824-2050
www.midnight-emissary.com

Printed in the United States of America.

2006 Edition
ISBN: 0-941380-06-8

TABLE OF CONTENTS

INTRODUCTION

The story you are about to read is true. The names of the individuals and organizations involved have *not* been changed.

To say that the information contained in this book is explosive, sensational and "mind blowing" is to couch reality in the mildest possible terms. It is all of the above — and more! *Above all, it is true!*

Fourth Reich of the Rich is the result of almost fifty years of in-depth research in which the author has striven, to paraphrase the words of the late Sir Winston Churchill, to seek and tell "the truth ... that alone ... that always ... that to the end."

We have nothing to fear from truth — if that, in fact, is what we are really seeking. Truth can only add to our knowledge and understanding of world affairs. Truth, alone, can provide a solid base upon which to build our world view.

If the conclusions reached in this book are, in fact, the truth, they should be accepted and taught as such. If, however, they are false, they can be shown to be error. As George Washington once said, "Truth will ultimately prevail where there is pains taken to bring it to light."

That civilization is presently faced with its greatest crisis of the Ages is beyond question. But why? These *effects* didn't just "happen" — they were *caused*. Something — some Force — brought them into existence and sustains them. In the following pages we will take a penetrating look at the effects, and then present some startling evidence regarding the *causes* for these *effects* — evidence that may totally revolutionize your outlook on world affairs. Hence the subtitle of this book, *The Missing Dimension in World Affairs*.

CHAPTER ONE

WHAT IS TRUTH?

"What is truth?" asked a high ranking official of the Roman Empire nearly 2000 years ago. That is a good question, but it is also one which the vast, overwhelming majority of people reject from their minds on initial contact.

Our minds are like fantastically complex computers. In the course of an average day's activities millions of messages flash in and out of our "mental computers" through the five senses — the senses of sight, hearing, taste, smell and touch — and millions of decisions are made based on the flood of incoming knowledge and our understanding of it. The process has become so automatic, so much of a reflex action that we are seldom consciously aware that these decisions are being made.

Unfortunately, most of us have the tendency to let ourselves drift through life while we make these automatic or semi-automatic decisions which, all too frequently, are based on misinformation, half-truths or even outright lies! As one author has said, "Drifting is an unconscious process. Often it is not until we are on the rocks that we know we are in danger. We are all constantly exposed to the actions of currents of opinion, habit, etc. which tend to carry us away insensibly from the position we ought to maintain."

But how about new or unfamiliar information that comes to our minds? How do we cope with knowledge that is not immediately "acceptable" to our mental computers? In most cases our highly developed, extremely sensitive mental "defense mechanisms" spring into action and flood our minds with 1001 apparently logical "reasons" why we should follow the path of least resistance and dispense with the new truth at the earliest possible moment.

As the late Sir Winston Churchill once said, "Most people, sometime in their lives, stumble across the truth. Most jump up, brush themselves off and hurry on about their business as if nothing had happened."

Is that *you*? If you really think about it, you will be forced to see the absolute truth of these comments and that they apply to you to one degree or another. That is just the way of human nature!

To most people the whole world is a jumbled mass of conflicting and confusing ideologies — without rhyme, reason or purpose!

That is true — *on the surface*! And who, nowadays, looks any further than the surface of any given situation? Few indeed!

The few who have had the integrity, tenacity and intestinal fortitude to dedicate themselves to a relentless search for truth and understanding have found it an immensely rewarding and satisfying pursuit! Truth is seldom if even found in any one place. As the prophet of old put it, the whole truth is found "here a little, there a little" (*Isaiah* 28:10). Like gold, truth is a rare and very precious possession. If only men, down through the corridors of time, had sought truth and integrity with the same fervor and diligence as they have lusted after the acquisition of gold, the whole world would certainly be a markedly different place in which to live.

The reason behind this apparent paradox is found clearly revealed in the pages of the Bible: "Light (truth) is come into the world, and men love darkness rather than light, because their deeds are evil. For everyone that does evil hates the light, neither comes to the light, lest his deeds be reproved" (*John* 3:19,20).

We know for sure — particularly in the light of recent events and revelations — that truthfulness and strong moral fiber are not qualifications required for high political office, whether it be at the city, state or federal level — or even in the White House itself! In fact, if anything such attributes would be a distinct hinderance, and even a severe handicap, to the incumbent of or seeker after any of the above exalted positions.

The American political scene is heavily overburdened with flim-flam men, con artists and "smooth operators" who have, over a period of just a few decades, stripped the great American nation of virtually all its dignity, self-respect and wealth. In spite of what has so very obviously been taking place, remarkably few people have even begun to stir to the realization that they have been the gullible victims of the most audacious con game in all recorded history.

One of the clearest and most readily understood lessons in human experience is the fact that appearance alone is no criterion of truth. We have all experienced situations in which "great buys" and "fantastic bargains" have turned out to be costly blunders. Most overlook the fact that this is particularly applicable when it comes to political legislation: welfare and other alleged "aid" programs illustrate the point!

How about the Press — is that honest? The shocking — but truthful — answer to that question was given by John Swinton (1830-1901), a New York editor, in a Five Minute Talk, “Journalists’ Gathering,” at the Twilight Club in New York, April 12, 1883: "There is no such thing as an independent press in America, if we except that of little country towns. You know this and I know it. Not a man among you dare utter his honest opinion. Were you to utter it, you know beforehand that it would never appear in print....

"It is the duty of a New York journalist to lie, to revile, to toady at the feet of Mammon, to sell his country and his race for his daily bread, or what amounts to the same thing, his salary. We are tools and vassals of the rich behind the scenes. We are marionettes.

"These men pull the strings, and we dance. Our time, our talents, our lives and our capacities are all the property of these men — we are intellectual prostitutes." (*The Great Quotations,* A Caesar Stuart Book, Lyle Stuart, New York, 1960. Page 671).

A *lie* cannot stand on its own. It must — by its very nature — be propped up by another lie. They, in turn, must be supported by additional lies. Such a practice quickly develops into a jumbled mass of deceit and chicanery in which truth becomes increasingly blurred with the passage of time.

"Oh, what a tangled web we weave when we practice to deceive!"

Truth, on the other hand, stands on its own — strong, immovable and permanent. It doesn't have to be "defended" by those who believe in it. It defends itself from all its adversaries — and emerges from attacks pure, simple and unscathed — *the truth!*

Henry Ford, the great auto pioneer, put it very succinctly: "The truth frequently seems unreasonable; the truth frequently is depressing; the truth sometimes seems to be evil; but it has the eternal advantage, it is the truth, and what is built thereon neither brings nor yields to confusion."

"To believe that we could be wrong about something — almost anything — is unfortunately a very ego-shattering experience for some (if not most) human beings. The exposure of myths and biases can be so psychologically disruptive that it is tantamount to complete ego destruction.

"When the security blanket is gone, so is the particular niche of comfort into which we can conveniently creep when some challenging new thought comes along to disturb our mental processes. We have our first line of defenses against truth, and they are far more effective than any radar set or military advanced-warning missile system. They unfailingly tell us that we are not wrong, but right after all!

"Most people stubbornly resist any new truth with a whole series of first-line defenses and several backup systems to boot! But when truth finally exhausts all their defenses, they are forced to resort to that one-and-only tired old excuse: 'Just who do you think you are? Where did you get your authority from?' If all else fails, people tend to fall back on this 'put-down.'" (G.T. Armstrong, *Good News* magazine, October 1975).

The more closely you scrutinize *truth* the more perfect and simple and pure it becomes — and the more penetrating and illuminating light it casts on affairs around it!

As you continue on into this book you will read many things that will interest you, educate you and with which you will find yourself in ready agreement. That is good! You will also find many facts which, at first sight, will have the appearance of rank idiocy. Your first inclination may well be to put the book down and dismiss the contents as "absolutely ridiculous," "nonsense," "fanatical" and "far out." That's understandable too: the author had the same reaction when he was first introduced to the same information! Remember, however, the admonition of *wise* king Solomon: "*He that answers a matter before he hears it, it is folly and shame to him*" (*Proverbs* 18:13).

As you read, be guided by the following two definitions of truth: (A) Truth is that which is "in agreement with reality; the eternal principle of right or the natural law of order; fidelity, constancy; agreement with a standard or rule; accuracy" (*Webster's Illustrated Dictionary*).

(B) An even more precise definition is given by Dr. Stuart Crane in one of his seminars: "Truth is an accurate representation of the subject under consideration, (1) As it relates to all other things; (2) As it always has been in the past; (3) As it universally holds in the present; and, (4) Shall hold without exception in the future. Error is not the opposite of truth. Error is anything except truth. If there are any exceptions, it is error."

Truth will always fit perfectly into the realities of the world — the society in which we live!

CHAPTER TWO

OUR PRECIOUS HERITAGE

On one thing all are agreed: the United States, as a nation, is totally unique in all of recorded history. It is by far the greatest nation which has ever appeared on the world scene; it is a nation of unparalleled freedom, one which — following World War II — had only 6.6 percent of the world's population yet enjoyed 50 percent of its wealth.

In the 1960s Clinton Rossiter, an historian and political scientist at Cornell University, writing in a *Life* magazine article on "The National Purpose," said: "The United States is rightly numbered among those nations for which a benevolent sense of national purpose — or, as I prefer, of mission — has been an historical necessity. We have been, like the children of Israel, a 'peculiar treasure.' Upon us destiny has bestowed special favor; of us it has asked special effort.... Men like Washington and Lincoln sensed this great truth and acted consciously upon it."

"We find ourselves," said Abraham Lincoln, "in the peaceful possession of the fairest portion of the earth, as regards fertility of soil, extent of territory, and salubrity of climate.... We find ourselves the legal inheritors of these fundamental blessings. We toiled not in the acquirement or in the establishment of them."

In his famous proclamation speech of March 30, 1863, Lincoln also said: "It is the duty of nations, as well as of men, to owe their dependence upon the overruling power of God. We have been the recipients of the choicest blessings of heaven. We have been preserved, these many years, in peace and prosperity. We have grown in numbers, wealth and power as no other nation has ever grown; but we have forgotten God! We have forgotten the gracious Hand which preserved us in peace and multiplied and enriched and strengthened us; and we have vainly imagined, in the deceitfulness of our hearts, that all these blessings were produced by some superior wisdom and virtue of our own."

Most of us in America grew up taking the nation's wealth for granted — as "par for the course," as something that is our "right," and not as something for which we should be eternally thankful and for which we will be held accountable for maintaining and developing.

It's good that we back off, at least momentarily, from all the "attention grabbers" with which we are surrounded daily and consider the power and luxury enjoyed by America in its heyday — and then compare it with the rest of the world.

As the 1940s ended the United States hit its peak and commanded a greater percentage of the world's riches than at any time in its history. During this period America had three times more gold reserves than the rest of the world combined. We produced 60 percent of the world's steel and drove 73 percent of the world's automobiles and trucks. We produced 51 percent of all the gasoline used around the world and owned 67 percent of all the phones on earth. Americans owned a much higher ratio of radios, refrigerators, freezers, washers, air conditioners and other luxury items than any other people on earth.

In productive capacity we far outstripped all others. In technical know-how we were in a league by ourselves. America was the *greatest*, a giant among pygmies — and the rest of the world looked on in awe, and held the United States in high esteem!

In the years since then something has gone terribly wrong. Now, instead of the nations of the world being at America's feet, most of them appear to be at America's throat, like ravening beasts, striving by every means at their disposal to drag America down. Lending their wholehearted support to America's enemies abroad are this country's own peculiar variety of vandals — organizations and individuals who constantly seek to discredit this country, to ridicule it and to undermine any authority America may still have in the world. Meanwhile, most of the politicians and civic "leaders" would appear to be cooperating with great zeal with these enemies of the state to bring about the destruction of the United States as we know it today!

When one looks objectively and analytically at the America of the late 40s and compares it with America early in the third millennium (and also in relationship to the other nations of the world) the contrast is staggering — *and rather frightening*! One is prompted to ask, "What is America trying to do, commit suicide?" For truly, America is being "weighed in the balance and found wanting."

America prides itself on being a "have" nation — a "developed" nation. In the United States today people "have" more money, more freedoms, more opportunities, more rights and privileges and more luxuries than any other nation in history. In fact Americans enjoy all the things which the people of just a few decades ago thought would result in a Utopian Society and yet, paradoxically, they are among the most mixed-up and unhappy people on earth.

America "has" more financial "experts" than any other nation, yet its personal and national debts boggle the mind; they are virtually beyond description. America "has" more medical experts than any other nation, yet about half the population suffers from chronic diseases. America "has" an abundance of expert marriage counselors, yet one out of every two marriages ends in divorce. And the majority of those marriage which last are held together by a tenuous thread and an uneasy truce.

America has "developed" a super technology to the point where it can send three men to the moon and bring them back safely to earth. It has "developed" the ability to communicate perfectly with men on the moon — and to receive perfect television transmissions from the moon — but, absurdly, the average man in the street is unable to communicate with his wife, his neighbor or even his own children. Fantastic, but true!

"It would be a foolish man who denied the plain facts," wrote James Reston in his column of January 1, 1970. "We are overpopulated, undercivilized, divided, corrupted and bewildered, 'destitute of faith and terrified of skepticism.' War, crime, pollution, racial tension, political cynicism and pessimism are our companions."

The spectacle of this great nation which does not know its own mind is as humiliating as it is dangerous. America's allies around the world are deeply concerned about what is happening to this country. They seriously question the ability (and even the intent) of the United States to deal effectively with any of its major problems

Yes, "it would be a foolish man who denied the plain facts." From a position of unprecedented power and world esteem, America has — in a remarkably few years — plummeted to a position of virtual moral, financial and spiritual bankruptcy.

Sixty years ago the image which America projected to the world was one of a colossally powerful, vibrantly alive, fantastically rich and benevolent giant who could confidently be trusted to lead the world through the challenges of the future and into the "sunlit uplands" about which Winston Churchill spoke during World War II.

In the process of time that image became tarnished, dented, chipped, smashed and broken. It is now totally unacceptable to even the most naive and gullible observer of the American scene from afar.

As the United States continues its journey into its third century as a nation, the new up-to-date image being received loud and clear by the nations of the world is a far cry from the one projected sixty years ago.

The new image is one of a lumbering, stumbling, bumbling, grumbling dolt who staggers from one crisis to another through a blinding haze of fear and indecision. It is one of a dissipated giant who throws crumbs (bought with borrowed money!) to his neighbors to keep them out of his hair while he engages in a mammoth orgy of crime and violence. It is the image of a terribly sick giant who, having exchanged his God-given Christian heritage for a bowl of humanistic Socialist pottage, has lost his sense of destiny and purged his mind of any trace of morality — a rebel whose reasoning processes are so devious, so scrambled as to be beyond comprehension. It is the image of a degenerate who can't be trusted because he doesn't trust himself; a giant who, in his traumatic neurosis, gulps down prodigious amounts of pills — pills to put himself to sleep, pills to wake himself up, pills to speed himself up and pills to slow himself down; plus pills and drugs to help him "escape" from the alarming reality of his ghastly predicament.

Many around the world find this an amusing — yet *frightening* — spectacle. It frightens them because their hopes and plans for the future were all based on the assumption that America (the fabled "land of the free and home of the brave") would remain the dominant power on the world scene. Nothing about the present American image serves to support their initial basic assumption, and that fact deeply concerns them.

Reviewing his fifty years year in the FBI, the late J. Edgar Hoover said: "Whether we like it or not the morals to which we subscribe as a people are vital for our survival as a free nation. Concerned citizens are beginning to wonder if we may not be in grave danger of rejecting those things which are the source of our nation's strength.

"Are we entering an age that must end in anarchy? Are we rearing a generation almost wholly lacking in self-discipline? In short, do we deserve our magnificent inheritance? Are we good enough to preserve the great Republic to which we have pledged our allegiance? Will we retain the capacity to do our duty as Americans?"

The late Police Chief Parker of Los Angeles also expressed pessimism about the future of our society. He said he was "very much concerned" about the way in which things are going. "It is very hard for me to believe that our society can continue to violate all the fundamental rules of human conduct and expect to survive. I think I have to conclude that this civilization will destroy itself as others have before it. This leaves only one question — *when?*

Will America collapse as some observers predict? Such an idea would have seemed preposterous sixty years ago, but now many view it as a distinct possibility.

ABRAHAM LINCOLN

Looking into the future Abraham Lincoln, with great clarity of vision and foresight, recognized that no foreign power — or combination of foreign powers — "could by force take a drink from the Ohio or make a track on the Blue Ridge in a trial of a thousand years.

"At *what point then is the approach of danger to be expected*? I answer, if it ever come, it must spring up among us, it cannot come from abroad. *If destruction be our lot, we must ourselves be its author and finisher. As a nation of freemen we must live through all time, or die of suicide"* (Abraham Lincoln, speech at Springfield, Illinois, January 27, 1837. Emphasis added).

Lincoln clearly understood that the only *real* danger facing the American nation, as it marched on into the future, was the corrupting of its people — or what has been called *the subverting of the American spirit.*

The subverting of the American spirit, which has been taking place with increasing intensity over the last 100 years, has undermined all the basic foundations upon which this great nation was built, and has turned it into a Sick Society.

When the American nation entered the Twentieth Century it was basically sound. It throbbed with life and vitality. Most people were deeply patriotic , loved their country, and lived by a definite standard of morality: they respected their country, their neighbor, and themselves! The home and family were held in high esteem. Men were masculine, women were feminine — and both sexes were content with their natural role and God-given responsibilities. As a result of these and other factors, the nation was essentially in a sound condition.

In the years since then all these pillars of a sound society have been eroding away. We have now reached the point where the average person is left without a set of clearly defined principles upon which to base their lives. We are left floundering in the quicksands of doubt, fear and indecision — a nation without any transcendent goals or a real purpose in being. As one person put it, America is "a nation which stands for nothing, but will fall for anything."

The result? The "fruit" is all around us for everyone to see. Look at any phase or facet of society, and you will see chronic disease gnawing away at the nation's vitals. The true state of the nation is reflected in its leading institutions — in education and in the churches, in literature and music, in government and in the home. It is mirrored in the financial mess in which the government and most individuals find themselves.

Yes, America today may be likened to a desperately sick man whose body is wracked with all kinds of deadly diseases. His eye sight and hearing are weak, his limbs are crippled with arthritis, his mental state is rapidly deteriorating, his heart is failing and cancer is gnawing away at his vitals. Yet, dumbly and naively, he is frantically trying to persuade himself that all is well — and that everything will work out alright in the end.

CHAPTER THREE

WHAT WENT WRONG?

What went wrong? What turned the famed American "dream" into the American nightmare? What has caused the land of the free and the home of the brave to become the land of the coward and of the knave?

What has come over us? What are the *causes* for the *effects* we see all around us in the world? Our homes and families are falling apart with mind-shattering rapidity. Our schools and colleges spawn alienated, frustrated, VD-infested pill poppers whose whole lives are wrapped up in "doing their own thing" — and let posterity be damned. Our courts force law-abiding citizens to lock themselves up in their own homes at night, while criminals are allowed to roam the streets, almost at will, to terrorize the populace. Governments (local, state and federal) grow and grow and grow. They tax and tax and tax. And they spend and spend and spend, while the nation groans under an awesome National Debt skyrocketing into multiple Trillions of dollars. Throughout every strata of society, lying, deceit, corruption, graft and hypocrisy are the orders of the day. No real soundness is found anywhere in society.

What has happened to us? Have we fallen victim to some strange National Curse? Or have we become infected with some exotic mental disease?

Did we fall accidentally into our present hideous national trauma — or were we pushed? Did it come about as a consequence of natural degeneracy or as the result of a *conspiracy*?

The idea of a massive conspiracy or "Hidden Hand" guiding the nations of the world towards total disintegration and collapse so that a Godless totalitarian One World Government may be established and ruthlessly enforced, is one worthy of serious consideration by every thoughtful person. In this book we propose to present forthrightly, and with thorough documentation, the reasons why belief in such a conspiracy is not only "rational" *but the only honest conclusion one can reach when confronted with all the evidence*!

The concept of such a conspiracy is not new — it has been written and spoken about extensively since the eighteenth century. Professor John Robison, the Abbe Barruel, Sir Walter Scott and Nesta Webster are among the historians whose works on the subject have been widely circulated and acclaimed. Many well-known people have expressed a belief in such a Plot: Winston Churchill, Henry Ford, Benjamin Disraeli, Charles Lindbergh and Taylor Caldwell are listed among the "believers."

Ironically, as we journey through our third century as a nation, with the evidence of such a conspiracy bombarding us from every point of the compass, it is the popular thing in circles of "higher learning" to heap scorn and ridicule on anyone "dumb" enough to harbor such an idea.

Those who are honest enough to look at the facts and have proven the existence of a conspiracy, are branded as "conspiracy nuts" and "right wing extremists" who have an "obsession."

The reader will note that individuals who specialize in other fields are never branded as being "obsessed." Their views are respected — as long as they stay away from the conspiracy "theory" of history.

Viewing the appalling and apparently never-ending parade of "blunders," "errors" and "mistakes" our government has made over the last sixty years, best-selling author Gary Allen states: "If we were merely dealing with the law of averages, half the events affecting our nation's well-being should be good for America. If we were dealing with mere incompetence, our leaders should occasionally make a mistake in our favor. *We are not dealing with coincidence or stupidity, but with planning and brilliance*" (*None Dare Call It Conspiracy*, p.8).

Oh, that the majority of people would read and ponder those words. Their truth should be chillingly obvious to everyone capable of logical deduction.

There have been many leading academicians in the United States who have openly professed belief in a "Hidden Hand" guiding the affairs of state in this country and other nations around the world. For example, the late Dr. Carroll Quigley, professor of history at the Foreign Service School at Georgetown University clearly stated: "*There does exist, and has existed for a generation, an ... international network which operates to some extent in the way the radical Right believe the Communists act.* In fact, this network, which we may identify as the Round Table Groups, have no aversion to cooperating with the Communists or any other group, and frequently do so. *I know of the operation of this network because I have studied it for twenty years and was permitted for two years, in the early 1960s, to examine its papers and secret records. I have no aversion to it or to most of its aims and have, for most of my life, been close to it and many of its instruments. I have objected, both in the past and recently, to a few of its policies ... but in general my chief difference of opinion is that it wishes to remain unknown, and I believe its role in history is significant enough to be known*" (*Tragedy and Hope*, Macmillan, 1966, p.950).

Another top-flight educator, the late Dr. Revilo P. Oliver, formerly professor of Classical Studies at the University of Illinois, declared that he was "absolutely certain" that such a conspiracy does exist (*Conspiracy or Degeneracy?* p.8).

Somewhere among the pages that lie ahead you will be faced with the very serious question of *Truth or Compromise*. It is bound to arise sooner or later — and probably a lot sooner than later!

Much of the evidence we will present will clash violently with what you have always thought, assumed or taken for granted from childhood. Your initial inclination may be to dismiss the evidence out of hand and to term it "absolutely ridiculous" and "nonsense" — or to use some other form of ridicule.

Let us dispense with such banality in dealing with the question of the International Conspiracy. Such childish behavior proves nothing — except, perhaps, the immaturity and intellectual dishonesty of the self-serving.

The only honest and totally sincere standard by which to make a decision is to *ask* and *answer* two questions: (1) Can it be proven? and (2) Does it fit the grim reality of the world in which we live?

As you read on, bear in mind the words of Benjamin Disraeli, a former British prime minister: "The world is ruled by very different personages from what is imagined by those who are not behind the scenes" (Coningsby, p.233). By the time you put this book down you will see the stark reality of those words — and that the fact of the Conspiracy is the only logical and understandable explanation for what is happening on the world scene!

CHAPTER FOUR

WHO RULES THE WORLD?

INTRODUCTION

Critics of the "conspiracy theory" of history rightly point out that to give such a conspiracy a sense of cohesion throughout many centuries, there necessarily would have to exist a centuries-old "guiding force" that would direct this conspiracy throughout different ages and make sure that it would be successful through changing mores, cultures, and societies throughout all time.

Up to now proponents of conspiracy theories have not shown this dimension that indeed a spiritual or immortal element of necessity must have inspired and guided this mysterious plot from ages immemorial. Some insight into this theory was given by a well-known conservative scholar who pondered these questions and reached an interesting conclusion. He wrote that a theory that a conspiracy "has been working consciously for many centuries is not very plausible unless one attributes to them a religious unity. That is tantamount to regarding them as Satanists engaged in the worship and service of supernatural evil, the directors of the (conspiracy) must see or otherwise directly perceive manifestations which convince them of the existence and power of Lucifer. And since subtle conspirators must be very shrewd men, not likely to be deceived by auto-suggestion, hypnosis, or drugs, we should have to conclude that they probably are in contact with a force of pure evil. That conclusion will give pause to the irreligious and skeptical" (Dr. Revilo P. Oliver, *Conspiracy or Degeneracy*, pp.39,40).

Let's explore this possibility:

EARLY REVELATIONS

In the Bible we are told that, "In the beginning God created the heaven and the earth ... and God saw *every thing* that he had made, and behold, *it was very good....*" (*Genesis* 1:1; 1:31). "Thus the heavens and the earth were *finished*, and *all* the *host* of them" (*Genesis* 2:1). The word "host" indicates that the angels were included in this creation, and that they were *"very good."*

But something awesome and far-reaching happened, for, in the third chapter of *Genesis*, we read of the appearance of the Serpent — or Satan. What happened between creation and the time Eve and the Serpent had their meeting? The answer to that question is revealed dramatically later on in the Bible — in *Isaiah* 14 and *Ezekiel* 28.

These passages reveal that at the time of creation, the Creator God had placed Lucifer, who "sealed up the sum, *full of wisdom, and perfect in beauty,*" over the angelic host (*Ezekiel* 28:12,14,15). Lucifer "was *perfect* in [his] ways" when he was *created* (v.15). The name Lucifer means "son of the morning" — the "shining one" or "shining star [angel, *Revelation* 1:20] of the dawn." He was the Light Bringer — a created spiritual being who had tremendous truth, knowledge, wisdom and understanding. Lucifer had been placed over many angels. It was his responsibility to direct them. He was the Illuminator of his day!

What was his attitude towards the responsibilities and power given to him by his Creator? *He wanted more power*! He became consumed by jealousy, vanity, lust and greed. He developed grandiose ideas — and conceived a plan to wrest control of the newly created Universe from his Creator.

The truth about his massive power-play begins to unfold in *Isaiah* 14. Starting in verse 4, we see the king of Babylon pictured as a grasping, conquering tyrant who was a curse to his subjects. He had the same attitude, the same philosophy as the rebellious angels portrayed in Jude, verse 6. There, we read of "the angels which kept not their first estate, but left their habitation." In actual fact the king of Babylon represented Satan: he was a tool of Satan — a pawn in his game plan.

This fact becomes crystal clear when we read verses 12-14. Here the lesser human type lifts to the great antitype — Satan — who controlled him. You will notice that things are said in these verses about the great former cherub, Lucifer or Satan, which could not be said about a mere human being: *"How are you fallen from heaven, O Lucifer, son of the morning! How are you cut down to the ground, which does weaken the nations?"*

Lucifer had said: "I [notice the big 'I'] will ascend into heaven [where God's throne is located]. *I will exalt my throne [position of rulership] above the stars [angels] of God.* I will sit upon the mount of the congregation in the sides of the north:

"I will ascend above the heights of the clouds; I will be like the Most High" (v.14).

As a result of his insubordination, God told Lucifer: "I will cast you as profane out of the mountain of God ... [since] your heart is lifted up *because of* your beauty, you have corrupted your wisdom *by reason of* your brightness ... *You have defiled your sanctuaries by the multitude of your iniquities..."* (*Ezekiel* 28:16,17,18).

One-third of the angels followed Lucifer in his rebellion. As a result, they became demons — and Lucifer, the former Light Bringer became Satan, or the Adversary. Having been cast out of heaven, they are now confined to the earth and its environs.

[The New Testament reveals that Satan is now "the god of this world" (*II Corinthians* 4:4), and that he "deceives the whole world" (*Revelation* 12:9). He also frequently appears as "an angel of light" (*II Corinthians* 11:14)].

The Bible also reveals that Satan rules the kingdoms of this world through a hierarchial system of "principalities" and "powers" — and "wicked spirits in high places" (*Ephesians* 6:12). The reader should notice that when Satan claimed to have control of "all these things" (the kingdoms of the world), Christ did not deny this reality (*Matthew* 4:9-11)].

Adam was given the assignment of taking care of the earth: "And the Lord God took man, and put him in the garden of Eden *to dress it and to keep it.*" He failed his assignment and, as a result, became a slave of Satan. He obeyed Satan rather than God. Mankind, with very few exceptions, has been following Satan's way — his philosophy — ever since.

As the population of the earth began to multiply people devoted themselves with remarkable diligence to following Satan's way. As a result, "God saw that the wickedness of man was great upon the earth and that every imagination of the thoughts of his heart was only evil continually" (*Genesis* 6:5). "The earth also was corrupt before God, and the earth was filled with violence ... for all flesh had corrupted his [God's] way upon the earth" (verses 11,12). The Bible tells us that as a result a worldwide flood (an event proved by archaeologists around the world, see *The Flood in the Light of the Bible, Geology and Archeology,* by A.M. Rehwinkle, *The Flood and Noah's Ark,* by Andre Parrot), was brought upon the earth by God. All the inhabitants of the earth, with the exception of Noah and his family, were destroyed.

NIMROD AND BABYLON

Following the Flood, everyone on earth knew God — and His way of life. They feared to do evil, at first. History records that for "many ages man lived under the government of Jove [God] without cities and ... all speaking one language.... Then discord began" (Hyginnius, p.114). As this group expanded they began migrating from the area of the mountains of Ararat where the Ark had landed (*Genesis* 8:4). "And the whole earth was of one language and of one speech. And it came to pass, as they journeyed from the east, they found a plain in the land of Shinar; and they dwelt there" (*Genesis* 11:1,2). Shinar, now known as ancient Babylonia (Breasted's *Ancient Times*), was a wonderfully fertile land.

These people could have continued to live under God's laws and enjoy the abundance and the peace they experienced at first. Instead, they decided to follow the hideous example of Adam and Eve and "do their own thing." The results were catastrophic!

Although the land continued to be productive, the wild animals began to multiply at a pace much faster than that of the people: many lived in terror of being attacked and consumed by these ferocious beasts.

It was at this juncture that Nimrod came on the scene as the "savior" of the terrified populace. Nimrod, the son of Cush, was a powerfully built black man who had developed a reputation as a "mighty hunter." Nimrod was known everywhere for his strength. He emancipated the people of the earth from their fear of the wild animals and, in doing so, became their leader.

Famous historian Alexander Hislop, in *The Two Babylons,* tells us that the "amazing extent of the worship of this man indicates something very extraordinary in his character; and there is ample reason to believe that in his day he was the object of high popularity. Though by setting up as king Nimrod invaded the patriarchal system, and abridged the liberties of mankind, yet he was held by many to have conferred benefits upon them, that amply indemnified them for the loss of their liberties, and covered him with glory and renown. By the time that he appeared, the wild beasts of the forests, multiplying more rapidly than the human race, must have committed great depredations on the scattered and struggling population of the earth, and must have inspired great terror into the minds of men....

"The exploits of Nimrod, therefore, in hunting down the wild beasts of the field, must have gained for him the character of a preeminent benefactor of his race. By this means, no less than by the bands he trained, was his power acquired, when he first began to be mighty upon the earth; and in the same way, no doubt, was that power consolidated. Then ... by gathering men together in masses, and surrounding them with walls, he did still more to enable them to pass their days in security, free from the alarms to which they had been exposed in their scattered life. Within the battlements of the fortified city no such danger from savage animals was to be dreaded; and for the security afforded in this way, men no doubt looked upon themselves as greatly indebted to Nimrod. No wonder, therefore, that the name of the 'mighty hunter,' who was at the same time the prototype of the 'god of fortifications,' should have become a name of renown.

"Had Nimrod gained renown only thus, it had been well. But not content with delivering men from the fear of the wild beasts, he set to work also to emancipate them from the fear of the Lord which is the beginning of wisdom (*Proverbs* 9:10), and in which alone true happiness can be found. For this very thing he seems to have gained, as one of the titles by which men delighted to honour him, the title of 'Emancipator' or 'Deliverer' (*The Two Babylons,* pp. 50,51).

Hislop goes on to tell us that "all tradition from the earliest times bears testimony to the apostasy of Nimrod, and to his success in leading men away from the patriarchal faith, and delivering their minds from the awe of God and fear of the judgments of heaven that must have rested upon them while yet the memory of the Flood was recent. And according to all the principles of depraved human nature, this too, no doubt, was one grand element in his fame; *for men will readily rally around any one who can give the least appearance of plausibility to any doctrine that will teach them that they can be assured of happiness ... though their hearts and natures are unchanged, and though they live without God in the world...*

"By the apostasy he introduced, by the free life he developed among those who rallied around him, and by separating them from the holy influences that had previously more or less controlled them, he helped them to put God and the strict spirituality of His law at a distance ... making men feel and act as if heaven were afar off from earth, and as if the God of heaven 'could not see through the dark cloud,' or did not regard with displeasure the breakers of His law. Then all such would feel that they could breathe freely, and that now they could walk at liberty. For this, such men could not but regard Nimrod as a high benefactor...

"According to the system Nimrod was the grand instrument in introducing, men were led to believe that a real spiritual change in heart was unnecessary, and that as far as change was needed, they could be regenerated by mere external means.... (He) led mankind to seek their chief good in sensual enjoyment, and showed them how they might enjoy the pleasures of sin, without any fear of the wrath of a holy God. In his various expeditions he was always accompanied by troops of women; and by music and song, and games and revelry, and with everything that could please the natural heart, he commended himself to the good graces of mankind" (pp.52-55).

All that Nimrod did seemed just great in the eyes of most people of his day, who, by their very nature, hated the laws of God (*Romans* 8:7) and wanted to follow the path of least resistance. They wanted to "live it up" and "do their own thing." They said, "Let us build us a city, and a tower, whose top may reach unto heaven; *and let us make us a name,* lest we be scattered abroad upon the face of the whole earth" (*Genesis* 11:4).

The people not only protected themselves from the wild animals by building a walled city; they also established an authority of their own — "let us make us a name." This was to be the central place of mankind's authority — the necessity of their obedience to God was not going to be recognized. Nimrod was their Boss. They began to build a tower to "reach unto heaven." With a tower that high, they could do as they wished, disobey God and still be safe from His punishment which had previously drowned the inhabitants of the earth.

Nimrod kept growing in power but the inborn desire of the people to worship had to be satisfied. Nimrod and his followers had deliberately turned against the true God. With the great power that he wielded, Nimrod set himself up as the priest of those things being worshipped by the people in order to gain a still greater hold over them. He gradually put himself in the place of the true God. The Bible tells us that Nimrod was a "mighty hunter before the Lord." Strong's Concordance shows us that the Hebrew word "paniym" translated "before" here should be translated "against." Yes, Nimrod was clearly against God (*Genesis* 10:8,9).

To whom did the people turn to worship when they rejected their Creator? We are told that they "changed the glory of the incorruptible God into an image made like .. creeping things" (*Romans* 1:23). They remembered the Serpent of the Garden of Eden (man's enemy); they would honor it, for had it not been through the Serpent that they had been promised the knowledge of good and evil? The Serpent had not commanded them to do anything. So it came about that the Serpent (Satan) was ultimately worshipped as the Enlightener (Illuminator) of mankind.

The sun, also, was a favorite object of worship because of the light and heat it gives. These two illuminators became associated together and, just as the Serpent was considered to be the illuminator of the spiritual world, so also was the sun the illuminator of the physical world. The most common symbol of the sun or sun-god is a disk with a Serpent coiled around it (Bunsen's *Hieroglyphics,* Vol. 1, p. 497). The Serpent is universally recognized as a symbol of the sun (*Druids,* p.437).

In *Revelation* 12:9 Satan is clearly identified with the Serpent: it now becomes apparent why sun worship is devil worship. Satan, by deceptively inspiring mankind, was associating himself with certain objects that mankind tended to worship in such a way as to receive the worship himself.

As shown in *Romans* 1:21-25, "When they knew God, they ... changed the glory of the incorruptible God into an image made like unto corruptible man and ... creeping things ... and worshipped the creature [created things] rather than the Creator."

These, then, were just a few of the false beliefs into which the people of Nimrod's day, who did not wish to worship the true Creator God, were being led. These were the beliefs promulgated by Nimrod and which gave him ever more power over the people. He became the priest of the Sun-god or Bol-Kahn, which means the priest of Baal. He was therefore the priest of devil worship.

Nimrod was a man of unbounded ambition. History tells us that he conquered all the peoples from Babylon to Lybia — or a large portion of the populated world of that day. Nimrod was the first ruler to form an army and establish economic, civil and social systems. He imposed his Satanic religion on all the vanquished peoples. In time, his pagan teachings spread to and held sway over all nations of the then known world.

It is not to be assumed that everyone was swayed and deceived by Nimrod and his deceitful teachings. There were always those who, like Noah, stood fast and worshipped the true God. In Wilkinson's *Egyptians*, Vol. 4, pp.330-332, we are told that Shem, another of Noah's sons, obtained the aid of a group of Egyptians to defeat Nimrod. After he was killed his body was cut up into small pieces and sent to many cities of the known world as a grim warning of what would happen to others who might "do as Osiris (Nimrod) had done, so should it be done to him; so should he also be cut to pieces" (*The Two Babylons*, pp.64,66).

It might be thought by some that Nimrod's death marked the end of the pagan worship which he initiated. This is not true. The warning against paganism did, however, have a very marked effect on would-be apostates. They realized that if one as powerful as Nimrod could be killed and disposed of in such a terrible manner, the same thing could happen to them if it was known that they were worshipping the same objects — idols. The people were afraid to worship these idols although they wished to do so. It will be readily understood that "if idolatry was to continue — if, above all, it was to make a step in advance, it was indispensable that it should operate in secret.... In these circumstances, then, began, there can hardly be a doubt, that system of 'Mystery' which, having Babylon for its center, has spread around the world" (Hislop, p.66,67).

These "Mysteries" were the guise that the pagans found whereby the hidden things of worship were represented by something else. In this way those initiated in the Mysteries would know in reality that they were worshipping the forbidden Sun or Serpent when they worshipped these new symbols, but the outsiders would not know. The whole thing would be a Mystery to them. According to Hislop, the purpose of these Mysteries was to "bind all mankind in blind and absolute submission to a hierarchy entirely dependent on the sovereigns of Babylon.

SEMIRAMIS

The individual who used the Mysteries to the greatest advantage was Semiramis, Nimrod's degenerate wife. She "is known to have impressed upon them [the people] the image of her own depraved and polluted mind. This beautiful but abandoned queen of Babylon was not only herself a paragon of unbridled lust and licentiousness but, in the Mysteries which she had a chief hand in forming, she was worshipped as Rhea, the great 'mother' of the gods, with such atrocious rites as identified her with Venus, the mother of all impurity" (Hislop, p.5).

Inspired by her true master, Satan, Semiramis wove together an intricate pattern of pagan worship which held the populace spellbound. It is important to note that not all her teachings were totally erroneous. They weren't. Many were based on truth, but were craftily twisted in such a way as to turn peoples' attention away from the Creator God and focus that attention on Semiramis and her Babylonian Mysteries.

That Semiramis and her associates enjoyed fabulous success is beyond dispute. Their whole system capitalized on the baser elements of human nature — a sure-fire formula for "success" in many undertakings!

In later years even the twelve tribes of Israel fell victim to the Babylonian Mysteries. In *Judges* 2:13 we read that they "forsook the Lord, and served Baal and Ashtoroth." "They set up their abominations in the house which is called by my [God's] name to defile it ... and they built high places [altars] to Baal" so that they could practice the idolatrous rites of the pagans (*Jeremiah* 32:33-35).

At one point the degeneration was so marked that Elijah — a servant of the true God — stated that the children of Israel "have forsaken your [God's] covenant, thrown down your altars, and slain your prophets with the sword; and I, even I only, am left and they seek my life to take it away."

Yes, Elijah thought that he was all alone in worshipping the true God: but he was wrong. A little later God said to him: "I have left me over seven thousand in Israel, all the knees which have not bowed to Baal, and every mouth that has not kissed him" (1 *Kings* 19:10,18).

The New Testament couldn't be more specific on the fact that this trend has held true over the intervening years. In *II Corinthians* 4:4, Satan (Baal) is described as "the god of this world who has blinded the eyes of those who believe not." In *Revelation* 12:9 we read that "Satan ... deceives the whole world." *II Corinthians* 11:14 states that "Satan himself is transformed into an angel of light" and that, on the religious front, he has ministers "who are transformed as the ministers of righteousness." Yes, Satan's ministers masquerade as the ministers of God to deceive the majority of people. In *Revelation* 9:11 Satan is described as "a king ... whose name ... is Abaddon [Destroyer]."

It was only when Jesus Christ came on the scene four thousand years after Adam than someone finally qualified to succeed Satan as ruler of the earth. We read the account of that epic battle in *Luke,* chapter four.

After Jesus had gone without food and drink for forty days, Satan "showed him all the kingdoms of the world in a moment of time." Satan then hit Jesus with what he considered to be his trump card: "All this power will I give to you and the glory of them: for that is delivered unto me; and to whomsoever I will give it.

"If you therefore will worship me, all shall be yours" (verses 5-7).

Notice carefully that Satan claimed that he had been given control over the whole earth, that it was under his authority — and that Jesus didn't deny that fact for a second. He knew it was true!

Notice, also, that Jesus didn't use human reasoning to try to combat Satan's offer. He went straight to the scriptures and gave Satan a command: "Get behind me, Satan: for it is written, you shall worship the Lord your God and him only shall you serve" (verse 8).

Now notice that Satan's next pitch was a curve ball. He quoted scripture straight out of *Psalm* 91:11,12 — and placed a Satanic twist on it. "If you be the son of God, throw yourself down from this pinnacle; for it is written, 'He shall give his angels charge over you, to keep you, and in their hands they will bear you up, lest at any time you shall dash your foot against a stone'" (verses 9-11).

Christ's reply clearly shows that this promise of protection by God only applied in the event of an accident — "lest you" or "in case you" have an accident. Jesus said: "You shall not tempt the Lord your God" by deliberately asking for trouble.

At last Satan has met his master. The spiritual "spell" he had held over mankind from the time of creation had been broken — completely smashed — by Jesus Christ. It was at this time that Christ qualified to succeed Satan by submitting totally to the government of God despite many trials and temptations.

Christ didn't assume that authority immediately. Instead, He had to die for the redemption of mankind. He had to be raised from the dead to become our Savior, and then ascend to heaven to act as our mediator before Almighty God.

CHRISTIANITY CATCHES FIRE

Following Christ's crucifixion many thought that "Christianity" — or whatever it was called during that period of time — was all washed up, a thing of the past.

"I'm going back to my job as a fisherman," cried the impulsive Peter. "We'll go with you," chimed in others of the disciples (*John* 21:3).

Following instructions from the risen Jesus Christ, whom they encountered shortly after the incident related above, they remained in Jerusalem waiting for a "promise."

Christianity "caught fire" on the Day of Pentecost, 31 A.D., when the disciples were imbued with powers and abilities far in excess of the norm (*Acts* 2:1-). About three thousand were converted that day (v.41). And "many wonders and signs were done by the apostles" (v.43).

The new dynamically alive faith swept the area around Palestine and began to spread further afield. It was even said that the apostles were "turning the world upside down" (*Acts* 17:6).

What must be kept in mind is that prior to this time Satan, the "god of this world" (*II Corinthians* 4:4), had turned the world upside down by his treacherous tactics. The apostles, under the direction of the risen Lord Jesus Christ, were busy setting it right side up once again. Throughout *Acts* there is a tremendous emphasis placed on the resurrection of Christ.

The church grew and expanded greatly. The gospel was preached and peoples' lives were dramatically changed: at last they could see the Big Picture, without having to view life from an upside down position. They were living the "abundant life" (*John* 10:10).

SIMON MAGUS

It was only logical that "that old serpent, called the Devil, and Satan, who deceives the whole world" (*Revelation* 12:9), would not sit still for such a (to him) catastrophic turn of events. From what appeared to be total victory in the crucifixion of Jesus, Satan was now faced with total humiliation by the new church inspired and directed, as it was, by the risen Jesus Christ. Here, at last, was real spiritual light — dynamic spiritual truth which revolutionized peoples' lives and produced the results which so many long for, but which so few truly enjoy: love, joy, peace, goodness, faith, self-control — and a real purpose for living!

Such a logical conclusion is well grounded in fact. Satan had a dedicated servant, a "trump card" waiting in the wings for just such an eventuality: his name was Simon Magus. Simon is first mentioned in scripture in *Acts* 8.

Simon was a priest of the Babylonian religion who operated out of Samaria. The Bible clearly shows that the inhabitants of Samaria were not Israelites: they were Babylonians whom the king of Assyria had placed "in the cities of Samaria, and [who] dwelt in the cities thereof" (*II Kings* 17:24). The following verses reveal that these people were not interested in obeying and serving their Creator. They were pagan to the core.

Acts 8 shows that over a long period of time Simon Magus had built himself quite a religious empire in Samaria. He "used sorceries and bewitched the people ... giving out that himself was some great one." All the people, "from the least to the greatest," were so swayed, so bewitched by his sorceries, that they proclaimed him to be "the great power of God" — God himself (*Acts* 8:9-11).

When the apostle Philip began to preach the gospel in Samaria, "the people with one accord gave heed unto those things which Philip spake, and seeing the miracles which he did" (vs. 5,6). They were very impressed by the miracles.

Shortly thereafter Simon, directed by his master, Satan, began to see the awesome potential of Christianity as a tool for his own aggrandizement.

Without repenting of his sin, changing his whole life and forsaking his pagan idolatry, Simon attempted to buy an apostleship in the Church. He wanted "this power" (vs.18,19) — or official endorsement to go out and preach lawlessness and rank paganism in the name of, or as if by the authority of, Jesus Christ.

The apostle Peter blasted Simon for being engulfed "in the gall of bitterness, and in the bond of iniquity." And, in the original Greek, Peter said that both he and his money could "go to hell" (vs. 20,23).

Nowhere is Simon said to have become a member of the true church — the body of Christ. He did, however, take the name of Jesus Christ and, at least nominally, a few of His teachings.

These he mixed with his Babylonian Mystery religion. He hung a "Christian" label on his new organization and set about establishing it as a universal religion. He was the Boss!

All these facts are clearly demonstrable from the pages of history: "... it need *not* be supposed that when Simon broke with the Christians he renounced all that he had learned. It is more probable that he carried some of the Christian ideas with him and that he wove them into a system of his own. Thus he became the leader of a retrograde sect, perhaps nominally Christian and certainly using some of the Christian terminology, but in reality anti-Christian and exalting Simon himself as the central figure which Christianity was giving to Jesus Christ" (*Hasting's Dictionary of the Apostolic Church,* Vol. 1, p.497).

"The amalgam of paganism and Christianity [that] was especially obvious in the Simonian system, is readily explicable in the teachings of Simon Magus who ... was brought into contact with Christian teaching without becoming a genuine member" (p.496).

From another source we learn that, "The author or first representative of this baptized paganism ... is Simon Magus, who unquestionably adulterated Christianity with pagan ideas and practices" (*Apostolic Christianity*, Vol. 2, p.566) and "subsequently attempted, with the aid and the sanction of Christianity to set up a rival universal [Catholic] religion" (p.514).

It is quite clear, then, that Simon had the mind or attitude of Satan: he was a liar, a deceiver and he lusted after total power.

The writings of the apostles are explicit in their condemnation of and warnings about the Simonian system of paganized "Christianity." It is mentioned repeatedly as being in full operation, and a deadly threat to real Christians. In *II Corinthians* 11:4 we read a warning about those who were preaching "another Jesus" and had "another spirit" (or attitude).

Satan's ministers (under the personal direction of Simon Magus) were "transformed *as* [if they were] the ministers of righteousness" (Christ's true representatives) and were leading the masses astray. It has always been a lot easier for human beings (with their human nature diametrically opposed to the will of their Creator, *Jeremiah* 17:9 and *Romans* 8:7) to follow the way of Satan rather than the way of God. Satan's way and human nature are highly compatible. To the natural, normal carnal mind the doctrines of Luciferianism (or

Illuminism) appear to be so "enlightened" — so "right." However, poison in a bottle labeled "honey" is still poison. Paganism is a package labeled "Christianity" is still poison and deadly paganism. There is only one way to be a Christian — God's way (*John* 10:7 and *Acts* 4:12).

Simon's Babylonian counterfeit "Christianity" (baptized paganism) dates from 33 A.D. — two years after the formation of the true Christian Church.

The *Acts of the Apostles* is the true history of the Christian Church up to 69 A.D. What happened immediately after that date is known in history as "the lost century" or the "age of shadows." It is a matter of historical fact that "of all the periods in the Church's history, it is the one about which we know the least... For fifty years after St. Paul's life a curtain hangs over the church, through which we strive vainly to look; and when at last it arises about 120 A.D. with the writings of the earliest Church Fathers, we find a church in many respects very different from that in the days of St. Peter and St. Paul" (Jesse Lyman Hurlbut, *The History of the Christian Church*). The famous historian Edward Gibbon states quite candidly in his *Decline and Fall of the Roman Empire,* that the "scanty materials of ecclesiastical history seldom enable us to dispel the cloud that hangs over the first age of the Church."

Note carefully the words "shadows," "curtain" and "cloud." It now becomes obvious that the "lost century" is a direct result of a massive cover-up and the destruction of evidence regarding its nature and purpose. We saw earlier that Satan is the prince of darkness and the one who attempts to destroy truth. Simon and his Satan-inspired followers were frantically busy deceiving the whole world once again (*Revelation* 12:9).

Continuing our probe into ecclesiastical history, we uncover many additional shocking facts which shatter numerous cherished beliefs. In the *Dictionary of Christian Biography*, Vol.4, p.682, we read that "when Justin Martyr wrote his *Apology* (152 A.D.), the sect of the Simonians appears to have been formidable, for he speaks four times of their founder, Simon ... and tells us that he came to Rome in the days of Claudius Caesar (45 A.D.), and made such an impression by his magical powers that he was honored as a god, a statue being erected to him on the Tiber, between the two bridges, bearing the inscription "Simoni deo Sancto" (the holy god Simon).

Could Justin have "made up" this story? Hardly! "There is very slight evidence upon which to reject so precise a statement as Justin makes; a statement he would scarcely have hazarded in an apology addressed to Rome, where every person had the means of ascertaining its accuracy. If he had made a mistake, it must have been at once exposed, and other writers would not have frequently repeated the story as they have done" (Hastings, Vol.2, p.496).

APOSTLE PETER NEVER IN ROME

It is a rather startling fact that neither secular or Biblical history contains any evidence that the *Apostle* Peter was *ever* in Rome. In fact, there is a superabundance of evidence which proves that Peter was never in Rome at any time.

The highly authoritative *Encyclopedia Biblica* plainly states that "Justin ... knows nothing of any presence of Peter in Rome at all."

There are many purely Biblical proofs that the Apostle Peter was never in Rome, and that he clearly was never in charge of the Christian Church in that gentile city. Here are just a few:

(1) Peter was appointed apostle to the Jews — the circumcision. Paul was the apostle in charge of gentile affairs. In 51 A.D. Peter was in Antioch where he got into a dispute with Paul because he (Peter) wouldn't sit with gentiles; very strange if he was bishop of Rome (*Galatians* 2:11-21);

(2) It was Paul who originally formed the Church *in* Rome in 55 or 56 A.D. Paul wrote to the Christians there: "I long to see you, that I may impart to you some spiritual gift, to the end that you may be established (*Romans* 1:11). If Peter had been instrumental in raising up a Christian congregation in Rome some years earlier, such a statement could only be interpreted as a massive personal insult to Peter.

Of course such was not the case, for Paul wrote to the Christians at Rome that "I have strived to preach the gospel, not where Christ was named, lest I should build upon another man's foundation" (*Romans* 15:20).

Notice also that, at the end of his letter to the Christians at Rome, Paul sent greetings to a total of 28 individual people, but makes no mention of Peter. Why? Peter just wasn't in Rome.

(3) When Paul eventually got to Rome, he immediately "called the chief of the Jews together ... (and) expounded and testified the Kingdom of God, persuading them concerning Jesus, both out of the law of Moses, and out of the prophets, from morning till evening."

Had Peter (a strongly partisan Jew) been bishop of Rome for years prior to this time, these Jewish leaders would certainly have known the basics of the Christian faith (*Acts* 28:17-23).

(4) Paul, towards the end of his ministry, wrote at least six letters *from* Rome, and Peter is never mentioned in any of them. Paul wrote that "all men [in Rome] forsook me ... only Luke is with me" (*II Timothy* 4:11).

"SIMON PETER" IN ROME

Of one thing secular history is abundantly and undeniably clear: there was a "Simon Peter" in Rome during the middle part of the first century — and he did wield tremendous influence on the religious scene in that gentile city.

Delving still further into the origins of the Babylonian Mystery religion, we come across many further enlightening facts which open up new avenues of understanding relative to the world situation.

Ancient history reveals that the pagan deities worshipped by the Babylonians and the Greeks were known as Peters: "Not only the gods but the Hierophatae [special gods], in most temples, and those priests in particular who were occupied in the celebration of the mysteries, were styled Patres" (Bryant, *Ancient Mythology*, Vol.1, p.354). Davidson's *Hebrew Lexicon* shows that the consonantal word P-T-R (Peter) means "to interpret."

The priests of the Babylonian and other mystery religions claimed to have the power to interpret the pagan mysteries.

In the *Luceii Fragments*, we find that the ancient Romans considered Neptune, Saturn, Mars and Liber as "gods" of Peter rank — i.e. chief gods. In the first century Rome was known as the "city of the gods." All the "gods" of paganism were strongly represented there.

When Simon Magus went to Rome he bewitched the inhabitants with his "magical" (demonic) powers and soon became known as Simon Peter — Simon the Interpreter (of the Babylonian Mysteries).

Simon, as we saw earlier, had taken the name of Jesus Christ — and much of the terminology of Christianity — and was using these tools to expand his own sphere of influence.

Peter or Pethor worship can be traced back to Mesopotamia where idolatry had its beginning and where Nimrod built the Tower of Babel. In *Deuteronomy* 26:4 we find that Balaam "of Pethor of Mesopotamia" was hired to put a curse on the nation of Israel. History tells us that this Pethor was a sacred high place "where there was an oracle temple, and hence called Pethor, and Pethora, which means place of interpretation, or oracle temple. Here was, no doubt, a college of priests of whom Balaam had been appointed chief."

Balaam was the chief Patora (Peter) of the Pethor (Peter temple) of Mesopotamia, the very home of idolatry and false religion. It is clear from his name that Balaam ("Conqueror of the People" in the Semitic language) considered himself to be the successor of Nimrod, the originator of the Babylonian Mystery religion. The Greeks called Nimrod Nicholas, which also means "Conqueror of the People."

It should also be noted that Nimrod was known by other names in other nations around the then known world: Janus and Mithras were among these names. Janus, a Peter-rank "god" to the ancient Romans "with a key in one hand," was pictured as being "the keeper of the gates of heaven and earth."

"Ovid speaks of him (Janus) ... his face is double to denote his double empire over the heavens and the earth — and that all things are open and shut to him at his will, that he governs the universe ... and that he presides over the gates of heaven" (*Classical Manual*, p.388)

Here was a Peter in Rome hundreds of years before Christ, and before the birth of the Apostle Peter, who claimed to be in charge of the "pearly gates." It will, of course, be noted that the

Catholic Church makes exactly the same claims for itself and its "Peter."

Sir James Frazer, in *Golden Boughs*, Vol.1, p.471, points out that "among the gods of eastern origin, who in the decline of the eastern world competed against each other for the allegiance of the west, was the old Persian deity of Mithra. The immense popularity of his worship is attested to by the monuments illustrative of it which are found scattered in profusion all over the Roman Empire. In respect both of doctrines and of rites the cult of Mithra appears to have presented many points of resemblance to the religion of the Mother of the gods, but also to Christianity."

Note that Frazer is writing about the situation that existed three or four hundred years after the apostles died. He clearly shows that by that time pure primitive Christianity (the teachings of Jesus Christ and the faith of the apostles) had all but faded from the scene. He also shows that the "new" church had adopted pagan festivals. As Frazer concludes, "the coincidences of the 'Christian' with the heathen festivals are too close and numerous to be accidental" (v.475).

No, it was not accidental! Satan's representatives were actively deceiving the people religiously once again. They were amalgamating all the old pagan religions into one, universal (catholic) church and were selling it to the public under a "Christian" label. To the untrained eye this counterfeit appeared to be genuine — "the real thing." It is only when the whole system is examined at close range that it is revealed to be the Great Babylonian Mystery Religion in a "Christian" wrapper (*Revelation* 17). For more detailed information on the Babylonian religious system, see *The Two Babylons* by Alexander Hislop. Also *Isis Unveiled and Secret Doctrine* by Madame Blavatsky.

If there are still any readers who entertain a flicker of doubt regarding the veracity of what they have just read, and are not totally convinced that the "Simon Peter" of Roman Catholicism is none other than Simon Magus — the "Peter" of the Babylonian Mystery religion of first century Rome — they should consider this startling admission by Werner Keller regarding the death and burial of "Simon Peter." The leading Catholic historian records that, "On the night of his death on the cross, Peter's followers buried his body. As in the case of Jesus on the hill of Calvary, it was wrapped in linen and *secretly taken to a pagan burial ground* on the via Cornelia, behind the stone structure of the arena. This pagan cemetery lay on a knoll called vaticanus (Vatican Hill): the Latin word 'vatis' means a 'prophet' or 'soothsayer.' In days gone by there had been an Etruscan oracle on the spot" *(The Bible As History,* p.368).

There can be very little if any doubt that this "Peter" was in fact Simon Magus, and not the Apostle Peter. A pagan cemetery would be the logical and appropriate place in which to bury Simon Magus. It should also go without saying that the true Christians would hardly search out a pagan burial ground — in fact the chief one — in which to inter their close friend.

Peter, of course, was a Jew who was an unyielding enemy of paganism. Jews were always buried in their own cemetery. The apostle Peter wouldn't have been "seen dead" in a pagan cemetery.

As time passed the "new" church continued its plunge into darkest paganism. Early in the fourth century Emperor Constantine adopted this Simonized "baptized heathenism" as the official religion of the Roman Empire. It now became "respectable" and was soon accepted as the church Christ founded.

History records that "the mere profession of the new faith became a passport to the emperor's favor and to office [and as a result] hypocrisy and selfishness took the place of that sincerity and devotion which had marked the primitive and persecuted Christians" (Myers, Rome: *Its Rise and Fall,* p.406). This church, in the fourth century, was a "study ... of disease; of moral lesions, corruption and abuses ... (and) there was an unholy rush into 'holy' orders in order to avoid taxation" (Thomson, *The Economic and Social History of the Middle Ages,* p.61).

From the same authority we learn that *"the Dark Ages were at least as much due to the corruption of the church as to the decay of Roman Civilization or the barbarian invasion.*

"So far from being constructive in its influence, the church in the Roman Empire was a dissolving and disintegrating influence of the first magnitude" (p.64).

As time went by "the church gradually usurped power over the state, and the result was not Christianity, but a more or less corrupt hierarchy controlling the nations of Europe, making the church mainly a political machine" (Hurlbut, p.80). This worldly church was a veritable cesspool of iniquity, heathen philosophy and spiritual whoredoms. Abominations of every description were the rule rather than the exception. Historical proofs of what really happened during the Dark Ages are so overwhelming that it is something every honest person must face squarely. This tragic chapter in human history wasn't written by humble, spirit-led followers of the risen Jesus Christ who were striving with every fiber of their being to serve their Savior. It was, in fact, penned by a closely-knit group of Satan-inspired, power-hungry rebels masquerading under a "Christian" label — but embracing all the Satanic rottenness of pagan Babylon.

The "fruit" of their lives — their doctrine, their philosophy and their private conduct — all combine to clearly demonstrate that this was not the true Christian church. "By their fruit shall you know them" (*Matthew* 7:20).

The Dark Ages was not just a period of stagnation — a time during which world affairs were held in a state of suspended animation. It was a period of steady degeneration across the full spectrum of human activity, during which knowledge and understanding developed from the beginning of time was either destroyed or deeply buried.

REFORMATION AND MARTIN LUTHER

After close to one thousand years of degeneration, the shackles of the Dark Ages were finally broken by the emergence on the European scene of the Renaissance — a revival of interest in art, science and literature — and, of course, the Reformation.

Multiple millions of people have assumed, over the years since then, that the Reformation was simply a religious movement. The image of thousands of earnest, totally dedicated men throughout Europe valiantly and devotedly striving for a return to "the faith once delivered to the saints" (*Jude*, v.3), is badly blurred if not completely out of focus. The truth is that religion was just one of the many factors involved in the Reformation. Other components included political, financial and intellectual considerations.

After many hundreds of years of religious and political servitude and heavy taxation, a powerful wave of nationalism began to sweep Europe. With it came a desire to be free from the dictates of the church, and a desire by many to manage their own affairs. Many of the Reformers used religion as a cloak behind which to further their own political ambitions.

In the beginning, the Reformers were mainly interested in getting rid of the monstrous depravities which permeated the Roman Church. Martin Luther remained in the church for several years following the nailing of his Ninety-Four Theses to the door of the Castle at Wittenberg. He attacked the sale of "indulgences" (the revenue from which was being used to build the giant "St. Peter's" Basilica in Rome) among other things. He did not attack Catholic doctrine.

The Reformation brought in its wake an increased interest in the knowledge of the Bible by the common man. "As soon as the revival of letters caused the contents of the New Testament to be known, it was seen that what passed for Christianity at the close of the fifteenth century was scarcely recognizable as such when placed side by side with what we know of Christianity at the close of the Apostolic Age" (Plummer, *The Continental Reformation*, p.17). "The nations of Christendom no longer looked to a holy and living God [but had] recourse to all the means that a superstitious, fearful and alarmed imagination could devise" (d'Aubigne, *History of the Reformation*, p.17).

Had all the leaders of the Reformation been totally sincere "seekers of truth" and had they lived up to their profession of "the Bible, the whole Bible and nothing but the Bible," they would not have fragmented into the many denominations of religious confusion we see around us today.

But that was not to be. Much of the "fire" and enthusiasm was soon gone. Instead of a growing love for and dedication to the One who is "THE Way, THE Truth and THE Life" (*John* 14:6), the unChristian attitudes of hate, strife, jealousy and persecution raised their ugly heads and rent the movement from top to bottom.

Ecclesiastical history is replete with examples of how many of these men "worked the angles," compromised, advocated the double-standard of situation ethics and politicked for their own advantage.

Many of the "Reformers" rejected pure Christianity and busied themselves with the formation of their own particular brands of Churchianity. It has been this Churchianity, and not Christianity, which has failed to lead mankind into a knowledge of what life is all about — the very reason why we exist.

CHAPTER FIVE

ILLUMINATI PART 1 — 1776-1876

Out of Germany was hatched a Diabolical Plot which has deceived untold millions, and which — at this present time — threatens to destroy Western Civilization.

In the years following the Reformation a new school of thought known as German Rationalism came to the forefront in circles of "higher learning." Rationalism developed first in Germany as that was the only country with comparative freedom of religion and thought. In other countries freedom of thought was verboten; church leaders persecuted or killed those who expressed their opinions.

Scholars were freed from the stifling restrictions placed on academic pursuits during the Dark Ages — and the winds of investigation and intellectual curiosity began to rustle refreshingly through the "hallowed halls" of universities. Many were motivated to challenge the cherished beliefs which had come to be accepted at face value by society at large.

From the beginning Satan was frantically busy among the leaders of these "emancipators." Having failed to keep all humanity bound with his Simonian form of "baptized paganism," Satan (the Great Deceiver, *Revelation* 12:9) tried another ruse.

These prideful "thinkers" could clearly see that corruption and depravity had decimated the church which had promulgated many of the ideas now proved to be totally fallacious. They saw that the worldly church held its adherents in subjection by means of fear and superstitious ritual. They falsely assumed that the myths and superstitions of the Dark Ages were based on the

Bible. When they proved that these superstitions were false, they assumed — without any real proof — that they had also proved the Bible false. As we clearly saw demonstrated in the last chapter, the teachings of that church were based on the Babylonian Mystery religion — not on the Bible.

The German Rationalists openly attacked all established beliefs with the deep-seated conviction that all religion was false (Hurst, *History of Rationalism,* p.27). One of their leaders arrogantly announced that "the turning point in history will be the moment man becomes aware that the only god of man is man himself" (Henri de Lubec, *Atheistic Humanist,* p.10). Another authority defined Rationalism as "that manner of thought by which the human reason is considered to be the only source and the only judge of all kinds of knowledge" (Hahn, *De Rationalismi*). Under an unending barrage of such "enlightened" scholarship, the "intelligentsia" of Europe were prepared by the second half of the eighteenth century for the advent of Illuminism — the secret society known as the Illuminati.

Illuminati? What is that? Most people respond to that question with a blank stare — a total lack of comprehension. A few respond with a ill-concealed sneer and a snide remark to the effect that, "You don't believe that garbage, do you?

Regardless of how various people may respond to that question, there is one fact of which we may be assured: the Order of the Illuminati was founded on May 1, 1776, by Dr. Adam Weishaupt, professor of Canon Law at Ingolstadt University, Bavaria. Weishaupt (born a Jew and a convert to Catholicism) was a former Jesuit priest who broke with that Order to form his own organization.

Many otherwise educated people have assumed that because the Illuminati is no longer an openly recognized organization called, say, "The Council of Illuminati Affairs" or "Iluminists International" that it, or more correctly the Satanically-inspired philosophy behind it, is no longer a threat to Western Civilization. Such an assumption would be naive in the extreme.

It would be equally naive and foolish to assume that the great apostate religious movement started under Satan's direction by Simon Magus in 33 A.D. had somehow "folded its tent and crept away into the night." No way! On the contrary, we should ex-

PLATE 1 — Founder of the Order of the ILLUMINATTI

pect to find Simon's operation very much to the fore in our society of today which is so obviously deceived — and so clearly under the direction of Satan (*Revelation* 12:9 and 2 *Corinthians* 4:4). It should also go without saying that the latter-day manifestation of Satan's Simonian church wouldn't peddle its deceitful wares under the banner of, say, "Simon's Spiritual Seduction Society," or "Satan's Church of Baptized Paganism." Such names wouldn't lead too many people to believe that such groups were truly Christian in origin.

There is evidence now extant that proves that the Simonian forces have joined the Illuminati (at the highest level) in an unholy alliance to achieve their mutual goal — total world domination (See *The New Montinian Church* and *The Vacant Chair*, both by the late Rev. Joaquin Saenz y Arriaga, Ph.D., a Mexican priest).

It is important that we clarify the meaning of the name of Weishaupt's Secret Society — the Illuminati. This is very significant.

The name implies that those who are members of the Illuminati are the only members of the human race who are truly enlightened and know "what it's all about." Weishaupt and his followers considered themselves to be the cream of the intelligentsia — the select of the elect — and the only people with the mental capacity, the insight and understanding to govern the world and bring it peace. Their avowed purpose and goal was the establishment of a "Novus Ordo Seclorum" or New World Order.

The name Illuminati is derived from the same root as the word Lucifer. Lucifer was the Bearer of the Light, a being of extrodinary brilliance (*Isaiah* 14:12).

The reader will note the direct parallel between the presumptuous, totally vain and arrogant attitude of Weishaupt and his followers and the attitude displayed by Satan (see the beginning of chapter four) when he, and the angels under his control, tried to take over the universe from their Creator. *Illuminism is clearly Satanism in one of its latter-day manifestations: their goals are virtually identical. In fact, Satan was the first Illuminist!*

Public attention was first drawn to the existence of the Illuminati and their diabolical plan for world conquest as the result of a bizarre accident in 1785. History records that a man named Lanze, an Illuminati courier, was racing on horseback from Frankfurt to Paris carrying documents relating to Illuminati activities in general, and specific instructions for the planned French Revolution in particular. The documents originated with Jewish members of the Illuminati in Germany and were addressed to the Grand Master of the Grand Orient Masons in

Paris. As the courier galloped through Ratisbon (Regensberg) he was struck by lightning and killed. All the papers he was carrying fell into the hands of the local police and were turned over to the Bavarian government. The authorities ordered the police to raid the headquarters of the Illuminati; this resulted in additional documents being captured.

The carefully documented evidence was brought to the attention of the various governments in Europe. For one reason or another, possibly Illuminati influence, they chose to turn a deaf ear to the warnings contained in these dreadful documents. Four years later the French Revolution exploded on the European scene in all its hideous fury.

SIR WALTER SCOTT

Sir Walter Scott, in the second volume of *The Life of Napoleon Buonaparte* (1820), indicates that the events leading up to the French Revolution were mostly orchestrated by bankers from Frankfurt.Their agents then led the mob in implementing the famous Reign of Terror. For additional documentation on the French Revolution, see the book of the same name by Nesta Webster.

The first "break," as far as the inside workings of the Illuminati are concerned, came when these "great intellectuals" were foolish enough to invite Professor John Robison to join their ranks. Robison, Professor of Natural Philosophy at Edinburgh University, was Secretary General of the prestigious Royal Society in that Scottish city: he was recognized by his contemporaries (and by Adam Weishaupt in particular) as one of the truly great intellectuals of his day. In inviting Robison into his elitist club, Weishaupt probably felt that the British professor would prove to be his "ace in the hole" in expanding Illuminati influence in the British Isles.

Weishaupt completely misjudged Robison's character. Instead of discovering a man with billowing vanity and an insatiable lust for power, he found a man of great integrity — one deeply concerned for the welfare of his fellow human beings, and for his own nation in particular. Robison was a man who couldn't be "bought."

Robison didn't fall for the lie that the goals of the Illuminati were pure and honorable. He kept his reactions to himself,

THE

LIFE

OF

NAPOLEON BUONAPARTE,

EMPEROR OF THE FRENCH.

WITH A

PRELIMINARY VIEW OF THE FRENCH REVOLUTION.

BY THE AUTHOR OF "WAVERLEY," &c.

——Sed non in Cæsare tantum
Nomen erat, nec fama ducis; sed nescia virtus
Stare loco: solusque pudor non vincere bello;
Acer et indomitus: quo spes quoque ira vocasset
Ferre manum, et nunquam temerando parcere ferro;
Successus urgere suos; instare favori
Numinis; impellens quicquid sibi summa petenti
Obstaret; gaudensque viam fecisse ruina.
LUCANI *Pharsalia*, Lib. I.

IN TWO VOLUMES.

VOL. I.

Exeter:
J. & B. WILLIAMS.
1820

PLATE 2 — THE LIFE OF NAPOLEON BUONAPARTE, EMPEROR OF THE FRENCH. (Title Page)

however, and played along with the conspirators. He was subsequently entrusted with top secret Illuminati documents and was thus able to scrutinize the inner workings of the secret society from close range. As a result, Robison wrote a startling book, *Proofs of a Conspiracy,* which was published in 1797. All of what is currently known about the early Illuminati comes from Robison's book and one written by the Abbe Barruel, *Memoirs Illustrating the History of Jacobinism,* published in 1798. Both books, though written by authors who were unknown to each other, give us a very clear picture of the organization. Both volumes quote extensively from *The Original Writings of the Order and Sect of the Illuminati,* an official report published by the Bavarian government in 1786, following a lengthy investigation. The following facts emerge:

Adam Weishaupt was born on February 6, 1748. His early training by the Jesuits had inspired him with an intense dislike of that Order. When he broke with the Jesuits he immersed himself in the subversive and anti-Christian teachings of the French philosophers and other writers who appealed to his innate sense of superiority.

The next five years were devoted to meditation, during which time Weishaupt devised a plan to overthrow civilization and establish what he termed a "Novus Ordo Seclorum," or New World Order. He constructed the very machinery for revolution itself.

On May 1, 1776, Weishaupt founded the Illuminati, the instrument by which he planned to accomplish his goal. All the members were required to adopt classical names. Weishaupt took the name Spartacus, the leader of an insurrection of slaves in ancient Rome; his chief assistant, Herr von Zwack, counselor to the Prince von Salm, became Cato; Baron Mengenhoffen, Sylla, etc.

Encyclopedia Britannica, 11th edition, 1910, tells us that the Order was divided into three main classes. The first included "novices," "minervals" and "lesser Illuminati;" the second consisted of freemasons, "ordinary" and "Scottish Knight;" the third or "mystery" class consisted of two grades of "priest" and "regent" and of "Magus" and "King." The King was, of course, Weishaupt himself!

PROOFS

OF A

CONSPIRACY

AGAINST ALL THE

RELIGIONS AND GOVERNMENTS

OF

EUROPE,

CARRIED ON

IN THE SECRET MEETINGS

OF

FREE MASONS, ILLUMINATI,

AND

READING SOCIETIES.

COLLECTED FROM GOOD AUTHORITIES

BY

JOHN ROBISON, *A. M.*

PROFESSOR OF NATURAL PHILOSOPHY, AND SECRETARY TO THE ROYAL SOCIETY OF EDINBURGH.

Nam tua res agitur paries cum proximus ardet.

EDINBURGH:

Printed for WILLIAM CREECH;—and T. CADELL, Junior, and W. DAVIES, LONDON.

1797.

PLATE 3 – PROOFS OF A CONSPIRACY AGAINST ALL THE RELIGIONS AND GOVERNMENTS OF EUROPE, CARRIED ON IN THE SECRET MEETINGS OF THE FREE MASONS, ILLUMINATI, AND READING SOCIETIES. (Title page)

32

mit ich indessen speculiren, und die Leute geschickt rangieren kann; denn davon hängt alles ab. Ich werde in dieser Figur mit ihnen operieren.

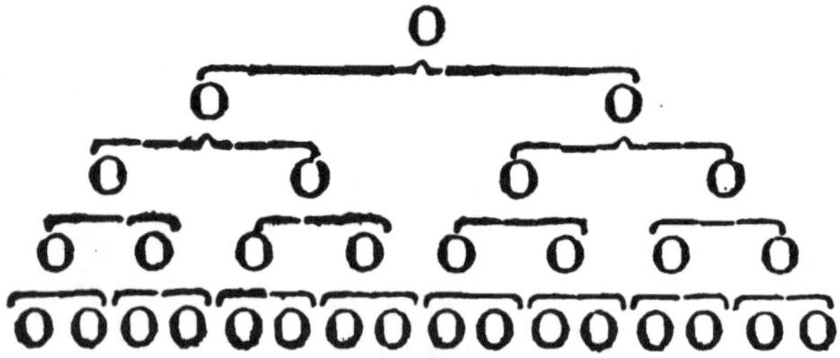

Ich habe zwey unmittelbar unter mir, welchen ich meinen ganzen Geist einhauche, und von diesen zweyen hat wieder jeder zwey andere, und so fort. Auf diese Art kann ich auf die einfachste Art tausend Menschen in Bewegung und Flammen setzen. Auf eben diese Art muß man die Ordres ertheilen, und im Politischen operieren.

Es ist ein Kunst dabey, dem Pythagoras etwas aus dem Ill. min. vorzulesen. Ich habe ihn ja nicht: ich habe keinen einzigen Grad in Handen, nicht einmal meine eigene Aufsätze.

Ich habe auch in des Philo Provinzen eine Art von Eid, Versicherung oder Betheuerung: bey der Ehre des ⊙o: beym ⊙, eingeführt. Man gebraucht sie nur, um sie nicht zu profaniren, bey den wichtigsten Vorfällen.

Wer

PLATE 4 — Diagram of Weishaupt's System. From *Nachtrag von Weitern Originalschriften der Illuminatensekte,* p. 32, muchen, 1787.

MEMOIRS,

Illuſtrating the

HISTORY of JACOBINISM

Written in FRENCH by

THE ABBE BARRUEL,

And tranſlated into ENGLISH by

THE HON. ROBERT CLIFFORD, F.R.S. & A.S.

Princes and Nations ſhall diſappear from the face of the Earth . . . and this REVOLUTION ſhall be the WORK OF SECRET SOCIETIES,

Weiſhaupt's Diſcourſe for the Myſteries.

PART I.

THE ANTICHRISTIAN CONSPIRACY.

Second Edition, reviſed and corrected.

LONDON:
Printed for the TRANSLATOR,
By T. BURTON, *No.* 11, *Gate-ſtreet, Lincoln's-Inn Fields*.
Sold by E. BOOKER, No. 56, *New Bond-ſtreet*.

1798.

PLATE 5 — *Memoirs Illustrating the History of Jacobinism*
(Title page)

CONTENTS.

PLATE 6 — *Memoirs Illustrating the Histroy of Jacobinism (Table of contents)*

CONTENTS.

PLATE 6A — *Memoirs Illustrating the Histroy of Jacobinism*
(Table of contents con't)

The initiates who made up the outer rings were told that the great purpose of the Illuminati was *"to make of the human race, without any distinction of nation, condition, or profession, one good and happy family."*

All initiates were required to take an oath to bind themselves "to perpetual silence and unshakable royalty and submission to the Order, in the person of my superiors; here making a faithful and complete surrender of my private judgment, my own will, and every narrow-minded employment of my own power and am ready to serve it with my fortune, my honor and my blood.... The friends and enemies of the Order shall be my friends and enemies; and with respect to both I will conduct myself as directed by the Order ... (and) devote myself to its increase and promotion, and therein to employ all my ability ... without reservation" (*Proofs of a Conspiracy*, p.71).

By way of warning as to the consequences of betraying the Order, the initiate took part in a ceremony during which he was warned that "If you are only a traitor and perjurer, learn that all your brothers are called upon to arm themselves against you. Do not hope to escape or to find a place of safety. Wherever you are, shame, remorse, and the rage of our brothers will pursue you and torment you to the innermost recesses of your entrails" (Nesta Webster, *World Revolution*, 1921, p.14).

By the time the member had reached the "inner circles" his oath of absolute secrecy and unquestioning obedience had become deadly serious. Only at this stage was he finally allowed to see the ultimate aims of the Order: (1) The abolition of all ordered governments; (2) Abolition of private property; (3) Abolition of inheritance; (4) Abolition of patriotism; (5) Abolition of all religion; (6) Abolition of the family (i.e. morality, marriage and the proper education of children, and (7) The creation of a New World Order or World Government.

Naturally, all members were never allowed to see the true goals of the Order. They were assured that the sole purpose for the society was to assure "the happiness of the human race."

Weishaupt had a subtle but clear-cut plan to destroy religion: "I have contrived an explanation which has every advantage; is inviting to Christians of every communion; gradually frees them from all religious prejudices; cultivates the social virtues; and animates them by a great, a feasible, a speedy prospect of universal happiness, in a state of liberty and moral equality, freed from the obstacles which subordination, rank and riches continually throw in our way. My explanation is accurate, and complete, my means are effectual and irresistible. Our secret association works in a way that nothing can withstand, and man shall soon be free and happy" (*Proofs of a Conspiracy*, p.64).

This plan proved extremely successful not only with the novices, but with men of all ranks and ages: "The most admirable thing of all," wrote Weishaupt to Cato, "is that great Protestant and Reformed theologians (Lutherans and Calvinists) who belong to our Order really believe they see in it the true and genuine mind of the Christian religion. *Oh man, what can not you be brought to believe*" (*World Revolution*, p.13).

Weishaupt was a master criminal of the type that appears at rare intervals in human history, one who alone can aspire to attaining mastery over the world by diabolical ingenuity and utter ruthlessness. He undertook to be all things to all men — and women — and promised everyone the fulfillment of their hopes and aspirations, no matter how contradictory. Weishaupt was the king of confidence men!

He demanded blind obedience to the party line as directed by himself. Lies, contradictions and deceit were the order of the day. He had no scruples about saying that he sought to lure dupes into his organization. "These people swell our numbers and fill our treasury; get busy and make these people nibble at our bait but do not tell them our secrets [they were not to be admitted to the secret degrees and knowledge of the conspiracy to enslave them, the true purpose of the Order]. They must be made to believe that the low degree that they have reached is the highest."

The Protestant princes and rulers of Germany were pleased with Weishaupt's plan to destroy the Catholic Church, and they sought to join the Order. These men brought with them control of the Masonic Order, into which they initiated Weishaupt and his co-conspirators in 1777. To prevent the rulers from realizing the true purpose of the Illuminati, Weishaupt limited them to the lower degrees.

On July 16, 1782, at the Congress of Wilhelmsbad, an alliance between Illuminism and Freemasonry was finally sealed. This pact joined together all the leading secret societies of the day — and united "not less than three million members all over the world." The actual effect of this merger on the subsequent history of the world has never been appreciated by historians.

"What passed at this terrible Congress will never be known to the outside world, for even those men who were drawn unwittingly into the movement, and now heard for the first time the designs of the leaders, were under oath to reveal nothing. One honest Freemason, Comte de Vireu, ... when questioned on the 'tragic secrets' he brought back with him, replied: 'I will not confide them to you. I can only tell you that this is very much more serious than you think. The conspiracy that has been woven is so well thought out that it will be, so to speak, impossible for the Monarchy and the Church to escape from it.' From that time on, says his biographer, M. Costa de Beauregard, 'the Comte de Vireu could only speak of Freemasonry with horror" (*World Revolution*, p.18).

During the next few years there was a movement which brought about the emancipation of the Jews in Europe. Prior to that time Jews had been barred from joining the Masonic Order: that ban was lifted. It was also decided to move the headquarters of Illuminized Freemasonry to Frankfurt, the stronghold of Jewish finance.

The Order expanded rapidly but was soon troubled by dissension. Krigge, one of Weishaupt's henchmen, who held the post of director of the provinces, attempted to usurp some of Weishaupt's "glory" and was relieved of his position. He left the Order.

People became intensely interested in the activities of the Illuminati as a result of the exposure of their diabolical plans. In 1778 four more leading members of the Illuminati left the Order and testified before a Court of Inquiry called by the Elector of Bavaria. Their public testimony removed all doubt about the Satanic nature of Illuminism. On October 11, 1785, the Bavarian authorities raided Zwack's house and discovered a mountainous array of Illuminati documents. These showed quite clearly that the Order planned to bring about a "universal revolution that should deal the death-blow to society.... This revolution will be the work of the secret societies, and that is one of our great mysteries."

The dreadful danger posed by the Illuminati became clear to the Bavarian government. They decided to let the documents speak for themselves and had them published and circulated as widely as possible. This official document was titled *Original Writings of the Order and Sect of the Illuminati*. The governments of Europe ignored the warning contained in it.

Shortly thereafter Zwack left the country and Weishaupt, with a price on his head, took refuge with one of his royal adepts, the Duke of Saxe-Gotha.

This apparent break-up of the Illuminati served well the cause of the conspirators. They now got busy circulating the news that the Illuminati was a thing of the past. This lie has been perpetuated ever since by "historians" anxious to cover up the truth about the Illuminati's subsequent activities.

It now became more important than ever that the words "Illuminati" or "Illuminism" be removed from public use. As the instructions to the degree of Regent put it: "The great strength of our Order lies in its concealment; never let it appear in any place in its own name, but always covered by another name, and another occupation" (Robison, p.195). We will now see how precisely those instructions have been carried out.

The Order of the Illuminati started when the American Revolution was already under way, and played no part in it. However, before the Colonies were united, the Constitution adopted, and our Republic established, fifteen Lodges of the Illuminati were formed in the thirteen Colonies. The Columbian Lodge of the Order of the Illuminati was established in New York City in 1785: members included Governor DeWitt Clinton, and later Clinton Roosevelt, Charles Dana and Horace Greeley. The following year a Lodge was established in Virginia with which was identified Thomas Jefferson. When Weishaupt's diabolical plans were exposed by the Bavarian government, Jefferson defended him as an "enthusiastic philanthropist."

A number of strong warnings were issued about the activities of the Illuminati in America. On July 19, 1798, David Pappen, President of Harvard University, issued a strong warning to the

A

V I E W

OF THE

New-England Illuminati:

WHO ARE INDEFATIGABLY ENGAGED IN

DESTROYING THE *RELIGION* AND GO-
VERNMENT OF THE *UNITED STATES*;

UNDER A FEIGNED REGARD FOR THEIR SAFETY—AND
UNDER AN IMPIOUS ABUSE OF TRUE RELIGION.

THE SECOND EDITION.

PHILADELPHIA:
PRINTED BY JAMES CAREY, No. 16, CHESNUT-STREET.

1799.

[*Copy-Right ſecured.*]

PLATE 7 — A VIEW OF THE NEW-ENGLAND ILLUMINATI: WHO ARE INDEFATIGABLY ENGAGED IN DESTROYING THE RELIGION AND GOVERNMENT OF THE UNITED STATES; UNDER A FEIGNED REGARD FOR THEIR SAFETY—AND UNDER AN IMPIOUS ABUSE OF TRUE RELIGION.

graduating class and lectured them on the influence Illuminism was beginning to have on the American scene. President Timothy Dwight of Yale University issued a similar warning.

Also in 1798, George Washington sent a letter to a G. W. Snyder in which he stated: "It is not my intention to doubt that the doctrine of the Illuminati and the principles of Jacobinism has not spread to the United States. On the contrary, no one is more satisfied of this fact than I am.

"The idea that I meant to convey was that I did not believe the Lodges of Freemasonry had, as societies, endeavored to propagate the diabolical tenets.

"That individuals of them may have done it, or that the founder or instruments employed to found the democratic societies in the United States may have had this object, and actually had a separation of the people from their government in view, is too evident to be questioned" (*The Writings of George Washington,* published by the U.S. Government Printing Office, 1941, Vol. 20, p.518).

The fact that George Washington was gravely concerned about the threat posed to the United States is amply demonstrated in his famous Farewell Address, delivered September 17, 1796. This document probably ranks second only to the Constitution in national importance.

Washington expressed his heartfelt wish that "heaven may continue to give you the choicest tokens of its beneficence ... [and] that the free Constitution which is the work of your hands may be sacredly maintained: that its administration in every department may be stamped with wisdom and virtue." He then declared the "apprehension of danger" that prompted him to "offer to your solemn contemplation, *and to recommend to your frequent review,* some sentiments which are the result of much reflection, of no inconsiderable observation, *and which appear to me all-important to the permanency of your felicity as a people...*

"But as it is easy to foresee that from different causes, and from different quarters, much pain will be taken, many artifices employed, to weaken in your minds the conviction of this truth: as this is the point of your political fortress against which the batteries of internal and external enemies will be most constantly and actively (though often covertly and insidiously) directed, it is of infinite moment that you should properly estimate the immense value of your national union to your collective and individual happiness...

"All obstructions to the executions of the law, all combinations and associations, under whatever plausible character, with the real design to direct, control, counteract, or awe the regular deliberation and action of the constituted authorities, are destructive of this fundamental principle, and of fatal tendency." Such "combinations and associations ... are likely in the course of time and things, to become potent enemies by which cunning, ambitious, and unprincipled men will be able to subvert the power of the people and usurp for themselves the reins of government: *destroying afterwards the very engines which have lifted them to unjust dominion...*

"One method of assault may be to effect in the forms of the Constitution alteration which will impair the energy of the system, and thus to undermine what cannot be directly overthrown ... *The jealousy of a free people ought to be constantly awake, since history and experience prove that foreign influence is one of the most baneful foes to Republican government...*

"The great rule of conduct for us in regard to foreign nations is, in extending our commercial relations, to have with them as little political connection as possible. As far as we have already formed engagement, let them be fulfilled with perfect good faith. Here let us stop...

"Why forego the advantages of so peculiar a situation? Why quit our own to stand upon foreign ground? Why by interweaving our destiny with that of any part of Europe, entangle our peace and prosperity in the toils of European ambition, rivalship, interest, humor or caprice?

"It is our clear policy to steer clear of permanent alliance with any portion of the foreign world..."

For one hundred and twenty years this document formed the basis of our foreign policy: as a result we prospered as no other nation in history.

One year after Washington spoke these powerful words Professor John Robison published his famous *Proofs of a Conspiracy,* in which he warned of Illuminati infiltration of Masonic lodges.

In 1796 John Adams, who had been instrumental in organizing Masonic lodges in New England, decided to oppose Thomas Jefferson in his bid for the presidency. He made a major issue of the fact that Jefferson — who had been minister to France (1785-1789), and was frankly sympathetic to the Illuminati-fomented Reign of Terror — was using Masonic lodges for subversive purposes.

John Quincy Adams wrote three letters to Col. William Stone giving details of the charges. The information contained in these letters is credited with having won his father (John Adams) the presidency. The existence of these letters was first brought to the public's attention by Commander William Guy Carr in *Pawns in the Game.* Until recently they were in the Rittenberg Square Library in Philadelphia. They have now mysteriously vanished.

It is difficult, if not impossible, to uncover a clear picture of Illuminati activities in the United States in the early part of the 20th century. This is due to the fact that Weishaupt's followers wholeheartedly believed in their leader's instruction that "the great strength of our Order lies in its concealment; let it never appear in any place in its own name, but always covered by another name and another occupation" (Robison, p.195).

To trace their activities further, we must look for prominent individuals and groups which adhere to the Satanic tenets of Illuminism. It is "by their fruits" that we shall know them. They will all be working toward the attainment of the goal of the Illuminati — the destruction of national sovereignty and the establishment of a New World Order.

In 1829 American Illuminists sponsored a series of lectures in New York by English Illuminist Frances "Fanny" Wright. She advocated the entire Weishauptian program including Communism made more palatable by the label of "equal opportunity and equal rights," atheism, emancipation and free love. Those present were informed that the Illuminati intended to unite the nihilist and the atheist groups with all other subversive organizations into an organization known as Communism. This new destructive force was to be used to foment future wars and revolutions. Clinton Roosevelt (a distant ancestor of FDR), Charles Dana and Horace Greeley were appointed a committee to raise funds for this new undertaking.

Roosevelt and his group posed as champions of the working class. They advocated "noble and worthy" causes and, at least in their early writings, stated that they were seeking to uphold the U.S. Constitution. They declared their intention to "kick the moneychangers out of the temple," and their opposition to monopolies. All these declared goals appealed to the "peasants."

Clinton Roosevelt was so taken by his own perceived importance that, in 1841, he published a book, *The Science of Government Founded on Natural Law*. In the preface of his small book, Roosevelt leaves no doubt in the mind of the reader with regard to his own superior wisdom: "A large work would have been more imposing in appearance, but the truth is, long works and long speeches are rarely made by men of powerful thought. The giant draws up by the roots the tree, which the pygmy hacks upon the lifelong day... The giant says the work is done and points him to his prostrate enemy." Yes, he was clearly an "Illuminated" one!

Roosevelt's book is clearly in line with Weishaupt's instructions that the "Superiors of the Order are to be regarded as the most perfect and enlightened of men; they must not even permit any doubts of their infallibility."

The title of the book is interesting also, for its adheres to Weishaupt's teachings. Weishaupt decreed that all arts, sciences, and religion must be abolished and replaced by "social(ist) science of government" as taught by himself and pronounced by him to the only true science. Weishaupt further stated that it must be based on "natural law."

In the *Science of Government*, Roosevelt outlined the plans of the Illuminati for the regimentation of mankind under the control of those who, like himself, are the "enlightened" ones. He revealed their plans to emasculate and then destroy the Constitution which he likened to a "leaky vessel" which was "hastily put together when we left the British flag." He declared his contempt for his Creator with his declaration that "there is no God of justice to order things aright on earth; if there be a God, he is a malicious and vengeful being, who created us for misery."

Just how well aware the latter-day Roosevelts were of plans to create such a New World Order is evidenced by the following passage from Roosevelt: *The Story of a Friendship*, by Owen Wister,

THE

SCIENCE OF GOVERNMENT,

FOUNDED ON

NATURAL LAW.

BY

CLINTON ROOSEVELT.

NEW YORK:
PUBLISHED BY DEAN & TREVETT,
121 FULTON STREET.
1841.

Entered according to Act of Congress, in the year 1841, by
CLINTON ROOSEVELT,
In the Clerk's Office of the District Court for the Southern
District of New York.

PLATE 8 – THE SCIENCE OF GOVERNMENT FOUNDED ON NATURAL LAW.
(Title Page)

Macmillan, 1930, p.52. It is an account of a conversation which took place in the late 1890s:

"'How long do you give the government at Washington to last,' I asked Teddy [Roosevelt] and [Cabot] Lodge as we sat lunching.

"Those two students and writers — and makers — of history, well versed in the causes which have led to the downfall of empires, kingdoms and Republics that have had their day and gone into the night, were both silent for a moment; then one of them said: 'About fifty years.'

"Which of the two set this limit, I do not recall; I remember only that the other did not contradict him."

In 1830 Adam Weishaupt died at the age of 83. In an effort to convince the world that Illuminism was dead and thus no longer a threat, he staged an impressive death-bed "repentance" and rejoined the Catholic Church.

In 1834 Giuseppe Mazzini, the Italian revolutionary leader, was appointed by the Illuminati as director of their revolutionary program around the world. He held the position until he died in 1872.

At about this same time an obscure intellectual named Moses Mordecai Marx Levy, alias Karl Marx, joined one of the branches of the Illuminati Conspiracy known as the League of the Just. In 1847 he was hired to write what became known as *The Communist Manifesto*. It was basically a statement of their overall plans for the future. Marx was of such little importance that for the first twenty years after publication his name didn't even appear on it. Marx was just a pawn in the game being played by the real powers behind the scene. Unbiased historians have long since recognized that there was nothing new or original in *The Communist Manifesto*: it was plainly a plagiarized rehash of the plans of Adam Weishaupt and his disciple Clinton Roosevelt.

The next important personality to emerge on the American scene as a leader of the Satanic Conspiracy was Albert Pike. He was chosen by Mazzini to head their operations in the United States.

Pike was born in Boston on December 29, 1809. His parents, though of modest circumstances, succeeded in sending him to Harvard. During the Civil War Pike served as a brigadier-general

Manifest

der

Kommunistischen Partei.

Veröffentlicht im Februar 1848.

Proletarier aller Länder vereinigt euch.

London.

Gedruckt in der Office der „Bildungs-Gesellschaft für Arbeiter"

von J. E. Burghard

46, Liverpool Street, Bishopsgate.

PLATE 9 — The cover of the first edition of the *Communist Manifesto*

GENERAL ALBERT PIKE, 33°
Sovereign Grand Commander of the Ancient and Accepted Scottish Rite of Freemasonry of the Southern Jurisdiction, U. S. A.

PLATE 10 — Albert Pike

PLATE 11 — Geuseppe Mazzini

in the Confederate Army. The Confederate authorities appointed him Indian Commissioner charged with conducting negotiations with the most savage tribes to raise an army of warriors. To aid him in the creation of the new army, he was made governor over Indian Territory. When the army, composed of Chickasawa, Comanches, Cherokees, Miami, Osages, Kansas and Choctawa came into being, it was placed under Pike's command. Among all the tribes he was known as "the faithful pale-face friend and protector."

Pike and his army of savages participated in an orgy of atrocities under the cloak of legitimate warfare. This barbarism was so terrible that the foreign powers intervened. Representations made by England, threatening intervention in the name of humanity, finally compelled Jefferson Davis to disband his auxiliary Indian troops.

Albert Pike was a diabolical genius of the first magnitude. He was a man of many talents who invariably used his abilities to destructive ends. Pike was very literate, being able to both read and write in 16 ancient languages. He was an avowed worshipper of Lucifer by name, who practiced necromancy and all forms of sorcery.

As top Illuminists, Pike and Mazzini worked in unison. Pike took control of the theosophical side of their operations, while Mazzini was in charge of the political. When the Grand Orient Lodges of Masonry become suspect as a result of Mazzini's revolutionary activities in Europe, Mazzini presented a Master Plan to Pike who was by then Sovereign Grand Commander of the Ancient and Accepted Scottish Rite of Freemasonry. Mazzini's plan was simple. Being a practical man, he understood that it was inadvisable to favor one rite to the exclusion of all the others.

In a letter to Pike, dated January 22, 1870, he wrote: "We must allow all of the confederations to continue just as they are, with their systems, their central authorities and their diverse modes of correspondence between high grades of the same rite, organized as they are at present, but we must create a super rite, which will remain unknown, *to which we will call those Masons of*

MORALS AND DOGMA

OF THE

ANCIENT AND ACCEPTED SCOTTISH RITE

OF

FREEMASONRY

PREPARED FOR THE

SUPREME COUNCIL OF THE THIRTY-THIRD DEGREE,

FOR THE

SOUTHERN JURISDICTION OF THE UNITED STATES,

AND

PUBLISHED BY ITS AUTHORITY.

CHARLESTON,
A.·. M.·. 5680

LUCIFER, the *Light-bearer!* Strange and mysterious name to give to the Spirit of Darkness! Lucifer, the Son of the Morning! Is it *he* who bears the *Light*, and with its splendors intolerable blinds feeble, sensual, or selfish Souls? Doubt it not!

321

PLATE 12 — *Morals and Dogma* (Title page). Also a reproduction of a section of p. 321

high degree whom we shall select. With regard to our brothers in Masonry, these men must be pledged to the strictest secrecy. Through this supreme rite, we will govern all Freemasonry, which will become the one international center, the more powerful because its direction will be unknown" (*Occult Theocrasy*, by Lady Queenborough, pp.208,209).

Historian Dominico Margiotta tells us that "it was agreed that the existence of this rite would be kept strictly secret and that no mention of it would ever be made in the Assemblies of the Lodges and Inner Shrines of other rites, even when by accident, the meeting might be composed exclusively of brothers having the perfect initiation, for the secret of the new institution was only to be divulged with the greatest caution to a chosen few belonging to the ordinary high grades" (*Adriano Lemmi*, p.97).

Pike organized this ultra-secret organization under the name of The New and Reformed Palladian Rite. He established three supreme councils; one in Charleston, N.C., another in Rome, Italy, and the third in Berlin, Germany.

Historian Dr. Bataille wrote that "this super rite, which is Masonic Luciferian spiritism, must not be confused with the machinery of high Masonry. Palladism is the cult of Satan [Lucifer] in the inner shrines of a rite superimposed on all the rites. It is a cult, a religion" (*Le Diable au XIX Siecle*, p.346). This fact will be proved beyond a shadow of doubt a little later.

Evidence gathered from a variety of sources strongly indicates that scientists working with the Illuminati had discovered the secrets of wireless telegraphy decades before Marconi invented the radio. Bataille, for example, wrote in 1894 that Gallatin Mackey (a top Illuminist) once "showed me that Arcula Mystica (Magic Box), of which there are only seven examples in existence, at Charleston, Rome, Berlin, Washington, Monte Video, Naples and Calcutta.

"When the Supreme Dogmatical chief wishes to communicate, for example, with the head of political action, he presses his finger on the Statuette Ignis and on the Statuette Ratio: these sink into their sockets and at the same instant a strong whistling is heard in Rome, in the office where Lemmi keeps his Arcula Mystica; Lemmi opens his box and sees the Statuette of Ignis sunk, while tiny, harmless flames issue from the throat of the silver toad. Then he knows that the Supreme Pontiff of Charleston wishes to speak to him. He presses down the Statuette of Ratio in his box and from then on the conversation between the two chiefs proceeds, each one speaking into the mouthpiece, while at the same time holding to his ear the small silver ball.

"At the end of the conversation, each chief replaces the golden statuette by pulling them up by the head.

"Each Sovereign Master of a Directory travels with his Arcula Mystica. The box is personally confided to him" (*Le Diable au XIX Siecle*, pp.391,392). It was the discovery of this secret that enabled intelligence officers to understand how seemingly unrelated "incidents" took place simultaneously around the world which aggravated a situation and developed into a war or revolution.

Albert Pike's most famous work is *Morals and Dogma*, published in 1871. Following the example of Clinton Roosevelt, the "Supreme Pontiff" of Universal Freemasonry "lets it all hang out" at the beginning of his book. He leaves no doubt as to what he has in mind:

"Force, unregulated or irregulated, is not only wasted in the void like that of gunpowder burned in the open air, and steam unconfined by science; but striking in the dark, and its blows meeting only the air, they recoil and bruise itself. It is destruction and ruin ... not growth and progress...

"The blind force of the people is a Force that must be economized, and also managed, ... it must be regulated by intellect.

"To attack the citadels built up on all sides against the human race by superstitions, despotisms, and prejudices, the force must have a brain and a law. Then its deeds of daring produce permanent results, and there is real progress. Then there are sublime conquests... When all Forces are combined, and guided by the Intellect [the Illuminated ones!], and regulated by the Rule of Right, and Justice, and of combined and systematic movement and effort, the great revolution prepared for by the ages will begin to march... It is because Force is ill regulated, that revolutions prove failures" (*Morals and Dogma*, pp.1,2).

The theological dogma of Albert Pike is laid out in the Instructions issued by him on July 14, 1889, to the 23 Supreme Councils of the world:

"That which we say to the crowd is: 'We worship a God, but it is the God one adores without superstitions.'

"To you, Sovereign Grand Instructors General, we say this, that you may repeat it to the Brethren of the 32nd, 31st and 30th degrees: 'The Masonic religion should be, by all of us initiates of the high degrees, maintained in the purity of the Luciferian doctrine.

"'If Lucifer were not God, would Adonay [the Christian God] whose deeds prove his cruelty, perfidy and hatred of man, barbarism and repulsion of science, would Adonay and his priests culminate him?

"'Yes, Lucifer is God, and unfortunately Adonay is also God. For the eternal law is that there is no light without shade, no beauty without ugliness, no white without black, for the absolute can only exist as two Gods: darkness being necessary for light to serve as its foil as the pedestal is necessary to the statue, and the brake to the locomotive...

"'The doctrine of Satanism is heresy; and the true and pure philosophic religion is the belief in Lucifer, the equal of Adonay; but Lucifer, God of Light and God of Good is struggling for humanity against Adonay, the God of Darkness and Evil'" (*Le Femme et l'enfant dans la Franc-Maconnerie Universelle*, by A.C. De La Rive, p.588, and *Occult Theocrasy*, pp.220,221).

Illuminist propaganda would have us believe that all those who oppose Christianity are atheists. This is a deliberate lie designed to hide the secret plans of those who are directing the Luciferian Conspiracy. They remain behind the scenes, their identity and true purpose hidden from even the vast majority of those they deceive into doing their will. They know that the final success of their diabolical plan to usurp the powers of world government through their New World Order depends on their ability to keep the truth hidden from people until it is too late to stop its execution.

In a remarkable letter dated August 15, 1871, which until recently was on display at the British Museum Library in London, Pike gave Mazzini details of the Luciferian plan for world conquest. In graphic detail he outlined plans for three world wars. He stated that in the third of these wars "we will unleash the Nihilists and Atheists, and we shall provoke a formidable social cataclysm which in all its horrors will show clearly to the nations the effect of absolute atheism, origin of savagery and of the most bloody turmoil. Then everywhere, the citizens, obliged to defend themselves against the world minority of revolutionaries, will exterminate these destroyers of civilization, and the multitude, disillusioned with Christianity, whose deistic spirits will from that moment be without compass [direction], anxious for an ideal, but without knowing where to render its adoration, will receive the pure light through the universal manifestation of the pure doctrine of Lucifer, brought finally out into the public view, a manifestation which will result from the general reactionary movement which will follow the destruction of Christianity and atheism, both conquered and exterminated at the same time."

CHAPTER SIX

ILLUMINATI PART II

Political and religious philosophers have long since recognized the fact that the most effective way in which to conquer a man is to conquer his mind. Education, then, is where the action is in the battle to conquer the world.

The leaders of the Illuminati Conspiracy realized from the beginning that if they were to succeed in their plan to conquer and rule the world they had to gain control of the schools, colleges and universities.

As Lady Queenborough pointed out in the 1930s: "A mind that is positive cannot be controlled. For the purpose of occult dominion minds must therefore be rendered passive and negative in order that control may be achieved. Minds consciously working to a definite end are a power, and power can oppose power for good or for evil. The scheme for world dominion might be doomed by the recognition of this principle alone, but, as it is unfortunately unrecognized, it remains unchallenged.

"Destruction, Materialism, Imposition. These are the three points of Albert Pike and they seem to be ruling the world today" (*Occult Theocrasy*, p.581).

Some years ago this author heard the president of a small, independent college state that at the turn of the 20th century the "educational system jumped the tracks of sanity and went careening off into the wilderness ... [and that since that time] educators have been funneling poison into the plastic, unsuspecting minds" of those entrusted to their care. Those statements are absolutely correct — except for one vitally important point: Education didn't "jump the tracks" — it was deliberately derailed. Let's understand the facts.

In *Tragedy and Hope,* the late Professor Carroll Quigley openly boasted that he had for many years been an elitist "Insider" and had first-hand knowledge of how the Conspiracy developed around the world. Regarding education in England, he said: "Until 1870 there was no professorship of fine arts at Oxford, but in that year, thanks to a Slade bequest, John Ruskin was named to such a chair. *He hit Oxford like an earthquake,* not so much because he talked of fine arts, but because he also talked about the empire and England's downtrodden masses, and above all because he talked about all three of these things as moral issues" (p.130).

JOHN RUSKIN

John Ruskin (1819-1890) was born in London, the son of prosperous wine merchant from whom he inherited a large fortune. His biographer, Kenneth Clark, tells us that Ruskin *"saw that the state must take control of the means of production and distribution, and organize them for the good of the community as a whole; but he was prepared to place the control of the state in the hands of a single man.* 'My continual aim has been to show the eternal superiority of some men to others, sometimes even of one man to all others.' He had a very low opinion of democracy... In spite of its materialistic philosophy, he would, I think, have approved of Communism; the peasant communes in China, in particular, are exactly on his model. He would not have thought the cure worse than the disease because he could not imagine a worse disease than the capitalist society of the nineteenth century" (*Ruskin Today*, pp.267,268).

In essence, Ruskin's doctrine was pure Illuminism! This fact was largely hidden behind a carefully erected facade. "Ruskin wrote to the Oxford undergraduates as members of the privileged, ruling class. He told them they were the possessors of a magnificent tradition of education, beauty, rule of law, freedom, decency, and self-discipline but that this tradition could not be saved, and did not deserve to be saved, unless it could be extended to the lower classes of England itself *and to the non-English masses throughout the world*. If this precious tradition were not extended to these two great majorities, the minority of upper-class Englishmen would ultimately be submerged by these majorities and the tradition lost. To prevent this, the tradition must be extended to the masses and to the empire" (Quigley, p.130).

Ruskin and his secret backers had thrown out some juicy bait and it was hungrily seized upon by the Oxford students, all of whom came from the "top drawer" of British society.

"Ruskin's message had a *sensational impact*. His inaugural lecture was copied out in longhand by one undergraduate, Cecil Rhodes, who kept it with him for thirty years. Rhodes (1853-1902) feverishly exploited the diamond and gold fields of South Africa, rose to be prime minister of the Cape Colony (1890-96), contributed money to political parties, controlled parliamentary seats both in England and South Africa.... Rhodes inspired devoted support for his goals in South Africa and in England. *With financial support from Lord Rothschild and Alfred Beit, he was able to*

CECIL RHODES

monopolize the gold mines of South Africa as De Beers Consolidated Mines and to build up a great gold mining enterprise as Consolidated Goldfields. In the middle of the 1890s Rhodes had a personal income of at least a million pounds sterling (then about five million [1890] dollars) which he spent so freely for his mysterious purposes that he was usually overdrawn on his account. These purposes centered on his desire to federate the English-speaking people *and to bring all the habitable portions of the world under their control. For this purpose, Rhodes left part of his great fortune to found the Rhodes Scholarships at Oxford in order to spread the English ruling-class tradition throughout the English-speaking world as Ruskin had wanted"* (pp.130,131).

Dr. Quigley went on to tell how many members of the British ruling class became "devoted disciples" of Ruskin and "devoted the rest of their lives" to carrying out his ideas.

On February 5, 1891, Rhodes' group joined with one from Cambridge University, led by William Stead, "an ardent social reformer," to "form a secret society of which Rhodes had been dreaming for sixteen years" (p.131). This secret society, following Weishaupt's pattern, had "outer circles" known as the "Association of Helpers." In 1909-1913 Lord Alfred Milner "organized semi-secret groups, known as round table groups, in chief British dependencies and in the United States. These still function in eight countries. They kept in touch with each other by personal correspondence and frequent visits, and through an influential quarterly magazine, *The Round Table,* founded in 1910, and largely supported by Sir Abe Bailey's money. In 1919 they founded the Royal Institute of International Affairs (Chatham House) for which the chief financial supporters were Sir Abe Bailey *and the Astor family* (owners of *The Times*).

After 1925, a somewhere similar structure of organizations, known as the Institute of Pacific Affairs, was set up in twelve countries holding territory in the Pacific area, the units in each British dominion existing on an interlocking basis with the Round Table Group and the Royal Institute of International Affairs....

"The power and influence of this Rhodes-Milner group in British imperial affairs and in foreign policy since 1889, although not widely recognized, *can hardly be exaggerated.*

"Similar Institutes of International Affairs were established in British dominions and *in the United States (where it was known as the Council on Foreign Affairs)* in the period 1919-27" (pp.132-135).

ROCKEFELLER'S GENERAL EDUCATION FUND

In the early 1900s one of the most despised names in America was that of Rockefeller. Old John D. Rockefeller had earned his reputation with unprecedented guile, deceit and greed. His name was synonymous with ruthless exploitation. He often stated that "*competition is a sin.*"

John D. Rockefeller in 1911

In a effort to change his image (*but not his character*) John D. hired Ivy Lee, one of the nation's leading ad men. At Lee's suggestion, Mr. Standard Oily (a notorious skinflint) carried a pocketful of dimes around with him and handed them to young children when he made rare public appearances.

As part of his "image improvement" program, Rockefeller set up a series of foundations and trusts. Outwardly, these were presented to the public as an effort on Rockefeller's part to better the lot of the American people, by financing projects in education, medicine, and religion. But, true to John D's "deep conspiratorial nature," there was always a catch!

As Gary Allen points out in *The Rockefeller File,* "he had an even more Machiavellian scheme in mind. He would 'give' money away to foundations under his control and then have those foundations spend the money in ways which brought even more power and profits to the Rockefeller Empire. The money 'given' away would be bread cast upon the waters. But bread that almost always had a hook in it. John D. was to refer to this as the 'principle of scientific giving" (pp.37,38).

This fact was clearly demonstrated when it came to Rockefeller's relationship with education. John D. enrolled the aid of Fred Gates, who earlier had enjoyed immense success as a front man for the Pillsbury flour company, to organize his General Education Board. The real purpose of this board was not, as some were led to believe at the time, to upgrade the standard of American education and so benefit the nation as a whole. Just like Clinton Roosevelt and Albert Pike before them, they showed their hand in their first publication. They followed a pattern laid out more than one hundred years earlier by Adam Weishaupt, who wrote that "it is necessary to gain the common people to our Order. The best means to that end is influence in the schools."

It would be difficult to express more precisely the objectives of Weishaupt's Conspiracy in the field of educational propaganda than was done in *Occasional Letter No. 1* of Rockefeller's General Education Board. It was issued in 1904:

"In our dreams, we have limitless resources and the people yield themselves with perfect docility to our molding hands. The present education conventions fade from their minds, and unhampered by tradition, we work our own good will upon a grateful and responsive rural folk. We shall not try to make these people or any of their children into philosophers or men of learning, or men of science. We have not to raise up from among them authors, editors, poets or men of letters. We shall not search for embryo great artists, painters, musicians nor lawyers, doctors, preachers, politicians, statesmen, of whom we have an ample supply.

"The task we set before ourselves is very simple as well as a very beautiful one, to train these people as we find them to a perfectly ideal life just where they are. So we will organize our children and teach them to do in a perfect way the things their fathers and mothers are doing in an imperfect way, in the homes, in the shops and on the farms."

All the important elements of Weishaupt's Illuminism are found in this letter. First, we see the pose of "philanthropy;" second, the intent to brain wash or "mold" the people; third, the elimination of tradition, science and real learning; fourth, the dictatorship objective; fifth, the intent to regiment the peasants in a caste system — "just as they are;" sixth, the plan to reduce national intelligence to the lowest common denominator and to destroy parental influence (and so break up the family); seventh, total contempt for the peasants; eighth, the element of subversion and Un-Americanism — the declared intent to overthrow accepted customs to serve the purposes of the Rockefellers and their cohorts, and, lastly, "perfectibilism," the "perfecting" of human nature, which was also Weishaupt's fake aim.

The corruptive influences that the Rockefeller Foundations, and others, have had on the American school system is thoroughly documented. When a Congressional Committee, headed by Carroll Reece of Tennessee, attempted to hold an open investigation into the activities of the foundations, they ran into a solid wall of opposition from the "powers that be" in the nation's capital, and it had to be disbanded (Quigley, pp. 954, 955).

Four years later the Committee's general counsel, Rene Wormser, wrote an expose on the subject: it was titled, *Foundations: Their Power and Influence*. Wormser stated that the facts this Committee developed *"leads one to the conclusion that there was, indeed, something in the nature of an actual conspiracy among certain leading educators in the United States to bring about Socialism through the use of our school systems....*

"A very powerful complex of foundations and allied organizations has developed over the years to exercise a high degree of control over education. Part of this complex, and ultimately responsible for it, are the Rockefeller and Carnegie groups of foundations."

Rockefeller and his allies understood that in order to control the educational system they had to gain control of the teachers' colleges. This they accomplished over a period of years by making large grants to the leading universities for the alleged purpose of helping them develop and grow. But, true to Rockefeller's "principle of scientific giving," there was a hook in every grant. Rockefeller fronts always ended up on the boards of the institutions being "helped." This gave them a big say in the way they were run.

John Dewey was a leading figure in their overall plans. As head of the Teachers' College at Columbia University he grew in influence on the national educational scene. In 1919, with Rockefeller money, Dewey founded the Progressive Education Association to spread the philosophy of his masters. As time went by Dewey was joined by Ruggs, Counts, Kilpatrick and other Socialists. They wormed their way into positions of authority and set about using the educational system as a tool to accomplish their political goals.

In their writings and speeches they made no effort to hide the fact that their main objective was to lead the American nation — like a flock of dumb, unsuspecting sheep — in a Piped Piper procession into a Socialist Utopia where they would, like in every fairy tale, "live happily ever after." A few quotations should serve to prove this point. In 1933, Dr. Harold Ruggs, in *The Great Technology*, revealed how they planned to bring America into the bondage of a Socialist state:

"A new public mind is to be created. How? Only by creating tens of millions of individual minds and welding them into a new social mind. Old stereotypes must be broken up and 'new climates of opinion' formed in the neighborhoods of America" (p.32).

"... through the schools of the world we shall disseminate a new conception of government — one that will embrace all the activities of men, one that will postulate the need of scientific control and operation of economic activities in the interest of all people" (p.271).

Dr. George Counts, a professor of education and a leading member of Dewey's "Frontier Thinkers," wrote that "the teachers should reach for power and then make the most of their conquest.... To the extent that they are allowed to fashion the curriculum and procedures of the schools they will definitely and positively influence the social attitudes, ideals and behavior of the coming generation" *(Dare the Schools Build a New Social Order?*, pp.28,29).

In the 1934 *Report on Education,* produced by the American Historical Association and sponsored by the Carnegie Foundation, Counts wrote that "the age of individualism and laissez-faire [freedom] in economy and government is closing and *a new age* of collectivism is emerging.

In *The New Republic*, July 29, 1936, Harold Laski, a leading British Socialist, stated that "stripped of its carefully neutral phrases, the Report is an educational program for a Socialist America."

Counts and his associates never denied this fact. In fact they stated that, to achieve their objective, basic "changes in our ideals" were needed (*Progressive Education*, April, 1932).

How are changes in the ideals of a nation brought about? Simply by changing *what* is taught in the educational system — and also in the churches and the mass media.

To accomplish the former goal, the new authorities in education had most of the basic textbooks scrapped or rewritten to plug the new Socialist line. Many new textbooks made their appearance in classrooms — all specifically designed to undermine traditional values and brainwash the students into an acceptance of Socialism, in which "Big Brother" Government would control every phase of peoples' lives.

The battle was on for the minds of the nation's youth, and the Socialists threw everything into their Blitzkrieg-type assault: no holds were barred. Newspapers, magazines and radio stations, all of which had been infiltrated by Leftists, took up the Socialist cause and the public was subjected to a subtle propaganda bombardment to further "the creation of a new social mind."

At first there were loud protests from those alert enough to realize that something was drastically wrong. The "progressive" educators changed their tactics: their attacks on the nation's heroes, customs and heritage were changed from being open to being implied and were thus much harder to detect by those who were not weighing and analyzing every word. From being nation-building institutions — foundational pillars in a basically sound society — the school and college systems were transformed into what is nothing more than incubators of degeneracy.

When we look at "education" today we see a situation which is very encouraging — even inspiring — *to our enemies!* The creators of "a new social mind" have done a thorough job!

The overview of the Education Establishment regarding American families and the children they produce has been laid out in no uncertain terms by their own spokesmen. These statements should suffice to demonstrate the point.

"The American family structure produces mentally ill children" — Ashley Montagu, (Lecture at Anaheim, California, November 9, 1970).

"Any child who believes in God is mentally ill" (Paul Brandwein, *The Social Sciences*, Harcourt Brace, 1970, p. 10).

"Every child in America who enters school at the age of five is mentally ill, because he comes to school with allegiance toward our elected officials, toward our founding fathers, toward our institutions, toward the preservation of this form of government ... patriotism, nationalism, sovereignty .... All these prove the child is sick, because the truly well individual is one who has rejected all those things and is what I call the true international child of the future" (Dr. Pierce, Harvard University, 1973).

REAPING THE CONSEQUENCES

One has only to listen to the average "man (or woman) in the street" — or question their beliefs (or lack thereof!) — to realize the stunning and frightening success of the Conspirators' onslaught on America through the educational system and other media of indoctrination.

Mostly, their reasoning processes have been so warped and bent out of shape by having liberal propaganda pumped into their plastic, unsuspecting minds from their earliest consciousness, that they have no real foundation upon which to base decisions relating to real life. They have not been trained to face up to real world situations — life as it really is! The educational process may have taught most people how to earn a living, but it has never taught them how to live. There is a vast difference.

Decades ago, Admiral Hyman Rickover summed up the situation very well: "America is reaping the consequences of the destruction of traditional education by the Dewey-Kilpatrick experimental philosophy. Dewey's ideas have led to the elimination of many academic subjects on the ground that they would not be useful in life... The student thus receives neither intellectual training nor the factual knowledge which will help him understand the world he lives in, or to make well-rounded decisions in his private life or as a responsible citizen" (*The Tablet*, August 11, 1959).

The awful truth of the Admiral's words should be startlingly evident when we honestly evaluate American society. The goals outlined in Rockefeller's *Occasional Letter Number One* have been achieved to a remarkable degree.

KARL MARX

Using Marx as a front, the Illuminati attempted to implement their plan for a world-wide revolution, but it proved a total failure. Marx's teachings never really fired the imagination of the people at any level of society — least of all the working class!

In London, in 1864, Marx organized the International Workingman's Association (later known as the First Socialist International). Their headquarters was moved to New York eight years later. Shortly thereafter they merged with the Socialist Party which was founded there in 1868.

In his own personal life Marx was a total failure. He was a leech who lived off other people: it is doubtful if he ever did an honest day's work in his life. His marriage resulted in six children. Marx, however, was so busy formulating theories to "uplift the downtrodden" that he never found time to support his own family. Three of his children died of starvation in infancy. Two others committed suicide: only one lived to maturity. When he died in 1883 only six people attended his funeral!

The Second Socialist International, founded in Paris on July 14, 1889, resulted from the realization that the "workers of the world" would not rally to the call of socialist leadership, but had to be manipulated through the organization and control of labor unions.

It was at this juncture that the Fabian Society and Lenin's Bolsheviks made their entrance on the world scene — and began to make real progress towards achieving the goals outlined by Weishaupt, Roosevelt, Marx and Pike. The only difference between these two groups were the methods they employed in working toward the same overall goal — the creation of a socialistic one-world society as envisioned by Marx (*A Manifesto*, Fabian Tract No.2, 1884). Since that time the Bolsheviks (Communists) have been working to bring it about by violent, revolutionary means. Of the Fabians, the *Encyclopedia Britannica*

(1973 edition, article on Fabian Socialism, Vol.20, pp.750,751) tells us that "the name is derived from that of the Roman General Fabius, the delayer, because of his deliberate, long-range strategy."

As a result, from the outset the Fabians worked toward the creation of a New World Order through the indoctrination of young scholars. They believed that eventually these intellectual revolutionaries could gain power and influence in the various opinion making and power wielding agencies of the world and so achieve their aims. Their tactics became known as "the doctrine of the inevitability of gradualism."

It should be noted that these were only two of the organizations through which the International Conspiracy was working. The real power has always been held by the bankers. Professor Quigley tells us that during the latter part of the nineteenth century the International Bankers, and their American counterparts, moved into "commercial banking and insurance on one side and into railroading and heavy industry on the other" and "were able to mobilize enormous wealth and wield enormous economic, political and social power. Popularly known as 'Society,' or the '400,' they lived a life of dazzling splendor. Sailing the ocean in great private yachts or traveling on land by private train, they moved in a ceremonious round between their spectacular estates and town houses in Palm Beach, Long Island, the Berkshires, Newport, and Bar Harbor, assembling from their fortress-like New York residences to attend the Metropolitan Opera under the critical eye of Mrs. Astor; or gathering for business meetings at the highest strategic level in the awesome presence of J. P. Morgan himself.

"The structure of financial controls created by the tycoons of 'Big Banking' and 'Big Business'... was of extraordinary complexity, one business fief being built on another, both being allied with semi-independent associates, the whole rearing upward into two pinnacles of economic and political power, of which one, centered in New York, was headed by J. P. Morgan and Company and the other, in Ohio, was headed by the Rockefeller family. When the two cooperated, as they generally did, they could influence the economic life of the country to a large degree and could almost control its political life, at least at the Federal level." They caused the "panic of 1907" and the collapse of two railroads, one in 1914 and the other in 1925 (Quigley, pp.71-73).

FEDERAL RESERVE SYSTEM

By the beginning of the Twentieth Century the American economy had grown so dynamic that the International Bankers were having great difficulty maintaining control of its development. Their power and authority was being challenged. A way had to be found to consolidate their position and thus ensure that their power would never be taken from them. They decided that a Central Bank had to be established — owned and operated by themselves.

For more than two hundred years these international banking families had dominated the European scene after establishing the Bank "of England" and other Central Banks in Germany, France, Italy, etc. Since their "coup of coups" in 1815, when they literally bought control of England for a few cents on the dollar, the Rothschilds dominated the banking scene (*Rothschilds, A Family Portrait*, by Frederic Morton). All their efforts to foist a Central Bank on the United States had met with failure. Our Constitution gave the Congress alone the authority "to coin money (and) regulate the value thereof."

Using the *created* financial panic of 1907 as an "example" of America's alleged great need of a centralized banking authority, a vast propaganda campaign was launched to sell the idea to the American public.

Some of the nation's leading bankers seemed opposed to the idea, but it was only a ploy. William McAdoo, Secretary of State and President Wilson's son-in-law, talked with these "opponents" of the plan to form a central bank: "These interviews with bankers led me to an interesting conclusion. I perceived gradually, through all the haze and smoke of controversy, that the banking world was not really as much opposed to the bill as it pretended to be ..." (*Autobio*graphy, p.225).

The Federal Reserve System (a Central Bank) came into being when the Federal Reserve Act passed Congress in late December, 1913. Under the Act, the International Bankers were granted the privilege of creating money out of nothing and of loaning it to the U.S. government at interest. The way had now been prepared for the looting of the American nation by the International Money Vultures.

"COLONEL" HOUSE

Around this time, the mysterious Colonel E. Mandell House (the rank was honorary!) came to the fore on the political scene: he was a front for the Internationalists. President Wilson said, "Mr. House is my second personality. He is my independent self. His thoughts and mine are one. If I were in his place, I would do just as he suggested" (*The Intimate Papers of Colonel House,* edited by Charles Seymour, Vol. 1, p.114).

In the Fall of 1912, immediately after the presidential election (in which Wilson was elected for his first term) a book was published anonymously titled *Philip Dru — Administrator*. "The Colonel was, in truth, the author" (pp.152-157).

In the book, House outlined plans for a Central Bank, income tax (both planks of the *Communist Manifesto*) and the establishment of "Socialism as dreamed of by Karl Marx" (p. 45). It is quite clear that "Socialism" and "Communism" are two of the names being used by the Illuminists in their thrust toward achieving their goal of world conquest.

For many years prior to this time the International Bankers had reaped vast fortunes in Europe by financing the various nations in their wars against each other. History records that these nations were being plundered, pillaged and bled dry by war debts to the bankers. *Only one group won in every war: the Big Bankers!*

"Give me control of the money and it doesn't matter who makes the laws," said Mayer Amschel Rothschild. With the advent of the "Federal" Reserve and the income tax that came along at about the same time, the way was cleared for a siphon to be inserted into the pockets of virtually every American — and for the vast resources of the American Republic to be manipulated and marshalled for the final thrust toward the accomplishment of their diabolical plan.

Many patriotic Americans recognized the grave dangers inherent in the Fed. Henry Cabot Lodge Sr. said it would make it possible for the bankers to "submerge the gold standard in a

PLATE 13 — President Wilson and Colonel House, September 1917

PHILIP DRU: ADMINISTRATOR

A STORY OF TOMORROW

1920–1935

"No war of classes, no hostility to existing wealth, no wanton or unjust violation of the rights of property, but a constant disposition to ameliorate the condition of the classes least favored by fortune."—MAZZINI.

NEW YORK
B. W. HUEBSCH
1919

PLATE 14 — *Philip Dru: Administrator* (Title page)

flood of irredeemable paper currency" (*Congressional Record*, June 10, 1932). Charles A. Lindbergh Sr., father of the famous aviator, stated that "the invisible government by the money trust ... will create inflation whenever the trust wants inflation" (*Congressional Record*, December 22, 1913). But, as usual, it seemed as if no one wanted to listen. The insight of these two great Americans was remarkable: since the Fed came into being, the National Debt has spiraled to $8,000,000,000,000 (2006). Present trends point toward a further explosion of debt during the next decade.

WORLD WAR ONE

What happened next is a demonstration of the totally deceitful tactics employed by the Conspirators, and their utter contempt for the American people. While Woodrow Wilson was campaigning for reelection on the slogan, "He Kept Us Out of War," his alter ego, Colonel House, was engaged in making behind-the-scenes agreements with Britain which assured America's entrance into the war.

As soon as Wilson was elected to a second term, the Insiders changed their tune and began to promote the idea that war was "inevitable." The sinking of the British munitions ship, the Lusitania, was resurrected and built up into an issue. Submarine warfare was also made an issue.

In his explosive best-seller, *The Lusitania* (Ballantine Books, 1974), Colin Simpson proves from British government documents that the famous ship had been turned into a munitions ship in the early part of the war, in spite of the fact that this was hotly denied at the time and for many years afterwards. Before the Lusitania left New York on May 1, 1915, with a large shipment of high explosives, German representatives in the United States went to great lengths to warn potential passengers that their lives were in danger if they made the trip. As they boarded the ship the warning was repeated verbally.

Six days later, off the coast of Ireland, the "floating bomb" was torpedoed by a German submarine. She sank within twenty minutes with the loss of 1,201 lives, many of them American.

It was obviously illegal for American citizens to be on the Lusitania, a warship. Those who made the trip were aware of the risk they were taking. In the resultant tidal wave of propaganda, the Germans were portrayed as murderous monsters and the incident was used as a tool to drag America into what the Internationalists hypocritically claimed would be "the war to end all wars." America entered the war on April 6, 1917.

The war proved to be a bonanza for the International Bankers and their friends. The expense of the war meant that the government had to borrow vast amounts of money from the bankers at high rates of interest. Men like Bernard Baruch and Eugene Meyer "cleaned up" as a result of having been placed in charge of key war projects.

On January 8, 1918, President Wilson addressed Congress and called for the formation of a League of Nations. This move was, no doubt, designed to begin the work of drawing the United States away from its long-held, and George Washington-inspired, policy of non-involvement with foreign nations. House and his unseen backers were thus busily setting the stage for another step toward the achievement of their ultimate goal, One World Government.

TROTSKY IN AMERICA

Toward the end of World War I, another piece of history was unfolding. After being thrown out of France and Spain, Leon Trotsky and his family arrived in New York aboard the steamer Monserrat on January 13, 1917. Although he was never known to have a job, the Trotskys lived in a fashionable apartment and travelled around in a chauffeured limousine. For some time the source of his wealth was unknown. It was later discovered to be international banking tycoon, Jacob Schiff.

Trotsky left New York aboard the S.S. Kristianiaford bound for Petrograd to organize the Bolshevik-led Russian Revolution. When the ship docked in Halifax, Nova Scotia, on April 3, 1917, the Trotsky party was detained by Canadian authorities under instructions received from the British Admiralty in London.

Within hours great pressure was brought to bear on Canadian authorities by high officials in both Washington and London, to gain the release of Trotsky. Official records of the incident, recently declassified by the Canadian government, reveal that the authorities knew that Trotsky's group consisted of "Socialists leaving [America] for purposes of starting revolution against present Russian government..." (*Wall Street and the Bolshevik Revolution*, by Dr. Antony Sutton, Arlington House, 1974, p.28). Trotsky and his group were quickly released.

Dr. Sutton (Hoover Institute, Stanford University) had access to government files on the incident. He goes on to throw a great deal of light on this period of history: "President Wilson was the fairy godmother [presumably on instructions from House and his backers] who provided Trotsky with a passport to return to Russia to 'carry forward' the revolution. This American passport was accompanied by a Russian entry visa and a British transit visa. Jennings C. Wise, in *Woodrow Wilson: Disciple of Revolution*, makes a pertinent comment: "History must never forget that Woodrow Wilson, despite the efforts of the British police, made it possible for Leon Trotsky to enter Russia with an American passport" (Sutton, p.25).

"In April, 1917, Lenin and a party of 32 Russian revolutionaries, mostly Bolsheviks, journeyed by train from Switzerland across Germany through Sweden to Petrograd, Russia. They were on their way to join Leon Trotsky to 'complete the revolution.' Their trans-German transit was approved, facilitated and financed by the German General Staff" unknown to the Kaiser (p.39). At that time Max Warburg, brother of Paul and Felix Warburg, leading instruments in shackling the Federal Reserve System on the United States, was in charge of German Intelligence. Max was also head of the Rothschild/Warburg bank in Frankfurt. *Very interesting!* Can anyone doubt that the International Bankers were running the whole show from behind the scenes?

Lenin and Trotsky joined forces (the original revolution, led by Kerensky, had begun in March) and within seven months — through cunning, corruption and deception — they were able to hire enough other criminals and make enough deals to impose, by brutality, what Lenin called "all power to the Soviets." The Bolsheviks snatched control of a few cities, the main one of which was Petrograd. It was years before Trotsky, Lenin and their murderous gang secured control of the whole country.

Russian General Arsene De Goulevitch, in *Czarism and the Revolution*, states that "the main purveyors of funds for the revolution, however, were neither crackpot Russian millionaires nor the armed bandits of Lenin. The 'real' money primarily came from certain British and American circles which for a time past had lent their support to the Russian revolutionary cause...

"The important part played by the wealthy American banker, Jacob Schiff, in the events in Russia ... is no longer a secret" (pp.223-232).

This was confirmed by the *New York Journal American* of February 3, 1949: "Today it is estimated by Jacob's grandson, John Schiff, that the old man sank about $20,000,000 [1917 dollars] for the final triumph of Bolshevism in Russia."

De Goulevitch writes that another Russian general claimed that the revolution was "engineered by the English, more precisely by Sir George Buchanan and Lord (Alfred) Milner... In private conversations I have been told that 21 million rubles were spent by Lord Milner in financing the Russian Revolution" (p.230). It should be noted that Milner (a Rothschild front) was a leading member of the Round Table organization whose "influence ... can hardly be exaggerated" (Quigley, pp.130-133). There can be no question that the real powers behind the scenes planned, created and financed the Russian Revolution.

As pointed out earlier, the same group was instrumental in setting up the Council on Foreign Relations in the United States. Since the days of Roosevelt's New Deal, the CFR has supplied most of the cabinet ministers that have "served" in nearly every administration.

There was considerable criticism in the American press immediately after the Bolshevik Revolution began, about its causes and effects. On November 28, 1917, Colonel House, "who had no official position in the U.S. government and had never been elected to office, cabled President Wilson just two weeks after the start of the Russian Revolution ... that 'it is exceedingly important that such criticism should be suppressed'" (*National Suicide — Aid to the Soviet Union,* by Antony Sutton, p.50).

Winston Churchill recognized the real power behind the Bolshevik Revolution — the Illuminati! In the *Illustrated Sunday Herald,* February 8, 1920, he wrote: "(From) ... the days of Spartacus Weishaupt to those of Karl Marx, to those of Trotsky, Bela-Kuhn, Rosa Luxembourg and Emma Goldman, this worldwide conspiracy ... has been steadily growing. This conspiracy played a definitely recognizable role in the tragedy of the French Revolution. It has been the mainspring of every subversive movement during the nineteenth century; and now at last this band of extraordinary personalities from the underworld of the great cities of Europe and America have gripped the Russian people by the hair of their heads, and have become practically the undisputed masters of that enormous empire."

The effects of the war and then the revolution on the Russian nation were devastating. When hostilities ceased Russia was in total shambles. The dead theories of Marx, and their application by his followers, proved disastrous. A collapse of the whole system seemed imminent.

Most of the population was starving when American aid, medicine and other supplies eased the pressure on Lenin's regime. This well-meaning gesture on the part of many sincere Americans only helped to consolidate the grip the Bolsheviks (now called Communists) had on the country. Without this aid it is almost certain that the Russian people would have thrown off their Red shackles which had been paid for by the International Bankers. In the years that followed American industrialists, bankers, and their associates from other countries poured capital into Russia. According to evidence presented during the Senate hearing on *The Export of Strategic Materials to the USSR*, October 23, 1961, the major American oil companies sent technicians and machinery in to develop the Russian oilfields. Many additional American experts were sent in to help the Communists consolidate their position by building railroads, steel plants and other vital industries.

GREAT DEPRESSION ... AND FDR

While the bankers and industrialists were busy building up the oppressive strength of the Soviet regime, they were also secretly planning to take the American people to the cleaners. After a trial run in 1921, they were all set to stage the Crash of 1929 and the Great Depression that followed.

On February 6, 1929, Montagu Norman, head of the Bank of England, arrived in Washington to confer with the Secretary of the Treasury, Andrew Mellon. Shortly thereafter the Fed reversed its easy money policy that had been in effect for more than six years, and began to raise the discount rate.

A timely warning went out to those in the know. Paul Warburg was quoted in the *Financial Chronicle*, March 9, 1929: "If orgies of unrestricted speculation are permitted to spread too far ... the ultimate crash is certain." During the following six months those in the know sold out of the stock market when prices were high and reinvested their money in silver and gold.

"When everything was ready, the New York financiers started calling 24 hour broker call loans. This meant that the stock brokers and their customers had to dump their stock on the market in order to pay the loans. This naturally collapsed the market and brought a banking collapse all over the country because the banks not owned by the oligarchy were heavily involved in broker call claims at this time, and bank runs soon exhausted their coin and currency and they had to close. The Federal Reserve System would not come to their aid, although they were instructed under the law to maintain an elastic currency" (*The United States' Unresolved Monetary and Political Problems*, by William Bryan).

Congressman Louis T. McFadden, outspoken Chairman of the House Banking and Currency Committee, understood the cause of the Great Depression: *"It was no accident. It was a carefully contrived occurrence... The International Bankers sought to bring about a condition of despair here so that they might emerge as rulers of us all"* (*The Speeches of Congressman Louis T. McFadden*).

As a result of the Crash, business was thrown into a state of chaos. Tens of thousands of companies were forced to close down. Millions lost their jobs and were forced to join the soup lines. Several millionaires lost all they had and committed suicide.

By 1932 the economy showed distinct signs of staging a major recovery. An air of hope and confidence once again began to flow through the nation.

Although the economic prospects looked promising the Internationalists had other plans for the American people. During the presidential campaign of 1932, Franklin D. Roosevelt presented a strong conservative image to the electorate. But rumors began to spread across the country that his platform did not represent his true views and intentions, and that basic changes in the entire economic, social and governmental systems were in the works. When Roosevelt was elected in November these rumors became rampant. The president-elect would neither confirm nor deny them. The 1932 election was the last one after which the actual inauguration took place the following March, rather than January. The long wait and the growing public uncertainty brought about what amounted to a "second depression — politically created — of paralyzing impact. The resultant public panic caused a nationwide run on the banks, forcing many to close their doors by the time of FDR's inauguration.

As a result, Roosevelt came to power in an atmosphere of great crisis which he, and the powers behind the scenes, had deliberately created. Roosevelt immediately undertook the long-rumored changes in our governmental system and way of life. Federal commissions and regulatory boards were given power to control at will almost every business transaction anywhere in America, and to enforce their will by imposing both civil and criminal penalties. Constitutional restrictions on the exercise of this kind of authority and force were swept away. Congress became subservient to a greater degree than ever before in our history; it did exactly what the president asked — impelled by the crisis atmosphere the president himself had created, and by the constant, cleverly-applied pressure of the Fabians and the Fabian-indoctrinated whom the president had installed in so many key Federal offices.

In short, the Roosevelt Administration attempted to inflict on the nation every last phase of Clinton Roosevelt's Illuminist blueprint for destroying our Constitution and form of government — on the pretext of establishing a "new social order," or New Deal as he ironically labeled it. They immediately placed the insignia of the Illuminati, in the form of the reverse side of the Great Seal of the United States, on our currency (their one d-llar notes), thus openly declaring the attainment of their conspiracy — their "Novus Ordo Seclorum" or "New Deal."

This insignia was adopted by Weishaupt at the time he founded the Order of the Illuminati on May 1, 1776. It was that event that is memorialized by the "MDCCLXXVI" at the base of the pyramid and not the date of the signing of the Declaration

PLATE 15 — Great Seal of the United States (obverse side)

of Independence, as the uninformed have supposed. This insignia acquired Masonic significance only after the merger of that Order with the Order of the Illuminati at the Congress of Wilhelmsbad, in 1782.

Note the wording on the insignia: "Annuit Coeptis" means "our enterprise [conspiracy] has been crowned with success." Underneath, we find the words "Novus Order Seclorum." This explains the nature of their conspiracy, the creation of a New World Order.

Notice that the "chief corner stone" (capstone) is missing from the top of the pyramid. In its place, we find the "all-seeing eye" which symbolizes Lucifer and the terroristic espionage agency which Weishaupt set up under the name of the "Insinuating Brethren."

It is highly significant that we find Jesus Christ described in the Bible as the head of the church. He is the One who defeated Lucifer (or Satan) through His death and resurrection. Christ is also described in *Mark* 12:10 and *Luke* 20:17 as "the stone that the builders rejected." As we saw in chapter five, the leaders of the Illuminati (*the builders of the New World Order*) rejected Jesus Christ and took Lucifer (or Satan) as their head — their Boss. No wonder they removed the "chief cornerstone" from their insignia and substituted the Satanic all-seeing eye!

Within months of coming to power, the Roosevelt Administration showed that it was very definitely in favor of the brutal Communist regime continuing to control Russia. After sixteen years of bungling, mismanagement and massive purges staged by Stalin — and in spite of colossal amounts of aid from the West — the Communist government was tottering precariously on the brink of oblivion. Had the Communists been left to their own devices, the regime would probably have fallen .

Such an event would have been a terrible blow to the plans of the Internationalists. They couldn't allow it to happen.

On November 17, 1933, the American government stepped in to save the force that was openly dedicated to the overthrow of every other government in the world. On that date Roosevelt formally granted diplomatic recognition to Soviet Russia, thus giving Stalin access to the credit and money markets of the world. In return, we obtained a promise that Russia would not interfere in our internal affairs. But as soon as Russia's first ambassador arrived on our shores, Communist cells and spy networks began to operate out of his embassy.

Roosevelt launched a massive attack on the Supreme Court during the years that followed. In 1937 he asked Congress for a law to limit the Court's historic authority to declare laws in conflict with the Constitution null and void. He also asked Congress for a law under which he could appoint six additional Justices — thus raising the total to 15. This would have loaded the dice in favor of the Insiders.

The public awoke suddenly to its danger and forced Congress to reject the changes that Roosevelt had demanded. The victory was, however, short lived. Within four years four justices had died or resigned because of poor health and were replaced by men thoroughly indoctrinated with the Fabian philosophy.

WORLD WAR TWO

As a result of the Insider-engineered Versailles Treaty which, in the words of Lord Curzon, was "not a treaty ... (but) simply a break in hostilities," war clouds were once again forming over Europe.

At the same time, as the International Bankers were bolstering the sagging Communist regime in Russia, they were also underwriting huge loans on both sides of the Atlantic for the new regime of Adolph Hitler. The financial backing for Hitler was handled by the Warburg-controlled Mendelsohn Bank of Amsterdam and later by the J. Henry Schroeder Bank with branches in Frankfurt, London and New York. It is interesting to note that the chief legal counsel to the Schroeder Bank was the firm of Sullivan and Cromwell, whose senior partners included John Foster and Allen Dulles (CFR) (*All Honorable Men*, by James Martin, p.51).

There is strong evidence that indicates that Hitler never had any intention of attacking Britain and engaging in a war with a power he greatly admired.

The Second World War was fought in such a way as to further the aims of the Illuminati and thus bring their plans much closer to completion. Following the Hitler-Stalin pact of 1939, Germany and Russia invaded Poland and divided that country among them. At that point Britain and France — at the urging of FDR and the Insiders — declared war on Germany but not on Russia. During the months that followed there was a "phony war" in which very little action took place. While Chamberlain was prime minister of England there was no shooting war. The leaders of both the German and British governments were aware of the plans of the International Bankers to have another major war, and they were negotiating in an effort to avoid it. Hitler wanted the British to join him in an all-out attack on Russia.

The controlled press in Britain launched a violent attack on Chamberlain. The powers that be wanted Chamberlain out of the way so that they could get a real war under way. Under the propaganda barrage Chamberlain was forced to resign. He was replaced by Winston Churchill. Immediately thereafter the shooting war started in earnest with a British air attack on

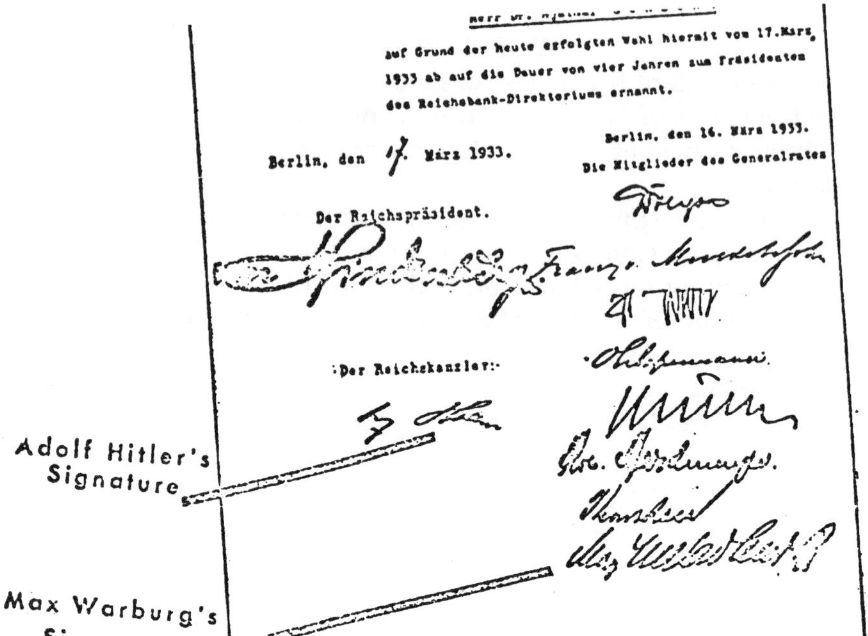

auf Grund der heute erfolgten Wahl hiermit vom 17. März 1933 ab auf die Dauer von vier Jahren zum Präsidenten des Reichsbank-Direktoriums ernannt.

Berlin, den 17. März 1933.

Der Reichspräsident.

:Der Reichskanzler:

Berlin, den 16. März 1933.

Die Mitglieder des Generalrates

PLATE 16

This amazing document, a routine appointment of H.H.C. Schacht as Administrator of Nazi Germany's money, was deliberately suppressed by Insiders at the time of the Nurenburg trials following World War II. It shows the REAL force behind Hitler — the International Bankers, represented by Max Warburg, the brother of Paul Warburg chief architect of the "Federal" Reserve System.

Germany (*Bombing Vindicated,* by J. M. Spaight, Principal Assistant Secretary to the British Air Ministry, published in 1944).

The following year the German High Command (unknown to Hitler) sent Rudolph Hess to Britain to contact Lord Hamilton and Churchill. Hess told the British that if they would sign a peace treaty they would get rid of Hitler and concentrate their military might on the destruction of Communism in Russia and other European countries. The British refused to agree to the offer made through Hess. Hess was then jailed and held in solitary confinement for more than forty years until his death in Spandau Prison in Germany.

Following their failure to negotiate a pact with Britain, the German generals persuaded Hitler to undertake an all-out attack on Soviet Russia, pointing out that until Russia was defeated Germany wouldn't be safe from a stab in the back.

Immediately after Germany's Blitzkrieg attack on Russia (June 22, 1941), instead of letting Hitler and Stalin destroy each other, the Roosevelt Administration began to pour billions of dollars of "lend-lease" aid into Russia in support of the brutal Communist regime. Propaganda promoted Stalin as our "noble ally."

Meanwhile, in the Pacific, policies put into effect by Roosevelt in 1936 were forcing the Japanese into a position where they would either have to fight — or capitulate. They decided to fight!

There is indisputable evidence that top government officials in Washington were fully aware in advance of the Japanese attack on Pearl Harbor (*The Final Secret of Pearl Harbor*, by Rear Admiral Robert Theobold, and *Warlords of Washington*, by Anthony J. Hilder — an interview with Col. Curtis B. Dall, a son-in-law of President Roosevelt). The truth is that FDR and his cohorts *wanted* a war with Japan and were doing everything in their power to induce the Japanese into launching an attack on the U.S.

One of the leading court historians described Roosevelt's mendacity as follows: "Franklin Roosevelt repeatedly deceived the American people during the period before Pearl harbor...

"The country was overwhelmingly noninterventionist to the day of Pearl Harbor, and an overt attempt to lead the people into war would have resulted in certain failure and an almost certain ousting of Roosevelt in 1940, *with the consequent defeat of his ultimate aims" (The Man in the Street,* by Thomas A. Bailey, Macmillan, 1948, pp.11,12). The American people had to be made to *want* war; the planned attack on Pearl Harbor, known to top officials in Washington but hidden by them from our Commanders in Hawaii, served the purpose perfectly. Yes, December 7, 1941, was "a day of infamy." That infamy was centered in Washington.

Although the war was ostensibly fought to "save democracy," the opposite was, in fact, the truth. There is abundant evidence which proves that the war, particularly in Europe, could have been won much more quickly had it been run on conventional lines. For example, Germany could have been attacked through the "soft underbelly" of Europe after Italy surrendered on September 8, 1943.

Instead of going straight for Germany's heart, the Allied High Command, under the direction of General Eisenhower (a protege of George C. Marshall who had been responsible, with others, for withholding news of the planned Japanese attack on Pearl Harbor from our commanders in Hawaii), withdrew most of the heavy equipment from the war front and began to turn the British Isles into a huge armed fortress. For the next nine months the British and American air forces pounded away at the centers of German industry. Many German cities were also reduced to piles of rubble. Very little action took place on the ground, in spite of the fact that many of the Allied commanders urged the political leaders to launch a massive assault on Hitler's Reich from the south and west.

What was the motivation for the refusal by the political leaders to reject such a logical plan? This writer believes that they clearly understood that such an offensive would have resulted in a clear-cut victory for the Allied Armies — and the occupation of all Germany and all eastern Europe. This would have defeated the real plans of the Insiders.

The real powers behind the scenes stalled for time, and concentrated on two main goals — the destruction of Germany by bombing and the building up of Communist forces in Russia. Only when the Communists, with a tremendous infusion of American supplies and war materiel, began to gain the upper hand over the Germans, did the Allies stage their Normandy invasion, and start their slow and very halting push toward the heart of Germany.

History records that General Eisenhower, the Allied Supreme Commander in Europe, under instructions from Washington, continually made "mistakes" and "blunders" which invariably helped the Russians. Eisenhower stopped the Allied forces (which had invaded from Italy) from crossing the Po Valley, then opened up another front in France. This gave Stalin more time in which to work his way west. It also opened up the Balkans for invasion by the Russians when the time came.

Shortly after the Allies reached Germany from the west, Eisenhower ordered a halt to the advance. After the Russians advanced from the east to central Germany, Eisenhower refused German attempts to surrender. It took three more weeks of brutal fighting for the Communist hordes to break through German defenses and reach Berlin. Can there be any doubt that it was all planned that way? (For additional details and documentation, see *Descent Into Slavery?*, pp.177-191).

OPERATION KEELHAUL

In 1945, in direct violation of their claims to be the defenders of freedom, the U.S. and British governments cooperated in the forcible and brutal repatriation of four million Russians after they had fled to the West. This agreement with Joseph Stalin (Operation Keelhaul) was a violation not only of the traditional Allied spirit of freedom, but also of the Geneva Convention.

The Operation Keelhaul file (1945) was classified secret in 1972, and is thus off-limits to investigators. Julius Epstein, in *Operation Keelhaul,* gives us many of the nauseating details of what has been called "probably the greatest single blot of all time on British and American diplomacy."

LENIN'S PREDICTION

One of the most amazing political predictions of all time was made in the early 1920s. It was made by Nikalai Lenin, the successor to Giuseppe Mazzini and Adriano Lemmi. It was a prediction of what would happen on the world scene; it was also the grand strategic plan of the Illuminati. Lenin stated: "First we will take Eastern Europe, then the masses of Asia, then we will encircle the United States which will be the last bastion of capitalism. We will not have to attack. It will fall like an overripe fruit into our hands."

The most important result of World War II was engineered at the infamous Yalta Conference which took place in early February, 1945. At this meeting the first step of Lenin's plan for the conquest of the world finally became a reality. All Eastern Europe was handed over to the Communists. Eleven sovereign nations were delivered into slavery by the stroke of a pen — the pen of our president, Franklin D. Roosevelt, with traitor Alger Hiss at his side. Three sovereign nations and part of Poland were given to Russia outright, to become part of Russian territory. Immediately, the people of those proud nations were shipped away in cattle cars by the millions to every corner of the

Communist empire. In an act of pure genocide, three entire nationalities were deliberately destroyed. Estonia, Latvia and Lithuania, as nations, are dead — with our approval and over the signature of the president of the United States, the alleged "land of the free and home of the brave."

Shortly thereafter Poland, the invasion and conquest of which had set off World War II, fell completely under Communist domination — a much more brutal form of oppression than that of Hitler. *In that respect, it can be said that all the "blood, sweat and tears" shed from 1939-1944 was in vain.* But that is not exactly true. The Conspirators were proceeding on schedule!

Lenin said: "First we will take Eastern Europe." At the Yalta Conference in 1945 his successor, Stalin, got Eastern Europe — as a free gift from the president of the United States.

It was now time for the second step, "then the masses of Asia." In 1945 the Communists in China were a small minority who had a foothold in only a few provinces. As the war ended, the Nationalist government of China — our firm ally throughout our war with Japan — turned its attention to ridding China of Communists.

Once again our government stepped in to aid the growth of Communist power and the fulfillment of Lenin's prediction. General George C. Marshall (yes, the same man who was responsible for not warning our Commanders in Hawaii, and who was one of those responsible for the holding back of the Allied advance in Europe) now turned up as our representative in China.

Marshall pressured Chiang Kai-shek, the Nationalist leader, to admit Chinese Reds to his government. When Chiang refused, all American aid was cut off. The Communists continued to be supplied from Russia. They also gained access to vast quantities of Japanese arms which had come under our control following Japan's surrender.

As a result of our embargo Chiang could no longer get gasoline for his tanks and planes. His forces were slowly driven back. On December 7, 1949 — the eighth anniversary of Pearl Harbor — Chiang evacuated his government to Formosa.

As a result of our betrayal of Chiang Kai-Shek, the way was now clear for the start of the Korean War, a war we were not allowed to win, a war in which one of the greatest American generals of the century, Douglas MacArthur, was disgracefully dismissed by President Truman because he would accept no substitute for victory. When the Chinese hordes entered the war, our policy makers afforded them a privileged sanctuary across the Yalu River in Manchuria, by prohibiting American Commanders from attacking Communist Chinese depots, bases and airfields there. Official Washington also ordered the American Seventh Fleet into Formosa Strait to prevent our ally —Chiang— from invading his lost mainland (which would have taken the pressure off our troops fighting the Chinese Communist enemy in Korea). Our government even refused Chiang's offer to fight alongside us in Korea.

Disclosure of some of these facts by patriotic Americans during the Korean War — coupled with the work of a few Congressional investigating committees — finally began to bring about some awakening among the American people about the dangers of Communism. This became a central issue in the presidential campaign of 1952.

EISENHOWER RHETORIC

Eisenhower campaigned with bold statements about "liberation, "rolling back the Iron Curtain" and "freeing the captive peoples." When Eisenhower became president many patriotic Americans naively assumed that drastic changes would be made in our foreign policy and that the country would quickly get back on the right track once again.

Many behind the Iron Curtain listened to the Eisenhower rhetoric — and, in the Fall of 1956, in Hungary, they acted.

In the magnificent uprising against their tyrannical Communist masters, the Hungarian Freedom Fighters, in a few days of sublime heroism, forced the withdrawal of Russian occupation forces from Hungary. This was the first major uprising in any Communist country since the Bolsheviks gained control of Russia. It was the first chance we had been offered to prove that "liberation" was more than an empty slogan to help win elections, and that victory over our enemies was more than a bygone dream. The world looked to us to redeem our pledges, to honor our commitment to the freedom we allegedly valued above all else. In this one brief moment we had a dazzling opportunity to roll back the Iron Curtain and free the captive peoples as promised by Eisenhower in his campaign rhetoric.

Resentment against Communist rule was at fever pitch throughout Eastern Europe. Had the uprising in Hungary succeeded, there would, no doubt, have been a wave of similar uprisings in almost every other Eastern Satellite. The whole area was a powder keg waiting to explode in Russia's face — if we sided with the brave Freedom Fighters.

We answered by spitting in their faces and dousing the fuse with ice cold water. The State Department sent a telegram to the Communists: "The government of the United States does not look with favor upon governments unfriendly to the Soviet Union on the borders of the Soviet Union" (*Congressional Record,* August 31, 1960, p 17407).

That was all Khrushchev needed. *The American State Department had confirmed its support of Communism.* Within hours, the Russians sent their tanks and troops back into Budapest, with orders to kill without mercy. In this way "our" State Department sealed the fate of millions of freedom-loving Hungarians who had been naive enough to believe Eisenhower's cheap campaign rhetoric. As the Red Army's tanks rumbled into Budapest on November 4, 1956, the radio station of the heroic Freedom Fighters broadcast one last, vain plea: *"People of the world, listen to our call. Help us not with words, but with actions, with soldiers and arms. Please do not forget that this wild attack of Bolshevism [Illuminism] will not stop. You may be the next victim. Save us ... our ship is sinking. The light vanishes. The shadows grow darker from hour to hour. Listen to our cry. Start moving. Extend to us your brotherly hands.... God be with you and us"* (*The Bridge at Andau,* by James Michener, pp.88,89).

After this there could only be silence!

In the same year, 1956, officials in Washington, in conjunction with the World Bank and the United Nations, blackmailed the British and French governments into handing over the Suez Canal, and various surrounding military bases, to Egypt under the threat that "full economic sanctions would be employed against both countries" if they refused (*The New Unhappy Lords,* by A.K. Chesterton, p.69).

Following the Suez Debacle it was the turn of the Cubans to be sold into slavery by the powers behind the scenes. The Communists had the Caribbean Island handed over to them on a plate by our State Department, which was greatly assisted by many of the "leading" newspapers in this country.

A young revolutionary thug named Fidel Castro — a known Communist — had a small group of bandit followers in the mountains of Cuba. Castro did not attract much public attention in the U.S. until 1957, when he was given a big build-up on the front page of the *New York Times*. In the same year William A. Weiland was appointed as State Department representative in the Caribbean area. Derogatory reports on Weiland at the time of his appointment brought no action from his superiors. Later, investigations by a Senate committee showed that Weiland "regularly disregarded, sidetracked or denounced FBI, State Department and military intelligence sources which branded Castro as a Communist."

Weiland and his cohorts "buried" all information that showed Castro's true colors and saw to it that the U.S. invoked sanctions against Batista who ran Cuba at the time. Castro was built up before the American public (just as Red Chinese "agrarian reformers" had been) as a heroic, patriotic well-meaning leader. As a result, the policies which permitted Castro's victory over Batista won public acceptance at the time.

Later, when Castro declared his dedication to Communism, the damage had been done. Cuba was in Communist hands. Can there be any doubt that the Bay of Pigs disaster a few years later was carefully planned that way?

THE VIETNAM TRAGEDY

We could go on to recite a long list of incidents in which official Washington aided and abetted the Communist cause — and hindered the cause of freedom — but we will spare you the trauma ... and conclude with one of our greatest national tragedies of all, the Vietnam War.

In the mid-1960s President Johnson, in spite of campaign promises to the contrary, ignored the stern warnings of military leaders to never become involved in a land war in Asia. In May, 1956, American troops began to pour into South Vietnam. At the height of the Vietnam conflict (April, 1969) U.S troop strength in Vietnam reached 543,000. The phony "war" was costing the long-suffering American taxpayer $30,000,000,000 a year.

It is a fact, stated many times by military men on the scene, that we could have defeated the Communists convincingly and won the war within a matter of just a few weeks ... had official Washington given the go-ahead. The decision to continue the war in a half-hearted manner for so many years was a purely political one.

Instead of winning the war, strict orders came from Washington *not* to bomb the enemy where it would hurt him — in his war plants, harbors, railyards, oil refineries etc. As a result tens of thousands of Americans were fighting — *and dying* — with one hand tied behind their backs, *on strict instructions from their own leaders*.

Vitally important facts regarding the Vietnam War are found in *National Suicide, Military Aid to the Soviet Union*, by Antony C. Sutton of the Hoover Institute: "The tanks, guns and trucks [for the Communist forces] came from the Soviet Union — and were produced in plants erected and equipped by American and European companies. The T-54 tank was used in force in 1972. The T-54 has a modified Christie-type suspension. The GAZ trucks on the Ho Chi Min Trail came from the Ford-built Gorki plant. *Both plants were equipped with new American machinery while the Vietnam War was in progress*. The amphibious PT-76 tank is manufactured in Volgograd — in a factory built by eighty U.S. firms. This is called 'peaceful trade' by the mystics in Washington.

"... the 'arsenal for revolution' was built by Western firms and has been kept in operation with 'peaceful trade.' When all the rhetoric about 'peaceful trade' is boiled out, it comes down to a single inescapable fact — the guns, the ammunition, the weapons, the transportation systems that killed Americans in Vietnam came from the American-subsidized economy of the Soviet Union.

"... both the Johnson and Nixon administrations irrationally and illogically chose to expand trade — the carrier for the technology required to fuel the North Vietnam side of the war — and so voted to continue the war.

"The more Hanoi stoked up the war, the more Soviet Russia received from the United States. American policy — wittingly or unwittingly — was guaranteed not only to maintain the Vietnam War but to expand it, increase our losses, and compound the problem of preserving South Vietnam" (pp.46-46).

To have won the Vietnam War would have been contrary to the plans of the Insiders. A victory would have dramatically improved the American image around the world. It would also have dealt a severe blow to Communism — and greatly bolstered the sagging psyches of countless millions of Americans.

Instead of winning, we built up their deep sea ports, the road and rail systems, the airports and other strategic areas of South Vietnam — and handed them over (lock, stock and barrel) to the enemy we had been aiding and abetting since long before the outbreak of hostilities. In addition, we left behind $5,000,000,000 in military equipment as a gift to the Communists.

Several extremely important objectives were achieved by our unseen rulers as a result of the National Catastrophe known as the Vietnam War:

(1) It greatly increased our indebtedness to the International Bankers, thus pushing us deeper into their grasp.

Economist C.V. Myers made a profound statement and summed up the truth in crystal clear terms: "The situation has gone so far that no matter who is elected [as president in 1968] he can produce no remedy now. If the Lord were to send an emissary of his own, this emissary could not stop the steamroller of destruction set in motion by the Johnson Administration. He could not stop it because if we concede that the Lord's laws are natural laws only, then all natural laws would have to be canceled and reversed if the emissary of the Lord could cure it. If he could cure it in any other way, he would have to defeat the Lord and all the natural laws that man has known since his birth on this planet" (*Conservative Viewpoint*, June, 1970).

(2) The trauma of the Vietnam War was used by the Conspirators to tear the nation apart through internal strife. Those who created the strife were heavily subsidized by the Insiders.

Jerry Kirk, a student at the University of Chicago, left the Communist Party in 1969 and, some months later, testified before the House and Senate Internal Security Committee. He stated: "Young people have no conception of the conspiracy's strategy of pressure from above, pressure from below, as well outlined in Jan Kozak's book, *And Not a Shot Was Fired*. They have no idea they are playing into the hands of the Establishment they claim to hate.

"The radicals think they are fighting the forces of the super-rich, like Rockefeller and Ford, and don't realize that it is precisely such forces which are behind their own revolution, financing it, and using it for their own purposes."

Kirk went on to describe an appearance made at the university by Stokely Carmichael, the leader of the revolutionary group known as SNCC: "Mr. Carmichael was obviously in the middle of something very important which made him more nervous and tense than in the past... He started speaking of things of which he said he could not have said before because his research was not finished...

"He repeated the line from the song he liked so well, 'Something is happening here, but you don't know what it is, do you, Mr. Jones?' He kept hitting on the theme that a very large monopoly capitalist money group, the bankers to be exact, was instrumental in fomenting (the) idea that the Jews are the ones actually behind the oppression of the blacks... In the agencies of this power, he cited banks, the chief among which were Morgan Guaranty Trust and Chase Manhattan. And the foundations connected with these monoliths" (Hearing of March 11, 1970, pp.226,227).

Within weeks Carmichael had been mysteriously removed from SNCC and the Black Panthers. He had learned too much!

In April, 1968, James Kunen was one of the leaders of the group which seized Columbia University. They were allowed to hold it for several days. Later, in *The Strawberry Statement*, Kunen related a very significant incident which happened during this period. On pages 130 and 131, we find: "In the evening we went up to the U. to check out a strategy meeting. A kid was giving a report on the SDS convention. He said that ... at the convention men from Roundtable International, the meeting sponsored by Business International for their client groups and heads of government, tried to buy up a few radicals.

"These men are the world's leading industrialists and they convene to decide how our lives are going to go. These are the guys who wrote the Alliance for Progress. They are the left wing of the ruling class... They offered to finance our demonstration in Chicago. *We were also offered Esso (Rockefeller) money. They want us to make a lot of radical commotion so they can look more in the center as they move to the Left."*

(3) The long, drawn-out agony of the Vietnam War also served to make the average American sick and tired of war and internal strife ... and thus much more susceptible to the propaganda put out by the One-Worlders. *This strategy is in complete agreement with their Master Plan as we will see in a later chapter.*

Among the tools being used in Illuminati propaganda is the traitorous Declaration of Interdependence — a document that has been signed by many of "our" representatives in Washington, in direct violation of their oaths of office (see p. 110).

REAGAN AND BUSH YEARS

During the 1980 presidential election campaign, at a time when the Carter administration was incapable of producing anything but debt, deficits and deceit, the "Great Communicator" Ronald Reagan came on the scene declaring that it was "time for a change." His campaign, wrapped in Old Glory, was filled to overflowing with America First rhetoric. He called for "a new beginning" for the United States and a return to traditional values. Reagan championed individual self-government and personal responsibility. He condemned Big Government, declaring that "Government is not the solution to the problem. Government is the problem." He condemned deficit spending and the wide array of socialist programs that were long-since part of government policy.

The American public believed Reagan and responded enthusiastically to his message. He was elected President, with George Bush as his number two man.

What many of the American electorate had forgotten — or had chosen to overlook — was the fact that, as a two-time (or two-timing!) Governor of California, Reagan had developed a notorious reputation of saying one thing and doing another; his actions rarely matched his rhetoric. The reality was that the

DECLARATION OF INTERDEPENDENCE

When in the course of history the threat of extinction confronts mankind, it is necessary for the people of The United States to declare their interdependence with the people of all nations and to embrace those principles and build those institutions which will enable mankind to survive and civilization to flourish.

Two centuries ago our forefathers brought forth a new nation; now we must join with others to bring forth a **NEW WORLD ORDER.** On this historic occasion it is proper that the American people should reaffirm those principles on which the United States of America was founded, acknowledge the new crises which confront them, accept the new obligations which history imposes upon them, and set forth the causes which impel them to affirm before all peoples their commitment to a Declaration of Interdependence.

We hold these truths to be self-evident: that all men are created equal: that the inequalities and injustices which afflict so much of the human race are the product of history and society, not of God or nature; that people everywhere are entitled to the blessings of life and liberty, peace and security and the realization of their full potential; that they have an inescapable moral obligation to preserve those rights for posterity; and that to achieve these ends all the peoples and nations of the globe should acknowledge their interdependence and join together to dedicate their minds and their hearts to the solution of those problems which threaten their survival.

To establish a **NEW WORLD ORDER** of compassion, peace, justice and security, it is essential that mankind free itself from the limitations of national prejudice, and acknowledge that the forces that unite it are incomparably deeper than those that divide it—that all people are part of one global community, dependent on one body of resources, bound together by the ties of a common humanity and associated in a common adventure on the planet Earth.

Let us then join together to vindicate and realize this great truth that mankind is one, and as one will nobly save or irreparably lose the heritage of thousands of years of civilization. And let us set forth the principles which should animate and inspire us if our civilization is to survive.

PLATE 17

conservatives got the rhetoric while the liberals got the action. -

Although there was a momentary increase in national pride and confidence during the Reagan-Bush years, they had a devastating impact on the financial well-being of the nation. During those eight short years, the National Debt increased a staggering 300 percent — from one to three trillion dollars.

With the advent of the Bush-Quayle administration in 1989, things went from bad to worse. Not only did the National Debt continue to skyrocket (at the end of their four years it was well over four trillion dollars), but Bush — for many years a member of both the Council on Foreign Relations (CFR) and the Trilateral Commission (TC) — did more than any other president in history to undermine the sovereignty of the United States. Both by their declarations and by their actions, members of the CFR and TC have repeatedly shown their dedication to the destruction of the United States as a sovereign nation and to its absorption into a One World Government.

November 3, 1992 the American voters rejected Bush's bid for a second term and elected Bill Clinton, 46, as their President.

THE TWO CLINTON ADMINISTRATIONS

Although *The Wall Street Journal* labeled Bill Clinton a political "outsider," that wasn't exactly true. He had friends in high places. Prior to becoming attorney general and then governor of Arkansas, Clinton had spent years at Georgetown University being schooled under the watchful eye of his mentor, Dr. Carroll Quigley. Later, as a Rhodes Scholar he attended Oxford University for further training in globalism. While in England, he led anti-American marches in London. During the same period, he spent time in Moscow and then in Prague, where he spent ten days with the family of one of that country's communist leaders.

After attending a Bilderberg meeting in Germany in June1991, Clinton suddenly emerged as the Democratic frontrunner in the 1992 presidential campaign. Seventeen months later he was firmly installed in the Oval Office.

Popularly known as "Slick Willie" and an individual with the morals of a degenerate alley cat, Clinton's presidency was marked by a long and varied series of scandals. Whitewatergate, Monicagate, Menagate, and Fostergate being just a few! There were also charges he helped in the coverup of drug-related murders in Arkansas. His presidency ended with the granting of clemency to a sordid array of criminals and other lowlifes. Numerous books and videos have graphically laid out the tawdry details.

THE GEORGE W. BUSH ADMINISTRATION

On January 20, 2001, multiple millions uttered a long sigh of relief as George W. Bush took over from Bill Clinton as president of the United States. Many on the Religious Right were ecstatic. And why not? Hadn't the new Commander in Chief told them he had turned his heart and life over to Jesus, and was a changed man? To them, it was as if everything political and spiritual had been miraculously rolled back to at least the early 1930s, a time when most positions of authority in the federal government were filled by men who had at least a basic respect for the United States and its Constitution. A time when values such as truth, character, self-government, personal responsibility, and law and order were still widely respected.

In their naivete many sincerely believed that under the new Bush administration the United States would experience a renaissance – a rebirth and revitalization of all those wonderful characteristics that were instrumental in making America the greatest nation in the history of mankind. Having failed to do their homework on the various characters involved, they blindly accepted as "gospel" the propaganda that spewed from the leaders of the hideously misnamed "Republican" party. Never having been trained to think, define terms, analyze and reach informed decisions, their wishful thinking far outweighed their mis-perception of political reality. Most truly believed that happy days were here again.

Most Americans are ignorant (many willfully so!) of the fact that the United States hasn't had a genuine constitutional form of government since March 9, 1933. As 1973 *Senate Report* (Number 93-549, 93rd Congress, First Session, Emergency Powers Statutes) states in its *Foreword*: "Since March 9, 1933, the United States has been in a state of declared national emergency." This continuing "state of ... emergency" confers "enough authority [in the federal government] **to rule the country without reference to normal constitutional**

processes...[and to control] the lives of all American citizens." These widely unrecognized emergency powers – under which the United States has been virtually transformed from a Constitutional Republic into a Socialist Democracy – have never been challenged by any "republican" administration.

With the arrival of the George W. Bush administration nothing changed in DC. Washington is still Washington. It's still politics as usual. Washington, DC (the District of Corruption) is a political cesspool filled with barracudas. One doesn't survive long is such a deadly environment unless they are sponsored by – and play ball with – the powers-that-be!

Political Reality 101, as the late George Wallace observed in the early 1970s, is that "there's not a dimes worth of difference between the two main political parties." As Establishment insider Dr. Carroll Quigley noted in 1966, "The policies [followed by both the Republican and Democratic Parties] are no longer subjects of significant disagreement, but are disputable only in details of procedure, priority, or method" (*Tragedy and Hope,* p.1248). Despite political rhetoric to the contrary, the steamroller of national destruction grinds relentlessly on, pulverizing everything in its path.

George W. Bush's roots are deeply embedded in the Eastern Establishment. For many decades the Bush clan has – in banking, business and politics – "played ball" with the Movers and Shakers. They have been rewarded handsomely as a result.

Upon his election as president, Mr. Bush surrounded himself with numerous Jewish advisors. These were led by Richard Perle, Paul Wolfowitz, and Douglas Feith. This rabidly pro-Zionist group were known as neo-conservatives or neo-cons. According to media reports, their primary goal was to "change the basic equation in the [Middle East] region." Iraq was number one on their hit list. This basic reality is further substantiated by a report titled *Rebuilding America's Defenses* published in 2000 by The Project for the New American Century. Months **before** George W. Bush was elected president, the report stated that "the United States has for decades sought to play a more permanent role in Gulf regional security. While the unresolved conflict with Iraq provides **[present tense, 2000]** the immediate justification, the need for a substantial force presence in the Gulf transcends the issue of the regime of Saddam Hussein ... **Further,**

the process is likely to be a long one, absent some catastrophic and catalyzing event – like a new Pearl Harbor." Very conveniently, such a "**catastrophic and catalyzing event**" took place the following year when on 9/11/01 the World Trade Center in New York was destroyed.

Six days later President Bush signed a 2½-page document marked "Top Secret." This "outlined a plan for going to war in Afghanistan as part of a global campaign against terrorism.

"Almost as a footnote, the document also directed the Pentagon to begin military options for an invasion of Iraq" (Glenn Kessler, *The Washington Post*, 1/12/02).

But here the Bush administration had a big problem. Such a dangerous venture couldn't be undertaken without what appeared to be a legitimate reason. As one clearly didn't exist, it had to be manufactured. Voila! Saddam Hussein's Iraq – which had been on its knees militarily and economically for almost a decade due to massive U.N. sanctions, and which never had any dealings with al Qaeda or 9/11 – suddenly "possessed weapons of mass destruction" and allegedly posed an imminent threat to world peace. As revealed in the infamous Downing Street memos, the president, not wanting to be confused by the facts, was adamant in his determination to attack Iraq. In other words, he was determined to "reshape the Middle East" as per the plan. Although hidden from public view, that "reshaping" had three main objectives: (1) Strengthen Israel by eliminating one of its enemies; (2) Seize Iraq's vast petroleum resources for American Big Oil, and (3) Clear the way for a "more substantial" American military presence in the Middle East. Six weeks prior to the invasion of the non-threatening, sovereign nation of Iraq on the Jewish festival of Purim (March 19, 2003), Jewish commentator Joe Klein stated: **"A stronger Israel is very much imbedded in the rationale for a war with Iraq. It is part of an argument that dare not speak its name"** (*Time*, 2/10/03). As Senator Ernest Hollings (D-SC) observed upon his retirement, "With Iraq no threat, why invade a sovereign country? **The answer: President Bush's policy to secure Israel**" (*Charleston Post and Courier*, 5/6/04).

Sclomo Brom, a former senior Israeli intelligence officer, revealed that "**Israeli intelligence was a full partner** to the picture presented by American and British intelligence regarding Iraq's nonconventional capabilities." **The Israelis "badly overestimated the Iraqi threat." This reflected the Zionist state's "one-dimensional perception" of Saddam's alleged threat** (*Los Angeles Times*, 12/5/03).

As the New York-based Jewish weekly *Forward* stated on April 16, 2004: "On the eve of the war, **Israel was a quiet but enthusiastic supporter of America's war plans**. Saddam Hussein's military power, it was universally agreed, made him one of the Jewish state's most dangerous adversaries... His overthrow was seen as eliminating Israel's most serious existential threat... [and Israel] eagerly cooperated ... sharing information on Iraqi capabilities and intentions ... meant to help the American action.... But because **Israel uniquely benefitted** from a war that is increasingly controversial in America and around the world, fears of speaking out have grown even stronger than they were before the war."

The immense power welded by Jews in our nation's capital was further highlighted when Israel's Hebrew-language radio station *Kol Yisrael* reported on a public argument between Shimon Peres and Ariel Sharon. It concluded with Sharon thundering: **"I want to tell you something very clear. Don't worry about America... [W]e the Jewish people control America and the Americans know it"** (AIP, Israel, October 3, 2001). This fact was further confirmed by a statement made a few years earlier by Avi Shavit, an Israeli journalist, who declared that "the White House and much of the America media [are] now in our hands" (*New York Times*, May 22, 1996).

'GOD TOLD ME ...'

Pressured by his Zionist "friends," and on the basis of deliberately-falsified "intelligence," Mr. Bush plunged ahead with his invasion of Iraq. Ari Shavit admitted a few weeks after the invasions that "the war was conceived by 25 neo-conservative intellectuals, most of them Jewish, who are pushing President Bush to change the course of history" (*Ha'aretz*, April 9,2003).

Despite his early claim of "mission accomplished" (May 1, 2003, which interestingly was the 227th anniversary of the founding of the Illuminati in 1776), the president soon found himself (and unfortunately his nation) "living on an ungrateful volcano" as warned against by Winston Churchill years earlier. Having also ignored his father's sage advice that "going in and occupying Iraq would incur incalculable human and political costs (as) the United States would be an occupying power in a bitterly hostile land" (*A World Transformed*, by G.H.W. Bush, p.489. 1998), George W. found himself in a quagmire to end all quagmires. Apparently during his years at Yale, from which he graduated with a degree in history, he wasn't bright enough to learn from the numerous lessons written so graphically in the history books.

Did he apologize? Not George W. Bush. No, sir! He "passed the buck,"stating that his decision to invade Iraq was directed by a "higher father" (Bob Woodward, *60 Minutes*, 4/18/04). This presidential belief in divine inspiration was confirmed during a visit to the Middle East in 2004, at which time *Ha'aretz* quoted the president as stating: "God told me to strike at al-Qaeda and I struck them. Then He instructed me to strike at Saddam, which I did. Now I'm determined to solve the problems of the Middle East (Quoted also in the *Washington Post*).

9/11 COVERUP

The events of 9/11/01 changed the world dramatically - and permanently. Within hours, the American people were subjected to a non-stop bombardment by the Establishment media: America Under Attack, America At War, America's New War, America Fights Back, America Unites. Day by day, these themes were pounded relentlessly into the minds of the American public. Within days the president declared his administration's "war on terrorism."

A multitude of important questions have been raised about probable White House/ CIA/Mossad/FBI involvement in the events of 9/11 and the widespread coverup thereof. In this overall context, this author is reminded of a statement made by Edwin Stanton, Abraham Lincoln's secretary of war, to the effect that "wars are not fought to defeat an enemy. Wars are fought to create a condition."

EXPLOSIVES PLACED IN BASEMENTS?

Many thoughtful and observant individuals who were directly involved - including members of the New York Fire Department, people who worked in the World Trade Center, and independent researchers - believe the federal government was somehow involved in the planning and execution of the attacks. They further believe that the collapse of the Twin Towers was caused, not by the two planes that crashed into the buildings but rather by explosives having been set off in the basements of each structure. Although the "mainstream" American media have dutifully chosen to ignore these assertions, a BBC commentator on the scene reported – on live TV – having heard two massive, distinct, and separate explosions just prior to the implosions of the towers. This independent and highly authoritative report serves to substantiate the testimony of firefighters and workers at the Twin Towers. This and other powerful evidence was presented to the commission allegedly investigating the terrorist attacks, but were carefully editing out of the "final report."

In the light of the fact that 9/11 may well have been a "black ops" exercise (an inside job) concocted to "create a condition," what could that desired "condition" have possibly been? Writing some 35 years prior to 9/11, Dr. Carroll Quigley may have provided us with a clue to the answer. On page 256 of his 1348-page book *Tragedy and Hope*, we read that changes that could take up to fifty years in peacetime can be brought about in five years during wartime

Did not Mr. Bush's phony war on terrorism produce "results" on the American scene that could never have taken place during a time of peace? You bet! Using the "war on terrorism" as their basic theme, the "republican"Bush administration – in unison with the mind manipulators of the Establishment media – did a masterful job of persuading the American sheeple they needed much more protection from "terrorists"and possible terrorist acts that could be perpetrated against them at any time. The grim situation "obviously" called for unprecedented government action to protect the nation from this immediate threat. Voila, the Bush administration stepped forward with the apparent "answer"– **the already-prepared-and-waiting-to-go Patriot Act and Homeland Security legislation**. Revealingly, our "representatives" on Capitol Hill weren't allowed to examine the contents of either of these draconian bills before voting for their passage. In time of "war" why bother about such trivialities? Of course, had a similar crime been perpetrated against the American people and their Constitution under a "democratic" administration, all hell would have broken loose. Under the "republicans," who are usually stridently vocal against expansion of government power, it sailed through with little public opposition. With almost total support from the "democrats," the potential chains and fetters of a totalitarian police state were successfully "sold" to the American public under the monstrously deceitful labels of "patriotism" and "security." As Adam Weishaupt so aptly put it, "Oh man, what can you not be brought to believe?" (*World Revolution*, p.13)

Homeland Security has been termed "the most significant transformation of the U.S. government since 1947 when 22 separate agencies were combined to become the Cabinet-level Department of Homeland Security." This legislation literally guts the Constitution and the Bill of Rights that have served our nation so well for more than 200 years. These draconian changes were slipped past a sleeping American public and a non-protesting Congress on a tidal wave of patriotic sounding rhetoric. Their full implementation await yet another "catastrophic and catalyzing event" like "another Pearl Harbor" or "another 9/11."

Is it not logical to conclude that it was all planned that way? America is thus being transformed into a Hitler-type Police State under the banners of "patriotism" and "national security." "We're from the government. We're here to help you."

Don't you find that extremely comforting?

But wait! That's not all. Our wonderful leaders in Washington (and Tel Aviv) are not slacking off in their herculean efforts on your behalf. As your devoted servants and protectors, be assured they are busy behind the scenes developing additional plans for your future. When the next "catastrophic and catalyzing" 9/11-like crisis explodes on the Americans scene, as it inevitably will in one form or another, our "honorable" leaders in Washington will immediately stress the "obvious need" for even sterner measures to fight the "war on terrorism." They will undoubtedly have previously devised strait-jackets and shackles waiting in the wings.

It is also important to note that George W. Bush has not talked about – or even openly acknowledged – most of our nation's real problems. We have heard no criticism of NAFTA, GATT, or CAFTA that have cost millions of Americans their well-paying jobs. We have seen no action to stop the massive influx of illegal aliens. There has been no condemnation of our unconstitutional fiat money system under which the United States has been financially raped by the international bankers. There has been no mention of how we are going to take care of the estimated forty trillion ($40,000,000,000, 000) in total federal debt obligations incurred since World War II. No concern has been expressed over the sell out of our national sovereignty. There has been no basic disapproval of the content of what is labeled "education" in our schools and colleges. No talk of seriously reducing the size of government as promised in his 2000 campaign - or of dismantling the various planks of the *Communist Manifesto* that are now in full force and effect in our nation. In other words, apart from a few minor changes in "procedure, priority, and method" the bipartisan rape of the United States by the New World Order continues unabated.

Two important questions: How will tens of millions of Americans react when finally forced to come face-to-face with the fact that an almost indescribable crime has been perpetrated against them by the villainous politicians of both main parties since the treacherous days of FDR? When they are compelled to face the fact that the media con artists or religious charlatans they so greatly respected aided and abetted in the crime - or stood by silently as our once great nation was plundered by the globalist vultures? When they have finally lost those things they assumed to be their "right"? When they find themselves reduced to feudal serfs on a global plantation as predicted by Dr. Carroll Quigley (*Tragedy and Hope*, p.324)?

Multiple millions have for years sneered and scoffed at the facts regarding the deadly threat posed by those exposed in the pages of this book. They sneered at reality. They poured ridicule and disdain on those they looked down on as "wackos" and "conspiracy theorists." Millions naively or wilfully chose not to believe that a crime of this magnitude could possibly be perpetrated upon a nation that prides itself on its ultra sophistication.

Stop and think! Could it possibly be true that **the real purpose** behind the Homeland Security and Patriot Act legislation is **not** the security of the American people in general, but is in fact ultimately designed to "protect" and make "secure" from unrestrained public wrath those criminal politicians in both parties - and their media co-conspirators - who have been instrumental in the execution of this dastardly crime?

It sure makes sense to me. How about you?

CHAPTER SEVEN

THE BILDERBERGERS

Is there really an international organization known as the Bilderbergers — made up of the elites from the worlds of banking, business, government and academia — which holds top-secret meetings each year in remote resorts in the United States and Europe, to plan what is going to happen on the world scene in the months ahead?

Some years ago, two concerned Americans who had heard about the possible existence of such a clandestine body wanted to have that question answered. One wrote to the White House requesting information, while the other wrote to a Senator seeking clarification.

The first letter was answered by the Justice Department to the effect that, "No one in the White House has any information regarding the Bilderbergers. Unfortunately, after some investigation, we have not been able to discover any information regarding the Bilderbergers either." The second letter — to Senator James L. Buckley — brought the following response: "Frankly, I don't subscribe to the theory that there exists an organization of international bankers called the Bilderbergers..."

It is vitally important that one thing be made perfectly clear at the outset of this chapter: either the people at the White House and the Justice Department, and the Senator from New York, were among the most totally ignorant, uninformed and "blind" people on the face of the earth — *or they lied*! There can be no alternative!

The truth is that, "Yes, Virginia, the Bilderbergers do exist." They are a type of international aristocracy who meet annually. Their original leader was H.R.H. Prince Bernhard of the Netherlands whose wife, Queen Juliana, was reputed to be the richest woman alive. Bernhard lost his leadership position as a result of his involvement in the 1976 Lockheed pay-off scandal, and the exposure of extra-marital affairs in Paris and elsewhere. He died in 2004.

The first secret meeting of these elitist internationalists took place, under the chairmanship of Prince Bernhard, at the Bilderberg Hotel in Oosterbeek, Holland, from May 29-31, 1954. Since then the meetings have been called Bilderberg meetings. Knowledge of the 1954 meeting, and the names of participants, was successfully "blacked out" by its organizers — with the full cooperation of those who control the mass media worldwide. One observer later said that the conference was "considered so important, even the `leaks' were watertight." Since 1954 hardly a word about the annual Bilderberg meetings has appeared in any of the leading newspapers, or on prime time TV network news programs. An almost total blackout! Why?

What conclusion can a rational, straight-thinking person draw from these facts? They are left with three possibilities: (1) These annual meetings are not really "news," and so are unworthy of coverage; (2) The media were unaware of these meetings and, so, couldn't report on them, or (3) There has been a conspiracy of silence among those who control the mass media to deliberately suppress any information about those meetings.

With a modicum of mental exertion the reader should be able to recall that, over the years, "great" publications like *New York Times, The Washington Post, Los Angeles Times, Newsweek, and Time magazine* have managed to find billions of feet of newsprint on which to print multiple thousands of "stories" that have little significance or public interest. Acknowledging this fact, the reader should ask themselves why these same publications can never seem to find space in which to inform their faithful readers about the Bilderberg meetings. No stories. No analysis. No photos. Nothing! Why? Former New York editor, John Swinton, gives us the answer: "We are tools and vassals of the rich behind the scenes. We are marionettes ... intellectual prostitutes."

On prime time television "news" programs, one never sees any of the well-known “anchors” pounding on their desks while thundering over the airwaves about the "public's right to know" about the

Bilderberg meetings. It is time we realize that these men are mere puppets (albeit, extremely well paid puppets!) who dance to the tune called by their masters behind the scenes. They are not interested in the truth. They are paid millions every year to parrot the party line and to project the image desired by the Big Boys who control the networks. A little investigation will reveal that these individuals are all internationalists — men who view the United States Constitution with contempt, and who are dedicated to the Illuminist concept of a One-World Government — or New World Order!

As Americans, we have been taught from childhood to believe that we live in a free country. But such is clearly not the case. During recent decades things have changed drastically. True, the old sentiments linger on in the hearts of some people but the reality of life in our nation has changed spectacularly. Chains of serfdom are being draped about our bodies and our institutions but, as a people, we seem so insensible and so numbed by the onrush of frightening historical events, that we appear unwilling or unable to move to defend ourselves! As Willis Carto wrote some years ago: "How the press ... loves to brag to its victims — its readers — about its freedom. Yes, the press may be free to lie and distort and suppress and deceive and malign, but is it free to tell the truth?" Many have good reason to believe that the truth is dead as far as the mass media is concerned.

'THE GREY EMINENCE'

The "credit" for getting the Bilderberg movement under way belongs to Joseph H. Retinger who, according to documents entered in the *Congressional Record*, September 15, 1971, p.E9620, "was generally regarded as the 'grey eminence' of European diplomatic circles." He "contributed much towards the intrigues of secret negotiations and organizations of power at the highest levels of statecraft. The eulogies bestowed upon him after his death in 1960 affirmed the notion that `he knew almost everyone that mattered in Europe and the United States.' `I remember,' recalled Sir Edward Beddingham-Behrens, `in the United States his [Retinger's] picking up the telephone and immediately making an appointment with the President; and in Europe, he had complete entree in every political circle, as a kind of right, acquired through the trust, devotion, and loyalty he inspired" (*The Times*, London, June 13, 1960, p.12).

Undoubtedly, Retinger was a front man, or `glorified' messenger boy, for the real movers and shakers behind the scenes. It was he who persuaded the Dutch royal family to take the lead in creating the Bilderberg organization. Readers who have studied the way in which the Rothschilds and other international banking families operate will recognize the fact that they very seldom, if ever, take the lead in promoting the ideas or concepts they wish to develop. They invariably use fronts or agents who have proven themselves to be thoroughly reliable and thus worthy of their trust. Historians recognize that such men as August Shoenberg (later known as August Belmont) who supported the North during the Civil War, and Judah Benjamin, Secretary of State of the Confederacy, were both Rothschild agents. Paul Warburg, of the well-known German banking family, who was the chief architect of the Federal Reserve System (which created a privately-owned banking monopoly in the United States) was also a Rothschild agent. The latter fact was confirmed by Colonel Ely Garrison, friend and financial advisor to Presidents Teddy Roosevelt and Woodrow Wilson. In *Roosevelt, Wilson, and the Federal Reserve Law*, Garrison stated: "Paul Warburg was the man who got the Federal Reserve Act together after the Aldrich Plan aroused such nationwide resentment and opposition. The mastermind of both plans was Baron Alfred Rothschild of London."

It is a significant fact that the big names in international finance have frequently played host to the secret Bilderberg meetings. In 1957 this "Invisible Government" met for the first time on American soil on St. Simons Island, Georgia. In 1964 they convened at Williamsburg, Virginia, a Rockefeller resort, and in 1971 at the Rockefeller-owned Woodstock Inn in the small, remote town of Woodstock, Vermont. In 1981, it was the turn of White Plains, New York to host the elitist group. In 2002, Chantilly, Virginia, had that "honor."

In Europe, the meetings are hosted by the Rothschilds in such places as the luxurious Hotel d'Arbois in the town of Megeve, in the French Alps. In 1962 and 1973 the meetings were held in Saltsjobaden, Sweden, and were hosted by the Wallenbergs, whose fortune has been estimated at well over 10 Billion dollars. In 2005 the

Bilderbergers met in Rottach-Egern, Germany. Can there be any doubt that those who control the Bilderberg organization are the "movers and shakers" in international affairs — those who make the truly big decisions?

A lot may be learned by noting the names of just a few of those who have attended these clandestine meetings over the years: David Rockefeller, Henry Kissinger, John R. Galvin (Supreme Allied Commander Europe), Queen Beatrix of the Netherlands, Queen Sophia of Spain, Katherine Graham (chairwoman of the Washington Post Co.), Robert L. Bartley (editor of the *Wall Street Journal*), Giovanni Agnelli (Chairman of Fiat), and Bill Gates of Microsoft. Bill Clinton was a Bilderberg "guest" before running for president. The same applied to Tony Blair before becoming British prime minister.

At the 1991 Bilderberg meeting held in Baden-Baden, Germany, after the first Gulf War, it was "repeatedly stated that ... there will be `other Saddams' in the years ahead who must be dealt with swiftly and efficiently.

"What the Bilderberg group intends is a global army at the disposal of the United Nations, which is to become the world government [George Bush's New World Order] to which all nations will be subservient...

"Crucial to making the U.N. a strong world government, `by osmosis,' in the words of some Bilderberg participants, is to bestow it with `enforcement powers'...

"`A UN army must be able to act immediately, anywhere in the world, without the delay involved in each country making its own decision whether to participate, based on parochial considerations,' said Henry Kissinger during one of the forums" (*Spotlight* Reprint, August, 1991).

It is illuminating (!) to note that practically all the attendees from the United States are members of the Council on Foreign Relations which, the reader will remember from chapter six, is a branch of the British-based, Illuminati-inspired Royal Institute of International Affairs (Chatham House).

Only politicians and others who have proven their unquestioning loyalty to the Rothschild/Rockefeller cabal are invited to Bilderberg meetings. They must be willing tools of the super-rich and totally dedicated to the creation of a New World Order. Nationalists and anti-Communist political figures are never allowed inside a Bilderberg meeting.

According to Bilderberg propaganda entered in the *Congressional Record* April 11, 1964, by liberal New York Senator Jacob Javitts,

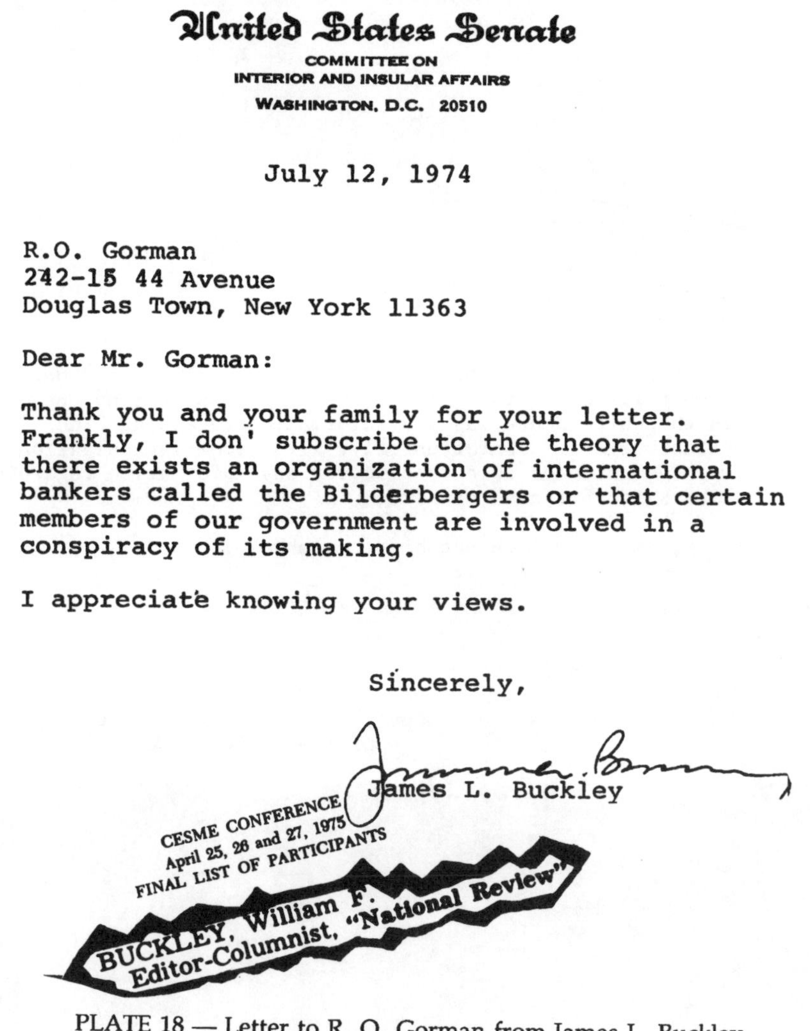

United States Senate
COMMITTEE ON
INTERIOR AND INSULAR AFFAIRS
WASHINGTON, D.C. 20510

July 12, 1974

R.O. Gorman
242-15 44 Avenue
Douglas Town, New York 11363

Dear Mr. Gorman:

Thank you and your family for your letter. Frankly, I don' subscribe to the theory that there exists an organization of international bankers called the Bilderbergers or that certain members of our government are involved in a conspiracy of its making.

I appreciate knowing your views.

Sincerely,

James L. Buckley

PLATE 18 — Letter to R. O. Gorman from James L. Buckley

The photographs following in this chapter are reproduced courtesy of American Free Press, 645 Independence Ave. SE, Washington, D.C. 20003.

DEPUTY ASSISTANT ATTORNEY GENERAL
OFFICE OF LEGAL COUNSEL

Department of Justice
Washington, D.C. 20530

Name & address deleted

APR 8 1975

Dear Ms. McArthur:

Your letter to the President of March 10, 1975, has been referred to this Office for reply, because no one in the White House has any information regarding "The Bilderburgers." Unfortunately, after some investigation, we have not been able to discover any information regarding "The Bilderburgers" either.

I am sorry I cannot be of more help.

Sincerely,

Mary C. Lawton
Deputy Assistant Attorney General
Office of Legal Counsel

PLATE 19 — Letter from Mary C. Lawton to Ms. McArthur

**PRINCE BERNHARD OF THE NETHERLANDS (right)
FOUNDER OF THE BILDERBERG SOCIETY
AND JOSEPH DESIRE MOBUTU (left).**

Upper Crust Only . . .

2002 - Chantilly, Virginia: This sign was posted at the entry drive to the Westfield Marriott Conference Center.

"Bilderberg is in no sense a policy-making body. No conclusions are reached. There is no voting and no resolutions are passed.

"The meetings are off the record. Only participants themselves may attend the meetings.

"Leading figures from many fields — industry, labor, education, government, etc. — are invited, who, through their special knowledge and experience, can help to further Bilderberg objectives."

The well-known British authority on international power politics, A. K. Chesterton, comments: "If the Bilderberg conferences reach no conclusions and recommend no policies, it is because the conclusions have already been reached and the policies determined, so that the delegates assemble to be told what the form is. They did not need to be given their orders. Once the form is declared they know well enough what is expected of them... (*New Unhappy Lords*, p.205).

That is precisely why the more things *seem* to change on the political scene, *the more they remain the same*! Political fronts may come, and political fronts may go under a variety of labels — democratic, conservative, liberal, moderate — but the elitist plan for a New World Order dictatorship rolls relentlessly on! The "leaders" of most nations of the world are but pawns in the game being played by the Bilderbergers and their Illuminist associates around the world.

Anyone naive enough to believe that the Bilderberg group is just a debating society which has no bearing or impact on world affairs should stop, think, and ponder these questions:

(1) If these meetings are as boring and uninteresting as the Bilderbergers would have us believe, would international bankers, billionaire industrialists, royalty, leading political figures, top scientists, military men and academicians, media magnates and other elitists tear themselves away from their usually hectic schedules, for close to a week, to travel up to half way around the world in order to attend? The possibility is extremely slim!

(2) If the proceedings are so dull and devoid of public interest, what is the point of having an army of up to 1,000 troops and security personnel turn the meeting places into veritable armed camps? None!

(3) If nothing truly significant and worthwhile is discussed, why do the organizers always insist on the residents of the resorts where they meet, having to leave their apartments (and other hotels in the area) while the meetings are in session?

(4) Why do they suspend the regular staff members at the resorts where they meet and bring in non-English speaking aliens to staff the resorts for the duration of their meetings?

(5) Why do the organizers have all the conference rooms "de-bugged" each morning, and before each afternoon or evening session?

Why the great emphasis on secrecy and security if the goals of the Bilderberg group are altruistic and above suspicion? Honest, sincere men are never afraid of light, as is so beautifully illustrated by the words of the Lord Jesus Christ: "And this is the condemnation, that light is come into the world, and men loved darkness rather than light because their deeds were evil.

"For everyone who does evil hates the light, neither comes to the light, lest his deeds be reproved" (*John* 3:19-20).

Yes, why so much secrecy? Is the reason not made perfectly clear in Benjamin Disraeli's book, *Coningsby*, in which he states that "the world is governed by very different personages from what is imagined by those who are not behind the scenes" (p.233)? Their goal, as the late Professor Carroll Quigley of Georgetown University, makes perfectly clear, is "nothing less than to create a world system of financial control in private hands to dominate the political system of each country and the economy of the world as a whole. This system [is] to be controlled in feudal fashion by the central banks of the world acting in concert, by secret agreements arrived at in frequent private meetings and conferences" (*Tragedy and Hope*, p.324).

In other words, the main goal of the Bilderbergers is nothing less than to advance the diabolical plan for a New World Order outlined by Adam Weishaupt and the Illuminati!

DAVID ROCKEFELLER'S ADMISSION

If the reader should doubt the veracity of what they have just read, they should soberly ponder the following quotation from David Rockefeller. It is taken from the opening speech at the June 5-9, 1991, Bilderberg meeting: "We are grateful to the *Washington Post, The New York Times, Time* Magazine and other great publications *whose directors have attended our meetings and respected their promises of discretion for almost forty years...*

[Rockefeller here admits that these "great publications" have, for "almost forty years," and under an oath of secrecy, deliberately lied to their readers about the plans of the Conspirators].

And the reason? "*It would have been impossible for us to develop our plan for the world if we had been subject to the bright lights of publicity during those years*. But the world is now more sophisticated [he really means more brainwashed by the media he thanked, and by the "educational" system his family helped set up!] and *prepared to march towards a world government* which will never again know war but only peace and prosperity for the whole of humanity [*Is this not an almost exact quote from Adam Weishaupt himself*? See chapter five]. The supranational sovereignty of the intellectual elite and world bankers is surely preferable to the national autodetermination practiced in the past centuries" (Quoted from *Lectures Francaises*, July-August, 1991, by *Hilaire Du Berrier Reports*, 20 Boulevard Princess Charlotte, Monte Carlo, Monaco).

No wonder the Bilderbergers have been scared of public exposure for more than fifty years!

COUNCIL ON FOREIGN RELATIONS

The main tool of the internationalist elite in the United States is undoubtedly the Council on Foreign Relations (CFR). The CFR was founded in 1921 under the direction of Colonel E. Mandell House, when it became apparent that the United States was not going to join the League of Nations, an early effort to create a One-World Government.

The principal figures behind the formation of the Council were banking barons J. P. Morgan, John D. Rockefeller, Paul Warburg and Jacob Schiff — the very same personalties who engineered the creation of the Federal Reserve System (1913), and who, in 1916, were responsible for the introduction of the graduated income tax to America. It is important to note that both of these (a Central Bank and a graduated income tax) are major planks of the *Communist Manifesto* published in 1848 — a work plagiarized from Illuminist Clinton Roosevelt's book, *The Science of Government Founded on Natural Law*, published by Dean and Trevett, New York, in 1841. It can therefore be truthfully stated that the United States became one-fifth Communist when these were implemented!

It is also important to note that it was Colonel House who authored the anonymous book, *Philip Dru — Administrator* (Intimate Papers of Colonel House, edited by Charles Seymour, pp. 152-157). In his book House outlined detailed plans for the creation of a One-World totalitarian government, i.e, "Socialism as dreamed of by Karl Marx" (p.45).

Research conducted by the late Dan Smoot, for many years an FBI agent, revealed that the Council did not amount to a great deal until 1927, when the Rockefeller family (through the various Rockefeller Foundations and Funds) began to pour money into it. Before long, the Carnegie Foundation (and later the Ford Foundation) began to finance the Council.

"In 1929 the Council (largely with Rockefeller gifts) acquired its present headquarters property: The Harold Pratt House, 58 East 68th Street, New York City" (*The Invisible Government*, p.7).

As Dr. Carroll Quigley points out in *Tragedy and Hope* (p.952), the CFR is a front for the International Bankers and the elitist Insiders! As documented earlier, the Council on Foreign Relations is the American branch of the Institute of International Affairs in England. Similar organizations operate in other nations worldwide.

The fact that the CFR is a secret organization is demonstrated by the following statement taken from its 1966 *Annual Report*: "It is an express condition of membership in the Council, to which condition every member accedes by virtue of his membership, that unless expressly stated by an officer of the Council to the contrary, all proceedings at the Council's afternoon and dinner meetings as well as study and discussion groups are confidential, and any disclosure or publication of statements made at such meetings or attribution to the Council of information, even though otherwise available, is contrary to the best interests of the Council and may be regarded by the Board of Directors in its sole discretion as grounds for termination or suspension of membership pursuant to Article 1 of the By-Laws."

"A country which expects to remain ignorant and free ... expects that which never has been and never can be." Thomas Jefferson

The roster of the CFR, said the *Christian Science Monitor*, September 1, 1961, "contains names distinguished in the field of diplomacy, government, business, finance, science, labor, journalism, law and education. What united so wide-ranging and disparate a membership is *a passionate concern for the direction of American foreign policy.*"

The "passionate concern" of the CFR is the creation of a One-World dictatorship. This is clearly revealed in its own publications. For example, in 1959 the CFR published a document titled *Study No. 7: Basic Aims of U.S. Foreign Policy,* in which it was stated: *"The U.S. must strive to build a new international order* ... including states labeling themselves as 'socialist' [Communist]." The study also urged that the United States "*maintain and gradually increase the authority of the United Nations*" and "make more effective use of the International Court of Justice, jurisdiction of which should be increased by withdrawal of reservations by member nations on matters judged to be domestic" (*Review of the News*, September 19, 1973)." This 1959 study (*please note it was issued by the CFR nearly fifty years ago*) also called for secret talks with the Russians about a disarmament agreement, as well as opening up contacts with Red China. The reader will, of course, note that the declared aim of the Council on Foreign Relations (a "New International Order") is identical with that of the Illuminati (a "New World Order"). This isn't coincidental!

WIVES AND PRESS BARRED

LA Times 4-25-75

West's Elite Discuss World Problems

From Reuters

CESME, Turkey—The rich and influential of the Western world gathered in secret here today with armed police on guard to ensure the privacy of their three-day discussions on major world problems.

The 107 delegates from 16 countries are at this Aegean resort for the annual meeting of the self-styled Bilderberg Conference. Set up in 1954 under sponsorship of Holland's Prince Bernhard, it aims to give leading figures from the non-Communist world an exclusive forum to exchange views.

Countries taking part are Belgium, Canada, Denmark, Finland, France, West Germany, Iceland, Ireland, Italy, Holland, Norway, Sweden, Switzerland, Turkey, Britain and the United States. Greece was invited but declined, Prince Bernhard said.

The delegates, who are not allowed to take their wives, include British Chancellor of the Exchequer Denis Healey, French banker Baron Edmond de Rothschild and NATO Secretary General Joseph Luns.

American participants include Arthur Hartman, assistant secretary of state for European affairs; Donald Rumsfeld, White House aide; George Ball, former undersecretary of state, banker David Rockefeller and World Bank President Robert S. McNamara.

Prince Bernhard has described the absence of wives by saying they would disturb the atmosphere of serious work.

No votes are taken or resolutions passed and the press is barred.

Prince Bernhard said the total secrecy was to allow delegates to talk frankly, without fear of uncomfortable publicity.

Turkish police armed with rifles checked all vehicles entering the luxurious, 1,300-bed hotel complex where the delegates are staying.

A conference spokesman said the delegates would spend half their time in open discussion—each speaker having a maximum of five minutes—and the rest in private talks.

Prince Bernhard has rejected suggestions that the conference amounts to a private club designed to preserve the economic status quo of the Western world.

Observers said that with such figures as prime ministers, foreign ministers, heads of international organizations, and leading industrialists and bankers attending, some understandings could be reached in private that would have a bearing on later public events.

PLATE 21 — *Los Angeles Times* newspaper article

The late Joseph Kraft (CFR) described the Council as a "School for Statesmen ... [which] has been at the seat of basic government decisions, has set the context of many more, and has repeatedly served as a recruiting ground for ranking officials" (*Harper's Magazine*, July, 1958). Kraft made it clear that the Council carefully trains its members in a specific line of strategy to be carried out when they become members of the elitist team in Washington.

In the House of Representatives on April 28, 1972, Congressman John Rarick stated: "The CFR is the Establishment. Not only does it have influence in key decision-making positions at the highest levels of government to apply pressure from above, but it also finances and uses individuals and groups to bring pressure from below to justify the high-level decisions for converting the United States from a sovereign, Constitutional Republic into a servile member-state of a One-World dictatorship."

Just as in 1966, when "insider" Professor Carroll Quigley blew the whistle on the International Banking Conspiracy, in 1975 it was the turn of CFR insider Rear Admiral Chester Ward to write (with Phyllis Schlafly) an expose of the CFR. In *Kissinger on the Couch*, Ward says that although he did not agree with the basic policies of the Establishment he remained on the inside for sixteen years. Why? Because "access to CFR `confidential' sources can provide more significant intelligence information than can be secured from the reports made available from our intelligence community."

Referring to previous books and exposes on the CFR, Rear Admiral Ward – based on his vast knowledge and understanding of the inner workings of the Invisible Government – makes this critical observation: "Previous attempts to document the CFR's influence have been ignored or smeared by the Liberal press as exaggerated. This is to be expected, considering the beachheads that key CFR members hold in all parts of the media, and especially because any attempt to tell about the power and activities of the CFR is bound to sound exaggerated.

"Actually, however, all the published accounts thus far have understated the CFR's influence, just as all previous accounts of Henry Kissinger's power vastly underestimate him" (p.148).

During the Korean War (December 9, 1950) the *Chicago Tribune* editorialized a stinging indictment of the Council on Foreign Relations, which has since proven to be remarkably accurate:

"The members of the Council are persons of much greater than average influence in the community. They have used the prestige that their wealth, their social position, and their education have given them to lead their country towards bankruptcy and military debacle. There is blood on them — the dried blood of the past war [1941-45] and the fresh blood of the present one" [the Korean War].

NONE DARE CALL IT TREASON

When one considers the writings, the spoken words and, above all, the *actions* of the many individuals in government service who have sprung from the ranks of the Council on Foreign Relations since its creation — and when we note their unrelenting dedication to the destruction of America's sovereignty and the establishment of a One-World, Humanistic, Socialistic Government — can there be any doubt that the members of the CFR are in flagrant violation of the Logan Act which forbids American citizens —

"a. without the permission or authority of the government;

"b. Directly or indirectly;

"c. To commence or carry on any verbal or written correspondence or intercourse with any foreign government or any officer or agent thereof; OR

"d. To counsel, advise or assist in any such "correspondence," i.e. in any verbal or written correspondence by a United States citizen with any foreign government or ... agent thereof;

"e. With the intent to influence the measure or conduct of any foreign government or any officer or agent thereof in relation to any disputes or controversies with the United States, OR

"f. *With the intent to defeat the measures of the government of the United States.*"

STATE OF NEW YORK)
: ss.:
COUNTY OF NEW YORK)

On this 2nd day of November, 1949, before me came ALLEN W. DULLES and FRANK ALTSCHUL, who being by me duly and severally sworn, each for himself, deposes and says: That he, the said Allen W. Dulles, is the President of the COUNCIL ON FOREIGN RELATIONS, INC., and that he, Frank Altschul, is the Secretary thereof; that they have been duly authorized to execute and file the foregoing Certificate by the concurring vote of a majority of the members of the said Corporation present, in person or by proxy, at an annual meeting thereof duly held on October 13, 1949, upon notice pursuant to Section 43* of the Membership Corporations Law.

Allen W. Dulles
President

Secretary

Subscribed and sworn to before me
this 2nd day of November, 1949.

Helen F. Johnson

PLATE 22 — **THE C.I.A. IS IN FACT THE ENFORCEMENT ARM OF THE C.F.R.** To prove this point one need not look any further than at the fact that Allen W. Dulles, head of the O.S.S. operations in Switzerland during WW II, later became president of the C.F.R. He was subsequently appointed to head the C.I.A. The signed document above shows Allen W. Dulles as president of the Council on Foreign Relations.

PLATE 23 **(opposite page) — POSITIVE PROOF THAT THE COUNCIL ON FOREIGN RELATIONS WILL LIE IF NECESSARY TO COVER UP THEIR CONNECTION WITH THE ROTHSCHILD-CREATED "FEDERAL" RESERVE SYSTEM IS WELL DOCUMENTED!**

The very first debate in history (on the CFR-"Federal" Reserve connection) came on May 28th, 1972, between John Temple Swing, Executive Director of the CFR, and Anthony J. Hilder, Public Relations Director of COBRA (Committee Opposing Bigotry and Racism in America). This debate took place over KABC radio, Los Angeles, on the Robert Vaughn Show, and hands and seals at the City of New York, the 25th day of July, A. D. Nineteen hundred and twenty-one.

In the presence of:

Edna M. Klein

Frank L. Polk (L.S.)
30 East 70th Street, New York.

(L.S.)
17 East 80th Street, New York.

(L.S.)
11 Myrtle Street, White Plains, N.Y.

Edwin F. Gay (L.S.)
1261 Madison Avenue, New York.

(L.S.)
7 West [illegible] Street, New York.

(L.S.)
Yonkers, N. Y.

(L.S.)
60 West 83rd Street, New York.

(L.S.)

STATE OF NEW YORK, :
: ss.
COUNTY OF NEW YORK. :

FRANK L. POLK, being duly sworn, says: that he is one of the above named incorporators; that no previous application has been made for the approval of the certificate of incorporation to incorporate the Council on Foreign Relations, Inc., except that an executed certificate in sub-

proved the tie-in between the CFR and the "Federal" Reserve.

In a grilling one-hour interview Hilder stated: "There's never been a Chairman of the Board of the Federal Reserve — the privately owned Federal Reserve Corporation — that hasn't been a member of the Council on Foreign Relations. Arthur Burns, MacChesney Martin and even Paul Warburg, who founded the Council on Foreign Relations, all have been members."

Then, in an attempt to cover up "that connection," Swing replied: "He didn't found the Council on Foreign Relations."

Hilder insisted: "He was one of the founders of the Council on Foreign Relations."

Obviously, in this denial that Paul Warburg had anything to do with the Money Monopoly, Swing had hoped to con the public once again about the existence of CFR collusion and co-operation with the Fourth Reich of the Rich.

Background Paper No.2
For Meeting of
May 21, 1970

CONFIDENTIAL: Not for Publication
Not to be quoted or cited.

COUNCIL ON FOREIGN RELATIONS

Discussion Group on
U.S.-Soviet Relations

SOVIET SOCIOLOGY AND SOVIET PERCEPTIONS OF THE UNITED STATES

Outline of Presentation

Paul Hollander
University of Massachusetts

I. The Major Characteristics of Soviet Sociology

1) Applied problem solving

2) Modest theoretical aspirations

3) Most of its practitioners untrained in sociology

4) Explicit subservience to political and social engineering objectives (scientific detachment not even an ideal)

5) Declining emphasis on "survivals" as a major explanatory concept of undesirable phenomena in Soviet society

6) Systematic and patterned neglect of certain areas of inquiry

7) A (sometimes) spurious sense of discovery (youthfulness of the discipline)

8) The increasing unintended demonstration of a convergence of social problems (in complex, urban, secular societies)

9) Contrasts: a) oriented to improve Soviet society, the efficiency of its institutions

b) an instrument in the ideological struggle (must provide theoretical critiques of capitalist societies, expose bourgeois theories of society, vindicate Marxism, etc.)

PLATE 24 — Outline of program for a CFR meeting

It is common knowledge that all public officials of the United States government must swear or affirm that they will defend their country and its Constitution "against all enemies foreign or domestic." Can there be any doubt that the government officials who are members of the CFR or Bilderberg organizations are in direct violation of their oaths of office when they attend clandestine meetings which are "considered so important that even the 'leaks' are watertight" — and where the topic is always the same: the dissolution of national sovereignty and the creation of Adam Weishaupt's New World Order?

The Constitution of the United States is abundantly clear on such activities. Article 3, Section 3: *"Treason against the United States shall consist only in levying war against them, or in adhering to their enemies, giving them aid and comfort..."*

Notice that there are three basic points to this law: (1) *What* is war?; (2) *Who* is the enemy?, and (3) *What* constitutes "aid and comfort"?

Read this law carefully. It mentions only the levying of war against the United States — it says *nothing* about our having to *declare* war on anyone, before arrests and trials for treason can take place.

To "levy war" is to muster strength for the purpose of seizure and control over our Nation. The Federalist Papers, especially No. 23, makes it crystal clear that *our Founding Fathers understood that "war" was not limited to military action.* They referred to "unforeseen" types of war. As a result, economic war, social war, psychological war, semantic war, etc. all fall within our Founding Fathers' meaning of the word "war." That establishes *what* war is!

It should be obvious that the real enemies of the United States are those individuals and groups which undermine our Constitution, our prosperity, our institutions, our families, our schools, and all those things that are near and dear to the hearts of every true American! As is being amply demonstrated in this book, these predators are waging *total war* against the United States on every level.

Principal among our real enemies are the liberals (Illuminists) and the other political, educational, social, economic, and religious termites who are gnawing away at our very vitals —

tional Communism stands clearly revealed as just one of the many tools used by the "Illuminated" Power Elite while working toward the accomplishment of their diabolical goals!

One question remains: what is "aid and comfort"? It is simply anything that helps the enemy to wage war: aid being tangible things and comfort being psychological (support, sympathy etc.). Ever since the advent of the Roosevelt Administration in the 1930s "our" government agencies have been literally showering "aid and comfort" on our enemies, both foreign and domestic. That fact has been responsible for the startling degeneration which we have witnessed in recent decades. It is the cause of the planned disintegration of our society!

In pondering these startling facts, it is good that we reflect on the immortal words of Sir John Harrington (1561-1612): ***"Treason doth never prosper, what's the reason? For if it prosper, none dare call it treason."***

FROM WHENCE IT GOT ITS NAME: Above is a photo of the Hotel de Bilderberg, the hotel that hosted the first Bilderberg meeting all the way back in 1954. Bilderberg meetings have been held every year since then, with the venue sites getting more lavish every year. Bilderberg has at times taken to meeting on islands, ostensibly because it's easier to keep reporters and photographers away so no one can document those participants who attend.

CHAPTER EIGHT

THE UNITED NATIONS — THE NEW BABYLON

"The last hope of mankind ... the only means to protect the world from the horrors of war." That was the banner under which the Internationalist Monstrosity known as the United Nations (a real bill of good!) was sold to the American people in 1945.

One thing must be established at the outset: the aims of the United Nations Organization are diametrically opposed to the best interests of the American people. The ultimate goal is to do away with the United States Constitution and our sovereignty, and merge this great nation into a mongrelized New World Order. This was basically admitted by none other than John Foster Dulles, who would later become President Eisenhower's first Secretary of State: "The United Nations represents not a *final* stage in the development of world order, but only a primitive stage. Therefore *its primary task is to create the conditions* which will make possible a more highly developed organization" (*War or Peace*, Macmillan, 1950, p. 40)

To understand how the UN came into being we need to go back to the conclusion of World War I. At that time, President Woodrow Wilson went to Paris with an entourage of Insiders — Paul Warburg, Colonel House, Thomas Lamont, etc. — with high hopes of establishing a base for their much-sought-after New World Order, through the formation of a League of Nations. Congress, at the strong urging of the American people, rejected the Treaty prepared in Paris. As a result, America remained fairly free of alien entanglements.

The Internationalists had lost a battle but were determined not to fail in their ultimate objective. Careful planning and organization was called for if the popular climate of rejection of such unconstitutional ideas was to be overcome. They decided on a multi-pronged offensive.

In the 1920s, the Internationalists formed a variety of front organizations all over the world to promote their plans for a One-World Government. In the United States their little publicized tool was the Council on Foreign Relations, which was dealt with in the preceding chapter. Since the days of the FDR Administration many CFR members have served in high government posts, and have been responsible for formulating National Policy.

Another powerful tool in the hands of the Internationalists was a new breed of "educators" masquerading under the name "Frontier Thinkers." These newcomers on the American education scene, sponsored by the Rockefeller, Carnegie and other foundations, were led by John Dewey.

Their specific job was to indoctrinate teachers and prepare teaching material designed to "influence the social attitudes and behavior of coming generations."

Dr. Harold Ruggs, a disciple of Dewey, unveiled their motives when he wrote: "A new public mind is to be created. How? Only by creating tens of millions of new individual minds and welding them into a new social mind. Old stereotypes must be broken up and new climates of opinion formed in the neighborhoods of America" (*The Great Technology*, p.32).

Their plan was simple: create a "new" breed of American by brainwashing the youth of the nation, by ridiculing traditional standards of conduct and by pumping alien, humanistic concepts into their plastic, unsuspecting minds under the guise of education. American schools were to be turned into brainwashing institutions so that future generations of Americans would "yield themselves with perfect docility" into the "molding hands" of the Conspirators! (See chapter 6).

Members of the Council on Foreign Relations lost no time in laying plans for the future. State Department publication 2349, *Report to the President on the Results of the San Francisco Conference,* by U.S. Secretary of State, Edward Stettinius, stated: "With the outbreak of war in Europe, it was clear that the United States would be confronted, after the war, with new and exceptional problems... Accordingly, a committee on Post-War Problems was set up before the end of 1939, *at the suggestion of the CFR.* The committee consisted of high officials of the Department of State." All but one were CFR members.

Following Pearl Harbor, the One-Worlders immediately capitalized on our entry into the war. A conference was called of all nations allied against the Axis powers. Meeting in Washington early in 1942, the representatives of 26 nations issued a "Declarations of the United Nations." Thus the term "Allied Powers" was superseded by "United Nations." In subsequent wartime propaganda the term served two purposes: (1) It helped develop support among the American people for our allies — including Russia, and (2) A more insidious aim — it served to condition the minds of Americans towards acceptance of the coming Adam Weishaupt-inspired New World Order.

Even before the founding meeting of the new United Nations Organization could be held, the Insiders began to sell out American interests. At the infamous Yalta Conference, early in 1945, President Roosevelt and his advisors granted Russia three votes in the General Assembly to our one. The veto provision was also written into the Charter at Yalta.

On April 25, 1945, less than two weeks after Roosevelt's death, the San Francisco Conference opened with representatives of 46 nations in attendance. They adopted the Charter the following day — and the United Nations was on its way. According to researcher Robert W. Lee, there were 42 "(m)embers of the U.S. delegation to the San Francisco Conference who were, had been, or would later become members of the Council on Foreign Relations" (*The United Nations Conspiracy*, Appendix C, p.243).

"At the conclusion of the ... Conference, the Charter of the United Nations was bundled off to a waiting plane and gingerly placed in a 75-pound fireproof safe equipped with a small parachute. Attached to the safe was a stern inscription: 'Finder — do not open! Notify the State Department, Washington, D.C.' Chief custodian was Conference Secretary, Alger Hiss..." (*Life* magazine, July 16, 1945). The Charter was on its way to Washington for ratification by the Senate.

The Establishment/Communist coalition spared no effort to get their favorite project past the American lawmakers. Their strategy was clear: "Great popular support and enthusiasm for the United Nations policies should be built up, well organized and fully articulate. But it is also necessary to do more than that. The opposition must be rendered so impotent that it will be unable to gather any significant support in the Senate against the UN Charter *and the treaties which will follow...*" (*Political Affairs,* the official theoretical journal of the Communist Party, USA, April, 1945).

This theme was taken up by the liberal press — and the American public was deluged by a flood of misinformation regarding the aims and purposes of the new organization. United States government officials instrumental in the founding of the UN kept from the public (and many of their representatives) the fact that, from its inception, the UN was designed to promote the cause of world socialism. The Soviet Union insisted that the headquarters of the United Nations be located in the United States.

The 17-acre site for the United Nations headquarters in New York was donated by, of course, the Rockefellers! It cost them $8,500,000. The cost of the UN building, $65,000,000, was taken care of by an interest-free "loan" from American taxpayers.

Ratification of the UN Charter was bulldozed through the Senate on a wave of oratorical praise, and so the United States became committed to a New World Order which subverted its own Constitution.

To many readers the last statement may appear ridiculous: it is, nevertheless, a statement of plain fact — as was clearly acknowledged by no less an Establishment Insider than John Foster Dulles. In an April 12, 1952, speech, Dulles declared: "The treaty-making power is an extraordinary power, liable to abuse. Treaties make international law and they also make domestic law. *Under our Constitution, treaties become the Supreme Law of the Land. They are indeed more supreme than ordinary laws, for Congressional laws are invalid if they do not conform to the Constitution, whereas treaty laws can override the Constitution.* Treaties, for example, can take powers away from the Congress and give them to the President. They can take powers from the States and give it to the Federal government, *or to some international body,* and they can cut across the rights given to the people by their Constitutional Bill of Rights."

The fact that treaties could place all Americans at the not-so-tender mercies of a future world government (or New World Order) was so clearly recognized by the legal profession following the ratification of the UN Charter that, in 1952, the American Bar Association passed a resolution recommending a Constitutional Amendment which would state: "A provision of a treaty which conflicts with any provision of this Constitution shall not be of any force and effect. A treaty shall become effective as internal law of the United States only through legislation in Congress which it could enact under its delegated powers in the absence of such a treaty."

NAMING NAMES

In 1950, the State Department published a very illuminating official report, *Post War Foreign Policy Preparation, 1939-1945,* which named the men in the U.S. government who did the planning and shaped the policies that led to the creation of the United Nations: Alger Hiss, Harry Dexter White, Virginius Coe, Noel Field, Laurance Dugger, Henry Wadleigh, John Carter Vincent, David Weintraub, Nathan Silvermaster, Harold Glasser, Victor Perlo, Irving Kaplan, Solomon Adler, Abraham Silverman, William Ullman, William Taylor and John Foster Dulles. All the above, with the exception of John Foster Dulles, were later identified in sworn testimony as Communist agents.

And John Foster Dulles? It is well known where his sentiments lay: he had been hired by Joseph Stalin to act as Russia's legal counsel in the United States. He was also closely associated with J. P. Morgan.

These, then, were the traitors who, in conjunction with Soviet Russia's official representatives, formulated the Charter of the United Nations at the Dumbarton Oaks and Yalta Conferences. No wonder some patriotic Americans got the distinct impression that our interests were being sold out at the end of the war. Seldom, in recorded history, has a nation been so deliberately deceived by its alleged representatives.

The few Americans who took the time to read the constitutions of both the USSR and the United Nations came to the spine-chilling realization that the latter is nothing less than a copy of the former. That fact is not surprising, considering the political hue of the characters involved in the drafting of the UN Charter. Nothing less could be expected.

In addition, the seals of both the UN and the USSR are also very similar. Again, no coincidence: the UN seal was designed by Carl Aldo Marzani, a well-known Leftist.

MASTERS OF DECEIT

The founders of the United Nations Organization — and their successors — have proven to be masters of deceit. They have managed to shield their real goals and objectives from the overwhelming majority of mankind by hiding behind an ever-increasing bombardment of propaganda labeled peace, justice, freedom and human rights.

Former United Nations Ambassador Adlai Stevenson openly acknowledged this monstrous hypocrisy when he was so bold as to encourage newsmen to project a false image of the UN to the world. Speaking to the United Nations Correspondents Association on February 14, 1961, Stevenson asked newsmen to "help us create the sense of our overriding human concern. Interpret us to each other not as plotters or as warmongers or as demons or demigods, but as puzzled yet aspiring men and women struggling on the possible brink of Armageddon to achieve a common understanding and a common purpose. *We are not like that, I have no doubt*. But I believe the majority of our delegates would accept such a description of their own attitudes. *The whole press corps working at the United Nations has a unique part to play in projecting this picture" (United Nations: Guardians of Peace*, State Department Publication 7225, September, 1961, p.36).

What these Illuminists clearly have in mind for our future is graphically portrayed in George Orwell's book, *1984*. Orwell would appear to have written *1984* with a considerable amount of inside knowledge and understanding of what the Internationalists have planned for our future. To date, Orwell has proven to be remarkably accurate in his predictions of things to come. His prognosis of the future almost directly parallels that of Dr. Carroll Quigley — a "system controlled in a feudalistic fashion" in which the individual's "freedom and choice will be controlled within very narrow alternatives by the fact that he will be numbered from birth and followed, as a number, through his educational training, his required military or other public service, his tax contributions, his health and medical requirements, and his final retirement and death benefits."

One of the false pictures being projected by the UN is that it is a "peacekeeping organization ... determined to save succeeding generations from the scourge of war ... and to reaffirm faith in fundamental human rights, in the dignity and worth of the human person, in the equal rights of men and women and of nations large and small..." (Preamble to the Charter of the United Nations).

Even a cursory glance at the record of the UN over its sixty years of existence will vividly demonstrate the fact that such high-sounding phraseology is just so much pious cant — devoid of any true and purposeful meaning. The simple truth is that never in history has there been a similar period so filled with war, terrorism and moral corruption. Since 1945 the world has seen more than 70 major outbreaks of violence: Korea, Vietnam, Hungary, the Middle East, Tibet, Biafra, Katanga, Bosnia and Iraq are just a few.

During the same period of time well over one billion people were enslaved by the Communists. The hypocritical UN has never raised a finger to prevent the enslavement of anyone, and it has never liberated a single individual from Communist tyranny. It hasn't tried to — for liberty is not the goal of the United Nations!

The recent changes that have taken place in Russia and Eastern Europe have taken place for two reasons — one economic, *the other political*. The "collapse of Communism" in the East opens up the way for still further massive Western economic aid and financial investment in those countries which were behind the Iron Curtain. It also begins to pave the way for the planned integration of East and West in the New World Order.

FRAUD OF "EQUAL RIGHTS"

The UN Charter makes various references to "equal rights" and "self-determination of peoples." Most Americans, unaccustomed as they are to examining words for their exact meaning,

have accepted these terms as being synonymous with protection of rights and liberties.

Merely to guarantee equal rights to everyone is no guarantee of rights at all. If the rights of all people were reduced to zero, all the people would have "equal rights."

When the UN Charter speaks of the "self-determination of peoples" (Article 55) the word "people" means the people of a nation as a collective body. There is no place for individualism and true freedom in the Orwellian world envisioned by the "Illuminated" Insiders.

The reader will, no doubt, see the direct parallel between the pious cant dispensed by Adam Weishaupt and that published by both the Communists and the United Nations.

CONGO BLOODBATH

A couple of examples should suffice to demonstrate the monstrous gall and unfathomable hypocrisy of the organization that was sold to the American people as "the last hope of mankind." On June 30, 1960, in the wake of a massive anti-"colonialism" and anti-"imperialism" blitz by the United Nations against the European powers which had developed and still controlled parts of Africa, the Congo was granted independence from Belgium.

With the arrival of "independence," two main power blocs emerged within the new African nation: one was led by Patrice Lumumba, a gin-drinking, hashish-smoking Communist thug who was called "a great African leader" by Nikita Khrushchev; on the other side was a group led by Moise Tshombe, the son of a successful businessman. Tshombe was a strong anti-Communist and an ardent advocate of the concepts of limited government and free enterprise. Tshombe and his followers wished to establish a government in the Congo based on the American model — a system of weights and balances.

Shortly after independence, the Congolese army mutinied against its Belgian officers. Lumumba immediately fired the officers and threw them out of the country. He promoted the mutineers, giving them huge increases in pay. Without professional military leadership, and incited by Lumumba and his Red advisors, the Congolese army went on the rampage — murdering, raping, plundering. European residents fled in terror, leaving behind everything they had worked so hard to accumulate. Their bank accounts were frozen. The lucky ones managed to get out of the country alive, with just the clothes on their backs.

The Belgian government ordered its troops back into the Congo to protect the lives and property of Belgians still there. In a mad rage, Lumumba declared war on Belgium and sought United Nations aid in fighting the Belgians. Belgium, in turn, called on the United States to help so that it couldn't be accused by the Communists of perpetuating its influence in that nation.

Washington refused to aid Tshombe, claiming that it would be best to call in the UN to help solve the problem. On July 14, 1960, the United States representative at the UN sided with a Russian resolution condemning Belgium. They demanded prompt withdrawal of Belgian troops and authorized the United Nations to send its own troops to aid Lumumba. Less than a week later, thousands of UN troops began pouring into the Congo. Belgium withdrew its troops immediately, leaving the new nation to the not-so-tender mercies of Lumumba's pillaging rabble and the United Nations' "peace-keeping forces." In one of many outrages, nuns were forced to dance naked and sing hymns in praise of the Messiah Lumumba before being taken and ravished and subjected to bestial tortures.

The UN arrivals did little if anything to assist those in real need or to restore law and order. For the most part they stood to one side and watched the territory pillaged ... and slip increasingly under Communist control.

It was during this period of virtual anarchy that Moise Tshombe led Katanga Province in its break with the Communist-dominated central government. He made a famous declaration: "I am seceding from Chaos."

Tshombe requested and received Belgian assistance in subduing the mutineers, and in restoring civil order. With Belgian aid, he reorganized the army — and peace was restored to the war-ravaged province. Within days, life in Katanga returned to near normal.

The policy of the Katangan authorities was reflected in a statement by interior minister, Godefroi Munonga: "I want my country, Katanga, to be a bastion of anti-Communism in Africa. I detest Communism and will not alter my opposition to it. Katanga will stay independent, no matter what. We will not give in."

What happened next should make any sane American stop in their tracks and reflect deeply on the declarations and actions of the United Nations — "the last hope of mankind."

Hiding behind a thick wall of deceit, the United Nations forces attacked peaceful Katanga, whose leaders were making efforts to unite the Congo along federal lines.

If the United Nations command thought that subduing Tshombe's anti-Communist forces would be an easy task, they were sadly mistaken. The Katangan leader's crash program to reorganize the army, though only in its early stages, had proved highly successful.

After initial setbacks, the Katangan forces fought back and kept the "peace-makers" from making further major gains. Frustrated by their lack of success, the UN mercenaries launched a campaign of terror against the civilian population of Katanga: murder, arson, rape and plunder were the orders of the day. Ninety percent of the buildings destroyed by UN bombs were civilian structures.

Miraculously, the Katangans held the United Nations' savages at bay and prevented their new country from capitulating. Then the tide began to turn in favor of the Katangans who, by then, were being joined by their white neighbors who volunteered to fight against the UN forces who were killing their black friends and destroying their property.

A week after its unprovoked attack on Katanga — and as a result of demoralizing setbacks — the UN butchers agreed to a face-saving cease-fire. Katanga remained proudly free!

As could be expected, the United Nations Organization put out a barrage of misleading statements, and laid a thick smoke-screen to cover up its atrocities in Katanga. There were, however, too many honest reporters on the scene — and too many gruesome photographs and startlingly graphic newsreel footage smuggled out of Katanga — for them to totally succeed in their work of deception.

Close to a year had slipped by when a top secret United Nations memorandum to high officials found its way into the hands of the American Committee for Aid to the Katangan Freedom Fighters. The memorandum laid out a detailed plan for a second and decisive attack on the anti-Communist province of Katanga. It also stated: "The US will judge itself bound, as in the past, by UN decisions and will supply the necessary transport aircraft and, later on, aircraft .... the State Department has based its policy on the UN and will in no circumstances disregard its obligations to the UN."

"ODDS ... OVERWHELMING"

On December 29, 1962, the "peace-keeping" barbarians from the United Nations, freshly supplied with American dollars and war materiel, launched their second attack on freedom-loving Katanga. A month later, when the invaders were storming his final stronghold, Moise Tshombe told his gallant troops: "You have fought bravely against the enemy three times in the last two and one-half years. The odds have become overwhelming against us."

Shortly thereafter the last flickering hope of independence and freedom in the Congo died.

Since that date virtually every other country on the African continent has been sold down the river and are now under the control of Socialist/Communist black stooges. These new nations — and their frequently awesome natural resources — are controlled in a variety of ways by the International Bankers. *Control, remember, is always the ultimate name of every game being played on the world stage*. The black Africans are mere pawns — very expendable pawns — in the "winner-take-all" global game of chess.

The descendants of the highly productive White Europeans who were instrumental in taming the Dark Continent and developing its enormous natural potential, have either been forced to leave the various countries, been terrorized into submission, or been murdered — all with the encouragement and support of the United Nations! As a result, nation after nation is reverting to its primitive, savage ways — the law of the jungle!

KOREA AND VIETNAM WARS

What the American "peasants" have never been told by their government is that the Under Secretary for Political and Security Affairs at the United Nations has been an official of the Soviet Union, without exception, since 1945: "The post of 'Political and Security Affairs' traditionally has been held by a Soviet national .... [who] is Senior Adviser to the Secretary General" (*New York Times*, May 22, 1963). This gives the Soviet Union direct and immediate access to all the plans for and activities engaged in by United Nations' forces anywhere in the world.

With this understanding, the light begins to dawn on all of the apparently "incredible" and "incomprehensible" events that took place during the course of both the Korean and Vietnam Wars.

Colonel F.P. "Bud" Farrell, USAF, Retired, who served in both of these wars, comments: "All of our military operations had to be forwarded by radio to the Soviet Commander of the United Nations Security Council ... before our forces went into action... The Soviet Commander delayed the battle plans until he relayed our battle planning information to Moscow....

"The enemy then relayed these battle plans to their Communist forces in the field. They knew beforehand when we were coming and how many of us there were. The enemy knew our every move at all times. *Our troops were led like sheep to the slaughter in both Korea and Vietnam*....

"Every president and every congressman since Truman has been aware of this treason by the United Nations Security Council against our military forces. The deaths, suffering and wounded — and prisoners of war — are to be laid at their feet. *This is treason at the highest level.*"

In Korea, for example, the overall military situation was so incredible that General Mark Clark speculated that "perhaps Communists had wormed their way so deeply into our government on both the working and planning levels that they were able to exercise an inordinate amount of power in shaping the course of America in the dangerous postwar era.

"I could not help wondering and worrying whether we were faced with open enemies across the conference table and hidden enemies who sat with us in our most secret councils" (*From the Danube to the Yalu*, Harper and Brothers, 1954, p.11).

Regarding the sanctuary granted Communist forces during the Korean War, General Douglas McArthur wrote: "I was ... worried by a series of directives from Washington which were greatly decreasing the potential of my air force. First I was forbidden 'hot' pursuit of enemy planes that attacked our own. Manchuria and Siberia were sanctuaries of inviolate protection for all enemy forces and for all enemy purposes, no matter what depredations or assaults might come from there. Then I was denied the right to bomb the hydroelectric plants along the Yalu. This order was broadened to include every plant in North Korea which was capable of furnishing electric power to Manchuria and Siberia. Most incomprehensible of all was the refusal to let me bomb the important supply center in Racin, which was not in Manchuria or Siberia, but many miles from the border, in northeast Korea. Racin was a depot to which the Soviet Union forwarded supplies from Vladivostok for the North Korean Army. *I felt that step-by-step my weapons were being taken away from me*" (*Reminiscences*, McGraw-Hill, 1964, p.365).

"That there was some leak of intelligence was evident to everyone. [General Walton] Walker continually complained to me that his operations were known to the enemy in advance through sources in Washington .... information must have been relayed to them, assuring that the Yalu bridges would continue to enjoy sanctuary and that their bases would be left intact. *They knew they could swarm across the Yalu River without having to worry about bombers hitting their Manchurian supply lines*" (pp.374,375).

In his book, McArthur cited an official pamphlet distributed by Chinese General Lin Piao, whose troops were fighting alongside those of North Korea: "*I would never had made the attack and risked my men and military reputation if I had not been assured that Washington would restrain General McArthur from taking adequate retaliatory measures against my lines of supply and communication*" (pp.374,375).

When the Korean armistice agreement was signed on July 27, 1953, General Mark Clark lamented the fact that he had "gained the unenviable distinction of being the first United States Army commander in history to sign an armistice without victory" (*From the Danube to the Yalu*, p.1).

The Vietnam War was basically more of the same — only worse!

Many recognize the fact that the United States could have won the Vietnam War within a week, and without the massive loss of life and limb (58,000 dead and hundreds of thousands of wounded) that resulted from it.

In Vietnam, we were deprived of victory by the issuance of the infamous "Rules of Engagement." Thanks to Senator Barry Goldwater (R-Arizona), this critical document was placed in the *Congressional Record* on March 6, 14, 18 and 26, 1985. As had been the case in the Korean War less than two decades earlier, these rules effectively emasculated American forces, thus preventing a victory. They prevented air strikes on targets vital to the enemy's war effort. The Joint Chiefs of Staff (JCS) pinpointed 242 such vital targets, but could not bomb them without permission from the secretaries of defence, Robert McNamara and Clark Clifford. This is not surprising: both McNamara and Clifford had sold their souls to the architects and builders of the New World Order. To their lasting shame, their treachery reflected their slavish dedication to their Illuminist masters.

It could be said that they were "following orders." But that is no excuse for their despicable betrayal of their own countrymen. "Following orders" was not held to a valid defense at the Nuremberg Trials following World War II, and it most certainly is not a valid defence for those holding high office in Washington — from the president on down — who betrayed our troops in Korea and Vietnam! As Colonel "Bud" Farrell said, their actions represented *"treason at the highest level."*

But then, as Sir John Harrington (1561-1612) so eloquently put it, "Treason doth never prosper, what's the reason? *For if it prosper, none dare call it treason."*

THE GULF WAR

The "Gulf War" of 1990-1991 was fought, as President George H. W. Bush clearly stated at the time, to advance the cause of the "New World Order." It had nothing to do with the long-term welfare of the United States, but it had everything to do with the balance of power in the Middle East. As this author wrote at the time, "under the terms of a secret agreement made between the American and British `elites'

(The Pilgrim Society) in 1897, America is pledged to come to the aid of the British Crown (or, in reality, Rothschild's City of London) whenever called upon.

"The secret agreement between the English and American Establishments, plus America's $3,400,000,000,000 debt to the Rothschild-controlled international bankers, ensures America's subservient compliance to their dictates. Hence our 1990 presence in the Gulf! America is now 'the City's' balance-of-power enforcer worldwide!" (*Midnight Messenger*, Issue #33, September-October, 1990, p.2).

WHO PAYS?

Who pays for the Illuminist-New World Order Monstrosity known as the United Nations? As you may have guessed, it is the US (Uncle Sap) which primarily gets ripped off for most of the expenses involved in maintaining this "last hope of mankind." When the United States began bankrolling the UN back in 1946, the US Congress opened a bank account in the name of: "The United Nations, New York, New York." Although few realize it, the check Congress signed "authorized to be appropriated annually to the Department of State, out of the Treasury, such sums as may be necessary for the payment by the United States of its share of expenses of the United Nations as appropriated by the General Assembly...." (*United States Code*, Title 22, Foreign Relations and Intercourse, Chapter 7, sec. 287, p.5639 [1970]. This US public law clearly states that the UN tells us how much we have to pay — and we pay it to them!

The UN budget is assessed against all members at scales broadly based on their ability to pay — which is simply an international application of the basic Marxist principle: "From each according to his ability, to each according to his need." The United States' share of the financial burden has always headed the list. It was originally suggested that the US kick in 50 percent of the budget, but that amount was negotiated down to 39.89 percent. Since that time our assessment has been gradually lowered. It now stands at 25 percent.

That figure is, however, misleading as it doesn't include our "voluntary contributions" to various "special programs" of the

UN. These "voluntary contributions" amount to more than our regular contributions (*Update*, a UN publication, January 1973).

What does Uncle Sap get for his massive investment in "the last hope of mankind"? According to an official government source, "the UN provides public forum for clarifying to a wide audience our position on issues of vital concern to us ... and for enlisting support for international action on matters of prime concern."

In fact what we are paying for is an expensive soap box for God-denying humanistic Socialists and One-Worlders to sell their anti-American Internationalist ideas in the United States. No wonder the Communists were so keen to have the UN headquarters located in America!

Every agency of the United Nations Organization carefully orchestrates its efforts towards the same goal — the establishment of a New World Order.

Some readers will no doubt take exception to that last statement. They will point to such operations as UNESCO and UNICEF, and ask, "Aren't these fine, outstanding organizations, and aren't they doing a tremendous job of helping people in need all around the world?"

On the surface that may appear to be true — but only because of lying propaganda disseminated by the UN and its friends. As far as UNICEF is concerned, the record clearly shows that ever since its inception this agency has mightily aided and abetted the Communist cause around the globe.

The case against UNESCO is eloquently stated in the following piece written by Paul Harvey. It was inserted in the *Congressional Record* in 1962:

Congressional Record

PROCEEDINGS AND DEBATES OF THE 87th CONGRESS, SECOND SESSION

UNESCO: Communism's Trap for Our Youth

PLATE 25 — Paul Harvey's article on "UNESCO"

EXTENSION OF REMARKS

OF

HON. JAMES B. UTT

OF CALIFORNIA

IN THE HOUSE OF REPRESENTATIVES

Tuesday, September 4, 1962

Mr. UTT. Mr. Speaker, under unanimous consent to insert my remarks in the Appendix of the RECORD, I wish to insert an article by Mr. Paul Harvey, news analyst, American Broadcasting Network, entitled "UNESCO: Communism's Trap for Our Youth."

I have long contended that UNESCO posed a threat to our American youth by imposing international control of our curriculum by an international organization which does not embrace the American ideals liberty and freedom.

This article points up the fact that UNESCO is not tolerated in the Communist countries, as these countries do not accept the precept of UNESCO. Therefore, this program is simply preparing the youth of the free world to the subjugation of international communism. I hope that every parent who has children in school will read this and demand that the UNESCO program be forbidden in our American schools.

The article follows:

UNESCO: COMMUNISM'S TRAP FOR OUR YOUTH

When your child comes home from school parroting some phrase about the "world society of the future—" are you going to tell him it's wrong for him to "love his neighbor"?

When he comes home talking of world brotherhood, are you going to contradict the Christmas message of peace on earth and tell him that all men are not brothers?

Now wait a minute.

When your child goes from house to house for UNICEF, collecting coins for underprivileged children overseas, are you prepared to tell him he should not be charitable to those who have less?

When his elementary school textbooks indoctrinate him with the philosophy of world government are you prepared to insist that world war is preferable?

Are you against world government just because the American Legion is against it?

I have been wrestling with these questions and seeking answers for several weeks.

I told you there was evidence that UNESCO was brainwashing patriotism out of our youngsters and substituting the United Nations for God.

I said if I found fire where I'd smelled smoke we'd go into it further. Well, I have gone into it further, I have burned a lot of late lights digesting and analyzing all the evidence, pro and con, concerning UNESCO, and I have reached a conclusion which I want to discuss with you, but you are going to have to wade with me through some of the preliminary evidence.

UNESCO is the United Nations Educational, Scientific, and Cultural Organization. It is an organization with thousands of publications too vast to enumerate.

UNESCO booklets are distributed through the National Education Association and the PTA to teachers and students.

UNESCO literature is issued through YMCA groups and churches, radio and TV programs, newspapers, magazines, civic groups, government agencies, but mostly directly and indirectly, it's philosophy of one-world government is aimed at the classroom.

Twelve persons connected with the administration of UNESCO have been identified in sworn testimony before congressional committees as Communists.

Seven have been connected with Soviet espionage.

Six others refused to appear before Government loyalty boards.

But now we are not challenging the loyalty or the motives of this organization. We are seeking to determine whether, whatever their intentions, a whole generation of young Americans is getting brainwashed for their own good or somebody else's.

Sometimes the defenders of the citadel, when they get desperate, become as vicious as the attackers.

The critics of UNESCO have sometimes let themselves get so worked up that they start flailing their arms, swinging in all directions, becoming at once ineffectual and slightly ludicrous.

Let us, instead, suppose that the world government idea is a good one.

Let us admit that all God's children would be better off living together than fighting and that the next generation of children all over the world should be reared to this understanding.

That national boundaries are not something to fight over and that a United Nations is the way to discuss our disagreements.

That it is unnecessary to spill any more blood defending the American flag if we all pledge allegiance to the U.N. flag.

That is what the UNESCO disciples believe.

They are not all Communists. They are decent citizens who are convinced that this is the better way and that is why they are indoctrinating your child today through UNESCO literature and UNESCO influence in his elementary school classroom.

But this is the rest of the story:

Russia is not thus indoctrinating Russian children.

This is the larger issue. This is the point well-meaning veterans organizations and others have missed. While we are allowing our youngsters thus to have their American allegiance brainwashed away so they do not consider Americanism worth fighting for anymore, the Russians in their schools (and I wouldn't say this if I couldn't document it with current evidence) continue to preach and teach their elementary school children that communism is the only efficient government.

That God does not exist.

That Russia will one day rule the world.

Now wait a minute.

I'm talking now to the mostly good American parents who have been convinced that UNESCO was the proper way to prepare the next generation of world citizens to live together.

Don't you see what's happening?

Through UNESCO—American schoolchildren are being influenced away from their national allegiance.

American schoolchildren are being indoctrinated with world government ideals while the Russians prepare their children to run that world government.

They are softening the patriotism of our next generation, while hardening their own.

The end result of this lopsided indoctrination is too obvious to require elaboration.

Ex-Senator William Benton, speaking to UNESCO, said, "We are at the beginning of a long process of breaking down the walls of our national sovereignty. In this UNESCO can be, and indeed must be, the pioneer."

But Red Poland has pulled out of UNESCO. And Red Hungary. And Red Czechoslovakia.

They will not use this "break down the walls" and love everybody stuff in their schools.

They will love communism and teach communism and only we, United States of Americans will dilute our patriotism until the American flag is a faded rag not worth fighting for.

You may have difficulty getting your school administrators to admit that they are using UNESCO materials even if they are. The best test is to learn directly from the students if they are being taught that "collectivism is inevitable," that "polygamy is acceptable," that "private property has no place inthe new order," that "we are all citizens of the world with an allegiance to all nations and to no one nation."

School teachers are vulnerable.

The president of the National Education Association, Dr. Lyman Ginger, says Russia "has an excellent school system." The basis for his judgment is that the Russian teacher is paid 1½ times as much as the Russian skilled worker. Of course, that fact loses its luster when you realize that the Russian factory workers have to work 80 hours and 49 minutes to buy one pair of shoes.

Yet many American teachers have felt that in adopting the international outlook they were being modern and imitating what their NEA president calls the Soviet Union's "excellent school system." Though Russia's schools are not teaching internationalism.

Communism over God. Russia over all.

Ask Mrs. Eleanor Roosevelt about her recent visit to Russia. Are Soviet schools incorporating the UNESCO program? Certainly not.

Are Russian schools teaching that one nation is just like any other nation and that we must all live together under a United Nations? Certainly not.

Our UNESCO literature is indoctrinating American children with the idea that we should have an international anthem. Would Russian schools thus teach Russian children? Certainly not.

Mrs. Roosevelt found the Russians demanding an indelible allegiance to their own country. Seeking in every way to strengthen their own country. Teaching their children, by the Pavlovian reflex method, precisely and only what the Soviet state wants them to believe. As Pavlov taught his conditioned dogs, they teach their children to hate the United States.

Is there nothing to encourage international peace in their curriculum? Nothing. The classroom is a nationalistic weapon of the Kremlin.

The UNESCO Seminar—which guides American teachers—states, "One of the chief aims of education everywhere is to develop those qualities of citizenship which provide the foundation upon which international government must be based." No, not "everywhere."

So before we rewrite our textbooks, as the UNESCO Seminar recommends, "on a view to improving them as aids to international understanding," let's be sure everybody else follows suit or the implication is obvious. We grow nationally soft while they grow hard and strong. Only a Russian citizen or a Soviet subversive would want that.

Now please don't come back at me with the many old pro-and-con arguments that have been weighed by the American Legion and the VFW and countless civic and discussion groups for years. I have, I believe, seen them all and I am not concerned with more hash from these leftovers.

We are not debating whether UNESCO's philosophy is good or evil.

We are not opposing the United Nations. We are not denouncing international cooperation.

We are not challenging the rightness or the wrongness of editing textbooks to put the U.N. in and rewriting history, to take the United States out and coaching our teachers to erase national boundaries from the minds of the next generation.

I only object to this one fact. It is not who is right that is of greatest importance, but what is right.

That while we are thus conditioning our children to salute a mongrel flag, Russia is conditioning her children to salute only the hammer and sickle.

Suppose you and I were trainers, training professional fighters and you taught yours to fight and I taught mine to dance the minuet, we'll have a real happy party. But

PLATE 25B

Russia is training fighters.

Now, you say, what can you do?

If you are concerned with preserving patriotism in the next generation of Americans then the youngster first must hear it at home.

Dad's constant complaining about unfair taxes and "crooks in Washington" does little to instill faith and confidence in our Government. It must be counterbalanced with a respect for the strengths of our Nation, rather than a constant exaggerated emphasis on its weaknesses.

After the youngster has heard a little star-spangled conversation around the house, it's time for the parents to attend PTA meetings and to take an active, intense, personal interest in what the school is teaching and what it is not teaching.

If you don't others will.

If you figure you can stay home and play cards on PTA night and "let George do it," you'd better expect the worst because George doesn't always agree with you.

The FBI has established that the Communists in the United States, under orders from Moscow, are making a concerted effort to work through respectable forums, including PTA groups. If you can't take an interest in directing your child's education, they will.

They are. Right now.

Much has been said about what Americans stand for. Equally important are the things Americans won't stand for.

And for goodness sake, understand this: Everybody who subscribes to the UNESCO philosophy of education is not a Communist. He may unwittingly be their tool, but a host of them are decent, honorable, entirely sincere parents like yourself who believe this is the best way to prepare their children for a future day when they must live with others in peace or perish in an atomic ash pile.

Don't try to shout them down, but try patiently to help them understand that Russia, as usual, is not keeping her part of this cooperative bargain.

Russia permits no UNESCO indoctrination of her youngsters.

Russia teaches "communism without compromise," and unless we prepare young Americans to believe in freedom without compromise, so that they will keep it strong and defend it against all enemies (foreign and domestic), we are dooming tomorrow's Americans to the fate of today's Hungarians.

But if we can revive in America's youth some of the faith of our fathers then this will again become the land of the free and the home of the brave and strong enough to keep your enemies at arms length which is quite enough to hope for in our time.

PLATE 25C

We must all agree with the statement made by former United Nations Secretary General U Thant: "Lenin was a man with a mind of great clarity, and his ideas have had a profound influence on the course of contemporary history.

"(Lenin's) ideals of peace and peaceful coexistence among states have won widespread international acceptance and they are in line with the aims of the United Nations Charter..." (*Los Angeles Times*, April 7, 1970).

The United Nations — with its headquarters in the "Tower of Babel" in New York City — is clearly playing a major role in the Satanic Conspiracy to once again enslave all peoples of the earth in a gigantic concentration camp, with the elitist International Banksters in total and unquestioned control.

One final word about the United Nations Organization. There are two highly significant religious symbols in the UN Headquarters building in New York. As you walk through the main entrance, you are greeted by a large naked male statue: this is Zeus — the supreme god of the pagan pantheon. He is representative of Satan (or Lucifer) the "god of this world" (*II Corinthians* 4:4. Also, see photo p. 161).

In a corner — at the right hand side of the main lobby — we find the "Meditation Room." This is a room that has a floor plan in the shape of a truncated pyramid, the symbol of the Illuminati (See p. 162. Also pp. 94, 95). You enter this room at the base.

On the back wall of the Meditation Room, in geometric design, are over one hundred occult symbols of various organizations: these include Masonry, Spiritism and all the ancient fertility cults.

In the center of the Meditation Room is a large polished black block. This is the ashlar and represents Freemasonry. The rough block represents humanity being formed and polished by the use of the compass and the square into a smooth, finished, even, rectangular block which is fit for use in a building. This is the Mason's symbol of taking the masses of humanity and forming them into a finished block under their control, thus building their New World Order. This is a modern-day application of Adam Weishaupt's doctrine of the "perfectibility" of man by his own efforts! Salvation by works!

Over the top of the black block is a small single floodlight mounted in the ceiling. This sends a single shaft of light onto the black block. This symbolizes the light of the sun (or the sun god) sending its semen or seed to fertilize the earth. This symbolizes prosperity and success for the plan of this building, through the black block — the ashlar.

As we saw in chapters 4 and 5, the sun represents Lucifer. The United Nations is clearly meant to grow into a One World Government, with a World Religion. Lucifer would, of course, be supreme over all!

If America is to be saved, it is abundantly clear that we must Get the US Out of the UN, and the UN Out of the US!

UN Photo

PLATE 26 — The naked figure of the Greek god Zeus standing in the main lobby of UN headquarters in New York City

PLATE 27 — The Meditation Room at the UN headquarters is shaped like a truncated pyramid (the Illuminati insignia) laid on its side.

Chapter NINE

THE EXECUTIVE ORDERS AND THE NEW CONSTITUTION

As we have progressed through the pages of this book we have unveiled and fully documented from its earliest beginnings, the overall story of the Luciferian/Babylonian/Simon Magus/Illuminati/-Round Table/Socialist/Communist/Capitalist conspiracy to seize control of all the countries of the earth, and to establish a totalitarian One-World government.

The close tie-in between all of these movements is no coincidence — it was planned that way by Satan (aka, Lucifer, the first Illuminist) who is the unseen ruler of this world (See Ezekiel 28:12; II Corinthians 4:4, and Revelation 12:9).

The reader must be aware by now of the clear, unmistakable pattern that flows through history — particularly modern history — now that the missing dimension has been supplied. Now, for the first time, national and world events which, when they occurred, seemed "incredible," "fantastic," "unbelievable" and "bizarre," now stand out in stark relief and assume real meaning. Now — at long last — world events fall into place and make sense.

As these facts are undeniably true, it is only reasonable that we can expect to find that the Insiders — whose lust for power and control over people is insatiable — have been frantically busy behind the scenes preparing unbreakable chains with which to shackle the people of the United States when the time is ripe.

If this concept appears to be so "far out" as to be beyond the bounds of reason or possibility, you had better brace yourself for one of the most traumatic, spine-chilling and hair-raising experiences of your life. Not only is this concept factual it is fully provable, as we shall now see.

What are Executive Orders? If a small random poll conducted by the author is any indication, there are remarkably few people in the United States who have even the foggiest idea what Executive Orders are — let alone how they are created or put into effect.

The most damaging of all the Executive Orders (EOs) is 11490, the so-called "omnibus" Emergency Preparedness Order that consolidated 23 previous EOs, which President Nixon signed on October 28, 1969.[1]

By virtue of EO 11490 then President Nixon declared a national emergency to exist on August 15, 1971, in connection with the nation's economy. At first glance, most of the EOs seem to be steps needed to enable the United States to prepare for and strike back in the event of a nuclear attack. This, however, is not the whole truth!

The 32 pages and 200,000 words of EO 11490 blanket every conceivable facet of today's gigantic and complex American society, and guarantee that regardless of events no part of it will ever be left without bureaucratic supervision from Washington.

More frightening than all its contents is the omission of a definition of the phrase "national emergency." The decision as to what constitutes a "national emergency" is left to the capricious whim of just one man: the President, whoever he might be.

Effect of Executive Orders: Although there are Presidential memoranda and previous EOs not specifically listed in this chapter, the author feels those excerpts referred to are the essential Orders that must be studied by all Americans if they are to acquaint themselves with this "sword of Damocles" hanging over all our heads. These Orders established the machinery which authorizes the President and his advisors to

---

1. The author acknowledges with thanks the assistance given by Liberty Lobby in developing the information presented in this section.

take control of every significant factor of the private sector of our society!

The Office of Emergency Preparedness (OEP) is responsible for assisting the President in all emergency preparedness activities. Its director is a member of the subversive Council on Foreign Relations! The OEP has eight regional offices and is the final authority in all matters relating to national security during the state of emergency. Although Congress directed the development of the preparedness program, the author believes our rapidly changing world and our shifting political bases can overnight transform a seemingly beneficial government edict into an absolute dictatorship. In this age of assassination the mantle of leadership could fall on any man at any time. The lure of total power contained in the Executive Orders might, in and of itself, invite a grab for power by radical elements within government.

History of Executive Orders: Under the Constitution of the United States, the President is vested with the executive power of the Government (Article II, Section 1, Clause 1), the power to "preserve, protect and defend the Constitution" (Article II, Section E, Clause 7), and the power to see that the laws are faithfully executed (Article II, Section 3). From these powers is implied the authority to issue Executive Orders. An Executive Order has never been defined by Congress. In use from the earliest days of the Republic, the Executive Order was at first employed mainly for the disposition of the public domain, the withdrawal of lands from federal reservations, and for other similar purposes. During World War I the use of the Executive Order was widened, as executive authority and power increased. In the early years Executive Orders were not numbered, and since there was no uniform system for recording them the total of the unnumbered orders is unknown. The validity of Executive Orders has been questioned many times, but a ruling as to the extent or limit to which they may be used has never been determined by the Courts or by Congress (Library of Congress, Legislative Research Service No. 398/117-9).

An Executive Order is not a law passed by Congress, nor a ruling promulgated by the Supreme Court or, any other court. It is a decree issued by the President and entered in the Federal Register which becomes a law 15 days after its entry — a law just as valid as if passed by the Congress and approved by the Supreme Court. The Expansion of the Executive Order into an action reflecting the growth of the power of the Chief Executive took place during the administration of Franklin D. Roosevelt. Roosevelt issued an Executive Order defining the outbreak of war in Europe as a "limited emergency" and was to remain in effect for the duration of the war, "and six months." At that time it became inoperative, although it remained on the books, available for the next "emergency."

In May of 1941 FDR declared a state of "unlimited national emergency" which was to remain in effect until the declaration ended. Another state of emergency was declared by President Truman in 1950 after Red China's intervention in the Korean War. Truman formally ended both the World War II emergencies in April of 1952, but expressly reaffirmed the 1950 declaration. Presidents Eisenhower, Kennedy, Johnson and Nixon also reaffirmed it as each took office.

Executive Orders can mean martial law: A declaration by the President indicating a "national emergency" exists has always stopped short of martial law, although the President has that prerogative. Undoubtedly it would be exercised in the event of an attack on the United States. The last use of martial law was in Hawaii a few hours after the attack on Pearl Harbor in 1941. It is interesting to note that the tendency of martial law to perpetuate itself was demonstrated in that case. The military retained basic control of Hawaii until the Supreme Court in 1944 ruled that the continued use of martial law, long after the disaster conditions had ended, was unconstitutional.

EO 11490 assigns emergency preparedness functions to federal departments and agencies:

WHEREAS our national security is dependent upon our ability to assure continuity of government, at every level, in any national emergency type situation that might conceivably confront the nation; and

WHEREAS effective national preparedness planning to meet such an emergency, including a massive nuclear attack, is essential to our national survival; and

WHEREAS effective national preparedness planning requires the identification of functions that would have to be performed during such an emergency, the assignment of responsibility for developing plans for performing these functions, and the assignment of responsibility for developing the capability to implement those plans; and

WHEREAS the Congress has directed the development of such national emergency preparedness plans and has provided funds for the accomplishment thereof; and

WHEREAS this national emergency preparedness planning activity has been an established program of the United States Government for more than twenty years;

NOW THEREFORE, by virtue of the authority vested in me as President of the United States ... it is hereby ordered as follows:

The next 32 pages outline the emergency functions to be performed by these departments and agencies:

1. Department of State
2. Department of Treasury
3. Department of Defense
4. Department of Justice
5. Post Office Department
6. Department of the Interior
7. Department of Agriculture
8. Department of Commerce
9. Department of Labor
10. Department of Health, Education, and Welfare
11. Department of Housing and Urban Development
12. Department of Transportation
13. Atomic Energy Commission
14. Civil Aeronautics Board
15. Export-Import Bank
16. Federal Bank Supervisory Agencies
17. Federal Communications Commission
18. Federal Power Commission
19. General Services Administration
20. Interstate Commerce Commission
21. National Aeronautics and Space Administration
22. National Science Foundation
23. Railroad Retirement Board
24. Securities and Exchange Commission
25. Small Business Administration

26. Tennessee Valley Authority
27. United States Civil Service Commission
28. Veterans Administration

Here are summaries of a few of the more significant sections:

Sec. 101. **Purpose.** This Order consolidates the assignment of emergency preparedness functions to various departments and agencies heretofore contained in the 21 Executive Orders and 2 Defense Mobilization Orders listed in Sec. 3015 of this Order ...

Sec. 3012 **Redelegation.** The head of each department and agency is hereby authorized to redelegate the functions assigned to him by this Order, and to authorize successive redelegation to agencies or instrumentalities of the United States, and to officers and employees of the United States ...

Sec. 3013. **Transfer of functions.** Any emergency preparedness function under this Order, or parts thereof, may be transferred from one department or agency to another with the consent of the heads of the organizations involved and with the concurrence of the Director of the Office of Emergency Preparedness.

Under the terms of EO 11490, the President of the United States can order that a national emergency exists, and can then:

- Take over all communications media
- Seize all sources of power (electric, nuclear, petroleum, etc.)
- Control all food resources
- Seize all forms of transportation
- Control all highways and seaports
- Seize railroads, inland waterways, and storage facilities
- Commandeer all civilians to work under federal supervision
- Control all activities relating to health, education, and welfare
- Register every man, woman, and child in the United States
- Shift any segment of the population from one locality to another
- Control all devices capable of emitting electromagnetic radiation
- Institute EXTRAORDINARY MEASURES with respect to any facility, system, or service essential to national survival
- Take over farms, ranches, or timberland properties so as to protect, manage, and utilize them effectively

- Demand emergency welfare services (food, clothing, and lodging) in private homes for those in need
- Regulate the amount of your own money you can withdraw from your bank or savings and loan institution
- Close the stock exchanges and freeze stock and bond prices.

All of these items listed, plus many others clearly enumerated on 32 pages incorporating nearly 200,000 words, pertain to every previous Executive Order ever issued unless specifically revoked.

EO 11615

Executive Order No. 11615 was issued by President Nixon on August 15, 1971. It provides for stabilization of prices, rents, wages, and salaries. Although the wage-price "freeze" was to last only 90 days, the Order established another bureaucratic agency called the Cost of Living Council.

This Council is almost certain to be with us for a long time, growing in power and size, with concomitant restrictions on the average citizen.

The Secretary of the Treasury is the Chairman of the Council, and the Chairman of the Federal Reserve System is an advisor to the Council.

Sec. 3 of EO 11615 delegates to the Council all of the powers conferred on the President by the Economic Stabilization Act of 1970. The working force of the Council is drawn from the Internal Revenue Service. As with tax matters, the Council is empowered by law to force any citizen to maintain appropriate records and produce these records on demand, under penalty of $5,000 fine.

EOs vs CONGRESSIONAL POWER

Attempts have been made to repeal the Presidential prerogatives inherent in the Executive Orders. The latest known attempt was in May, 1971, when Sen. Charles McC. Mathias, Jr. (R-Md.) said, "We must reject the concept of national emergencies declarable by the President at his discretion in peace time without termination dates. It is up to the Congress to recover by legislation the constitutional role that it has allowed that executive to usurp. We must reassert the principle that emergency powers are available only for brief periods when Congress is unable to act for purposes directly related to the emergency at hand."

In the context of the unlimited power represented by the Executive Orders, it is interesting to note that in a speech before the Senate Banking and Currency Committee on March 23, 1953, the unelected President of the United States, Bernard Baruch, made an impassioned plea for "Stand-by Mobilization Legislation." The majority of his recommendations appeared in subsequent Executive Orders.

It is also significant that Executive Order 10952, signed by President Kennedy in 1961, and still in effect today, transferred all civil defense functions to the Department of Defense while Adam Yarmolinsky served as it first director. In a speech opposing the transfer, Senator Fulbright made a statement chilling in its implications: "Whereas civil defense can be considered as a purely national responsibility, civil emergency planning requires close cooperation between the NATO allies..."

WHAT IS A NATIONAL EMERGENCY?

Only the President knows for sure, and he has unlimited option. Crime on the streets would appear to be an area where the President could well declare not enough was being done to control anarchy. There would be ample justification today: Violent crime has increased 176% in the last decade. What is to prevent the President declaring a national emergency and confiscating all the guns in the hands of individual citizens?

Under the terms of Executive Order 11490 the President could order the transfer of any segment of our population from one locality to another, thus effectively and legally integrating. If any citizen, or group of citizens objected, the rest of the Nation would never know it because all communications and all mass media would be under the control and direction of government!

The Constitution of the United States ranks above the Executive, the Legislative, and the Judicial branches of government. It must remain that way.

THE NEW CONSTITUTION

As the Executive Orders have been created by the Insiders to deal with the coming catastrophic "National Emergency" —

which will be the direct result of the undermining of our society by the conspirators — it is only reasonable that we could expect the Insiders to have gone one step further and prepared the groundwork for the introduction of a New Constitution for the United States of America. Our expectations are not to be disappointed.

For many years a high percentage of the trustees of the Ford Foundation have been members of the Council on Foreign Relations. In 1953, the Ford Foundation established the Fund for the Republic.

Under the direction of Paul G. Hoffman and Robert M. Hutchins, both notorious leftists, the Fund for the Republic went to work suppressing in every possible way the strong spirit of anti-Communism that had erupted after the Alger Hiss scandal and the frustrations of the Korean War. In 1959, they set up the Center for the Study of Democratic Institutions in Santa Barbara, California.

In October, 1970, this "very prestigious" organization published in its *Center* magazine an article entitled "Constitution for the United Republics of America." The Institute announced that for six years prior to its publication some of the greatest minds in the country had been working on this document. The prime mover behind it was Rexford Guy Tugwell, a radical, who had been closely associated with Roosevelt's "New Deal."

It is very difficult for a patriotic American to truly grasp what the Insiders have planned for him and his country, which is supposedly the "land of the free."

The new plans call for the abolition of the United Sates Constitution and the establishment of a ruling elite made up of Insiders.

The following is just a sampling of what the conspirators plan:

Article I, Part A, Section 11: "Education shall be provided at public expense for those who meet appropriate test of eligibility." (No private schools allowed. All the peasants must be brainwashed into acceptance of the party line.)

Article I, Part B, Section 8: states that "the bearing of arms or the possession of lethal weapons shall be confined to the police, members of the armed forces and those licensed under law." (Gun control to keep the peasants in check.)

Article II, Section 1: "There shall be Newstates, each comprising no less than 5 percent of the whole population. Existing states may continue and may have the status of Newstates if the boundary Commission, herein-after provided, shall so decide."

Article IV, Section 2: "There will be a National Planning Board of fifteen members appointed by the President." (Total control by the Insiders).

Article V, Section 1: states that the Presidents will be elected for a term of nine years. Section 2: there will be two Vice Presidents. Section 3: "The Chancellor of Financial Affairs shall supervise the nation's financial and monetary systems, regulating its capital markets and credit-issuing institutions..."

Article VI, Part A, Section 1: states that the Senate will be made up of "former Presidents, Vice-Presidents, Principal Justices, Overseers, Chairmen of the Planning and Regulatory Boards ..."

Other members will be "appointed by the President," and in Section 2, "membership shall be for life."

Article VI, Part B, Section 9, Subsection 8: "To assist in the maintenance of world order and, for this purpose, when the President shall recommend, to vest jurisdiction in international legislative, judicial and administrative agencies."

Article VI, Part B, Section 9, subsection 10: "To assist other peoples, who have not attained satisfactory levels of well-being, to delegate the administration of funds for assistance, whenever possible, to international agencies; and to invest in or contribute to the furthering of development in other parts of the world." [The American taxpayer will be worked, starved and bled dry in order to redistribute our wealth to the world. This is pure Marxism: "From each according to his ability, to each according to his need."]

Article X, Section 2 calls for such things as "the Planning Board," "the Overseer," "the Watchkeeper," and "the Regulator."

When Mr. Tugwell, the prime author of this document, was asked how it would be possible to get this constitution adopted, he replied:

"... It *could* happen that the present system of government would prove so obstructive and would fail so abysmally to meet the needs of a continental people and a great power that general recognition of the crisis would occur. There might *then* be a redrafting of the basic law, and, if so, then it might be that this model we have worked out over a number of years might be taken into account." (*The Center Magazine,* p. 52, Vol 3, No. 5).

In summing up the New Constitution, *National Spotlight* of March 29, 1976, stated: "Tugwell and his cohorts declared that the U.S. Constitution is an ambiguous document concocted 200 years ago and inadequate for the present day. The new constitution would abolish states and substitute a smaller number of regions, called republics. They wouldn't be republics in any rational sense of the word. (They) ...would be mere administrative eunuchs, having little real power beyond the paperwork assigned them from above." The "illuminated" ones on top would be calling the tune. Citizens would be reduced to mere numbers as forecast by Dr. Carroll Quigley: "...his (the individual's) freedom and choice will be controlled within very narrow alternatives by the fact that he will be numbered from birth and followed, as a number, through his educational training, his required military or other public service, his tax contributions, his health and medical requirements, and his final retirement and death benefits."

Chapter TEN

THE MONEY CHANGERS

If we are to believe the highly authoritative *Guinness Book Of Records*, the greatest robbery in recorded history took place in Germany in 1948. The total "take" was in excess of nine million dollars.

On this occasion, Guinness is wrong — totally in error! The greatest and most audacious robbery of all time has been taking place in the United States of America since 1914. To date, the loot has amounted to multiple Trillions of dollars.

This statement will, no doubt, sound absurd and unbelievable to most readers. Please bear with us, and see the truth unfold clearly and unmistakably in the pages that follow.

"We have in this country one of the most corrupt institutions the world has ever known. I refer to the Federal Reserve Board and the Federal Reserve Banks, hereinafter called the Fed...

"They are *not* Government institutions. They are private monopolies which prey upon the people of these United States for the benefit of themselves and their foreign customers...

"In that dark crew of financial pirates there are those who would cut a man's throat to get a dollar out of his pocket..."

Who spoke those words? A wild-eyed, raving fanatic on a soap box in Pershing Square? A deranged idiot on a psychedelic trip? A frustrated member of the working class unable to keep up with the staggering rate of inflation?

No, these words were spoken on the Floor of the House of Representatives by none other than the Honorable Louis T. McFadden who, for more than ten years, served as Chairman of the Banking and Currency Committee. He was in a perfect position to know the facts!

To deny that we, as a nation, are ensnared in a hideously complex and ever-deepening financial crisis would be the height of folly. The signs are everywhere evident — a multi Trillion dollar National Debt, high unemployment, massive welfare rolls, a jittery stock market and many state, city and personal budgets floundering hopelessly in a stormy sea of red ink!

HISTORICAL PERSPECTIVE

Did this catastrophic financial crisis just "happen" — or was it deliberately created? Did we just "fall" into it — or were we pushed?

To clearly understand these vitally important questions we must go back to the very beginnings of our nation and trace the history of our economic affairs. We must go directly to the speeches and writings of men such as Washington, Jefferson, Jackson and Lincoln — men who were directly responsible for making American history. We must trace historical events through original documents in order to ascertain the truth. In this way we will find the causes for the effects we see all around us today. When we get the facts and begin to see the perfect correlation of cause and effect, the once dry, dull and uninteresting pages of history will leap into life and become truly meaningful. We will also be forced to the inevitable conclusion that a great deal of effort has been expended by "the powers that be" to hide these plain truths from the American public.

In the beginning .... A number of extremely important events occurred on the world scene around the time the first European settlers were coming to the New World: the Renaissance, the invention of printing, the Protestant Reformation and the publication of the King James Bible combined to have a profound impact on the lives and attitudes of the pioneers.

The discovery of a huge, empty continent open for colonization presented the opportunity to start life anew in an uncrowded land that held out the promise of vast wealth. It also offered the opportunity to escape from the various forms of persecution to which they had been subjected in Europe, and to live under much freer conditions. The fact that America was a perilous two months' boat journey from Europe restricted the number of people who headed West to those who had a real "yearning to breathe free."

The defeat of the Spanish Armada signaled the decline of Spanish power and the rise of England as a world force. As a result, the settling of the New World was, at least in the beginning, largely a British affair.

AT FIRST ... FINANCIAL FREEDOM

The British Crown was pleased to have private citizens undertake settlements and granted them charters more or less on their own terms. Each Colony was allowed to make its own laws, provided they were not inconsistent with the laws of England. At first the British Parliament did not have any authority over the Colonies. The Colonial constitutions were never restricted. Had the Crown attempted to encroach on the rights of the Colonists they would have met with tremendous resistance. The Colonists were content to have a close relationship with England, but refused to be dictated to in terms of policy.

Among the powers granted to the Colonies was the right to create their own money — legal tender. At this point in history paper mony was just coming into widespread use. The Colonies began using this convenient form of money, and paid it into use by way of public expenditure until there was enough in circulation to allow necessary changes without restraint. They were sound currencies, issued by the authorities without interest having to be paid to private bankers!

It would be difficult to overemphasize the role played by the Bible in these early, formative years. Books were very few and far between and were eagerly sought after. The Bible was by far the most widely published book in existence. Its contents were enthusiastically studied and listened to by most of the populace; it was accepted as the Word of God — and became the law of the land! Although its contents may not always have been perfectly understood it was, nevertheless, for many years the final arbiter in most disputes. As a result, society was generally established on Biblical principles — thrift, diligence, integrity, close families and faith in an Almighty, Creator God.

A combination of Biblical knowledge and personal experience taught the people to have a distinct distrust of money changers and bankers. As will be clearly demonstrated, this lack of trust was amply justified!

As the seventeenth century drew to a close an event of monumental importance took place in Europe — an event which was instrumental in changing world history. The details are laid out in *The Breakdown Of Money,* by Christopher Hollis:

"In 1694 the Government of William III was in sore straits for money. A company of rich men under the leadership of one William Paterson offered to loan William £1,200,000 (6 million dollars) at eight percent on condition that 'the Governor and Company of the Bank of England,' as they called themselves, should have the right to issue notes to the full extent of its capital. That is to say, the Bank got the right to collect £1,200, 000 in gold and silver and to turn it into £2,400,000, lending £1,200,000, the gold and silver, to the Government, and using the other £1,200,000, bank-notes , themselves. Paterson frankly admitted that this privilege which had been given to the Bank was a privilege to create money out of nothing. 'If the proprietors of the Bank,' he wrote, 'can circulate their own fundation of twelve hundred thousand pounds without having more than two or three hundred thousand pounds lying dead at one time with another, this Bank will be in effect as nine hundred thousand pounds or a million in fresh money brought into the nation.' In practice they did not keep a cash reserve of two or three hundred thousand pounds. In 1696 we find them circulating £1,750,000 worth of notes against a cash reserve of £36,000.

"Intelligent critics saw that the experiment had proved that it was perfectly possible to manufacture mony without any metallic backing, but that it was dangerous and iniquitous to allow the privilege of that manufacture to be in private hands..."

Big changes were in the works when this newly formed private bank, masquerading under the name "Bank of England," began to create and issue its own private money. Its proprietors soon began casting envious glances in the direction of the fast developing American Colonies. Not content with the profits they made through regular trade with the Colonists, these bankers launched a deliberate, carefully-thought-out drive to exploit and control the industrious Colonists. It was this campaign, more than any other factor, that was the basic cause of the War of Independence. The writings of Benjamin Franklin, which continually stress the absolute importance of honest and sound money, also lay bare the real motives behind England's economic war on America.

FOREIGN INTERVENTION BEGINS

In 1720 we see the beginning of foreign control over the issuance of our money. "An instruction was issued (from the British government) ... to every Governor in America to consent to no Act for emitting Bills of Credit except for the support of government, without a suspending clause, till the King's pleasure should be known" (*Bancroft's History of the Colonization of the United States of America*, page 263).

One of the results was that "in 1738, the New England currency deteriorated in value as compared to British money" (p. 263). In spite of this fact, the "period was marked by unrivaled prosperity of the Colonies. The population which had doubled within twenty-five years grew rich through industry" (p. 265). Here is proof positive that hard work, a locally controlled and a carefully managed currency were largely responsible for the fast development and prosperity of the New World! It will be noted that as long as the Colonies had a good supply of their own currencies in circulation they didn't need to pay interest to European bankers for the "privilege" of using their currency!

"From the (British) Board of Trade in March, 1751, a Bill was presented (to Parliament) to restrain Bills of Credit (Colonial Currency) in New England, with the added clause of giving the authority of law to the king's instructions on that subject.

"...the obnoxious clause (King's power of law) was abandoned; yet there seemed to exist in the minds of 'some persons of consequence' a fixed design of getting sanction by Parliament to the King's instructions.

"The Board of Trade was all the while maturing its scheme for Controlling America" (pp. 367 and 368). As a result, the Colonists were forced to borrow money, at interest, from the bankers to put in circulation.

In 1764, the prohibition by the English authorities against the New England Colonies issuing their own currencies was extended to the rest of the Colonies. "The interference of home government (under the direction of the bankers) in prohibiting paper issues had more than immediate results; it provoked opposition; was regarded as an unjustifiable interference, and helped to develop the growing discontent with government by England" (*The Financial History of the United States,* Dewey).

There is no doubt that some of the Colonies made mistakes and had suffered as a result. Yet, the Colonists went to war to retain their sovereign right to create their own money. As Gertrude Coogan points out in her very informative book, *The Money Creators*, "Our early history books strangely omit the fact that some years prior to 1773 the British Parliament had busied itself annulling the laws under which the American Colonies had exercised their fundamental right to create and issue their own money. Much is said about taxation without representation, but what underlies that phrase is omitted. The fact is that the Bank 'of England' manipulators, *having gained control over British industry through frequent depressions*, cast their greedy eyes on the commerce and industry of America, and set to work to lay hold on the money of the Colonies and, hence, the industry of the Colonies" (p. 181).

The reason why the British abolished the right of the Colonies to create and issue their own money is simple: the bankers did not want the Colonists to be able to trade among themselves without paying tribute to them on the promises of the Bank of England, which they were forcing the Americans to borrow for use in trading among themselves. The objective was clear: by forcing Americans to pay interest, the European money changers wanted to enslave the Colonies in a mountain of debt. As Benjamin Franklin clearly stated: "The plan of our adversaries is to render the Assemblies in America useless .... It is in our interest to prevent this" (*The Works of Benjamin Franklin,* Federal Edition, published by Putnam, p. 307).

The effort to usurp the rights of the Colonists was conducted along lines that would serve the interests of the International Bankers, and bring Americans to their knees economically.

Exorbitant prices were placed on goods shipped to the Colonies, in spite of the fact that there was overproduction in England. As England demanded to be paid in specie (gold or sliver coins), the Colonies were drained of these precious metals which they obtained by trade with other nations.

An embargo was placed upon trade with nations other than England. This move made it impossible for Americans to obtain the specie with which to pay British manufacturers who, by this time, had been reduced to the position of mere factory managers for the bankers. In this way Americans were forced to borrow from the Bank of England and to build up bonds and interest in acknowledgement of their debt.

The writings of Benjamin Franklin bear witness to the enormous corruption which pervaded the British government and nation at that time. He wrote to Joseph Galloway from London on February 17, 1768, that "this whole venal nation is now at market (being sold to the highest bidders), and will be sold for about two million, and might be bought out of the hands of the present bidders (if he would offer half a million more) by the very Devil himself."

The first Continental Congress convened on September 5, 1774. A month later the delegates issued their Declaration of Resolutions. They also formed an "Association of the various Colonies" for the purpose of boycotting British goods. England retaliated by forbidding trade with her own Colonies.

Although, in Jefferson's words, there wasn't ever a "whispered" disposition to make a formal break with Britain at that time, the situation quickly changed. On August 23, 1775, King George III issued his Proclamation of Rebellion. The crisis quickly mushroomed and headed towards the "date with fate" — the Declaration of Independence on the Fourth of July, 1776.

Sixteen months later the Continental Congress agreed on the Articles of Confederation. From the time the first Congress met on March 2, 1781, to the time the Constitution of the United States was ratified in 1789, this document was the basis of the government.

It is vitally important that we bear in mind that all during this period the fight for control of the American currency was where the real action was!

In 1775 the Continental Congress authorized the respective colonies to issue paper currency in defiance of Britain. The European Money Changers were so infuriated by this move that they set about to destroy the value of this new money. They printed up a huge amount of counterfeit Continental money and flooded the Colonies with it. As a result, the value of these "bills of credit" was greatly debauched. The counterfeiting campaign was so successful that in 1779 "the entire issue had to be recalled in order to save the system from immediate collapse" (*History of Money in America*, Del Mar, 1899, p. 104). A year later the Continental bills were only worth one fortieth of their original face value (p. 107).

BANK OF NORTH AMERICA

The Independence of America attained, and the Constitutional Government established, a new chapter in our history begins. The fact that we had attained political freedom did not prevent the European Bankers from using their great wealth and influence in an immediate attempt to nullify Article 1, Section 8, subsection 5 of the Constitution which gave Congress the power "to coin Money, (and) regulate the Value thereof." With the aid of Alexander Hamilton (an avowed Monarchist, and one who strongly favored the European system of Central Banks) and Robert Morris, the new Congress was persuaded to interpret the Constitution "as having implied powers" never intended by its authors. By deceiving the corrupt part of Congress, control over our currency issuance (and also, as a result, power over our wealth and government) was given to our just-defeated enemies. As a result, in 1781 the Bank of North America was founded, modeled after the Bank of England.

Never was a great historical event followed by a more feeble sequel. A nation rises to claim for itself liberty and sovereignty. It gains both of these ends through enormous sacrifices in blood and wealth. Then, when victory has been gained and secured, it hands its national credit over to private individuals to do with it as they will!

It should be noted that all of this was done in spite of strong opposition from Jefferson, Madison and others. Jefferson clearly understood the dangers inherent in such an arrangement: "There is scarcely a king (or a would-be king) in a hundred who would not, if he could, follow the example of Pharaoh — get first all the people's money, then all their lands, and then make them and their children servants forever" (*The Works of Benjamin Franklin*, p. 368). Evidence presented elsewhere in this book proves the penetrating insight possessed by Jefferson!

Fortunately, the Bank of North America was never recognized by the majority of the States. Within a short period of time Hamilton and his backers realized that the States didn't intend to give up the better half of their sovereignty to an internationally controlled money creating bank that would have the power to control the entire nation.

When the Bank of North America "folded" in 1790 they were ready with another plan. In 1790 the foreign debt of the United States was approximately $12,000,000: this money had been borrowed from Spain, France and private capitalists in Germany and Holland. The domestic debt was $42,000,000. The total debt of all the States was about $21,000,000.

Following the ratification of the Constitution in 1789, George Washington made the blunder of accepting Robert Morris's advice to appoint Alexander Hamilton Secretary of the Treasury. In 1790, following the death of Franklin, Hamilton — the proven friend of the Money Creators — proposed that the public debt (amounting to approximately $75,000,000) be converted into interest bearing bonds. In December, 1790, he introduced a report in the House of Representatives which would charter the Bank of the United States. This was to be a privately owned corporation with the sole right of issuing currency for the United States. The corporation was to be exempt from taxes, and the U.S. government was to be responsible for all its transactions.

This bank charter, which was clearly in defiance of the Constitution, was keenly debated in both Houses. The basic issue was whether the United States should control the issue of its money (as was specifically provided for in the Constitution), or whether this awesome power would be turned over to private bankers.

Thomas Jefferson stated boldly that: "The Incorporation of a bank and the powers assumed by this Bill have not ... been delegated to the United States by the Constitution.

"The Bill delivers us up bound to the National Bank, who are free to refuse all arrangements, but on their own terms, and the public not free, on such refusal, to employ any other bank" (*Writings of Jefferson*, published by H. W. Derby, New York, 1861, Vol. 7).

Hamilton, who was the servant of the "apostles of debt" (debts which meant interest had to be paid to the bankers!), rather than the people whose Constitution he had sworn to uphold and defend, had to find a way to subvert the Constitution if his Bankers Bill was to pass.

During previous years he had built up close friendships with men who were now in key positions in Congress — men whose opinions carried a lot of weight. He hinted that vast fortunes could be made by them if they bought up public obligations at discount prices and then helped him convert them into interest-bearing bonds. In spite of strong opposition from various Constitutionalists, Hamilton succeeded in getting the Bill passed. Although he recognized that the Bill was unconstitutional and that "it is in all cases the duty of the government to dispense its benefits to individuals with as impartial a hand as the public interest will permit" (Madison's Veto Message framed at Washington's request, *Writings of Madison*, Vol. 6, pp. 41, 42), President Washington was coerced into signing the Bill on February 25, 1791. Those politicians who went along with Hamilton's deceitful plan to turn public debt into interest-bearing bonds made a financial killing as a result!

After the International Banksters had used Hamilton to effect the legalization of their scheme, they threw him to one side. A few years later he repented of his treachery and wrote to Oliver Wolcott, the new Secretary of the Treasury: "My Dear Sir: No one knows better than yourself how difficult and oppressive is the collection even of taxes very moderate in amount, if there is a defective circulation. According to all the phenomena which fell under my notice, this is our case in the interior part of the country...

"For these and other reasons which I have thought well of, I have come to the conclusion that our treasury ought to raise up a circulation of its own. I mean by the issuing of treasury notes.

"This appears to me an expedient equally necessary to keep the circulation full ... it will be easy to enlarge without hazard to credit. Alexander Hamilton."

It should be noted that during these years there were many States that were unwilling to recognize the authority of a Central Bank that had been given unconstitutional powers to create money. They chartered State Banks. When the charter of the "Bank of the United States" expired in 1811 there were close to ninety of the State Charter banks in existence: they were all strongly opposed to the concept of a Central Bank.

The charter of the Central Bank (the misnamed Bank of the United States) was not renewed. Instead, it was decided that if private money creation powers were granted at all, a number of independent banks should be chartered. In doing this Congress chose the lesser of two evils.

Many historians realize that the war of 1812 — the second war with England — was primarily the result of efforts by the international financial interests to create chaos on the American business scene, and thus force the United States Congress to grant another charter to the Bank of the United States. After a bitter struggle they succeeded in their aim! In 1816 another misnamed "Bank of the United States" — also privately owned and with the unconstitutional power to create money — was granted a Charter for twenty years.

JACKSON'S FAMOUS VETO MESSAGE

During the presidential campaign of 1828, General Andrew Jackson came out strongly against the concept of a central bank controlled by the international money tycoons. He said to the bankers: "You are a den of vipers. I intend to rout you out and by the Eternal God, I will rout you out." He also stated: "If the people only understood the rank injustice of our money and banking system there would be a revolution before morning."

Jackson was elected President. In 1832 he was re-elected.

On July 10, 1832, President Jackson presented to the Senate his veto message on rechartering the "Bank of the United States Bill." *In it, he crystallized for all time all the arguments that should be offered against giving the fiscal power and resources of this great nation into the hands of a private monopoly.* He stated:

"Having considered (the Bill) with solemn regard to the principles of the Constitution ... (I) come to the conclusion that it ought not to become a law .... Some of the powers and privileges possessed by the existing bank are unauthorized by the Constitution, subversive to the rights of the States, and dangerous to the liberties of the people ... It enjoys an exclusive privilege of banking under the authority of the General (Federal) Government, monopoly of its favor and support, and, as a necessary consequence, almost a monopoly of the foreign and domestic exchange.

"(The Act) seems to be predicated on the erroneous idea that the present stockholders have a prescriptive right to not only the favor but to the bounty of government ... for their benefit does this act exclude the whole American people from competition in the purchase of this monopoly."

If the Bank were rechartered in perpetuity, "the present stockholders and those inheriting their rights as successors (would) be established (as) a privileged order, clothed both with great political power and enjoying immense pecuniary advantages from their connection with government ....

"Should its influence become concentrated, as it may, under the operation of such an act as this, in the hands of a self-elected directory whose interests are identified with those of the foreign stockholders, will there not be cause to tremble ... for the independence of our country in war? Their power would be great whenever they might choose to exert it ...

"Should the stock of the bank principally pass into the hands of the subjects of a foreign country, what would be our condition?

"All its operation ... would be in aid of the hostile fleets and armies without.

"Controlling our currency, receiving our public monies, and holding thousands of our citizens in dependance, it would be more formidable and dangerous than the naval and military power of the enemy ....

"It is maintained by some that the bank is a means of exercising the Constitutional power 'to coin money and regulate the value thereof.' Congress has established a mint to coin money and passed laws to regulate the value thereof. The money so coined with its value so regulated, and such foreign coins as the Congress may adopt, *are the only currency known to the Constitution.*

"But if they (Congress) have the power to regulate the currency: *it was conferred to be exercised by themselves, and not to be transferred to a (private) corporation.*

"If the bank be established for that purpose, with a charter unalterable without its consent, Congress have parted with its power for a term of years, during which the Constitution is a dead letter.

"It is neither necessary nor proper to transfer its legislative power to such a bank, and therefore unconstitutional.

"It is to be regretted that the rich and powerful too often bend the acts of Government to their selfish purposes .... *In the full enjoyments of the gifts of Heaven and fruits of superior industry, economy and virtue, every man is equally entitled to protection by law;* but when the laws undertake to add to those natural and just advantages, artificial distinctions, to grant titles, gratitudes, or exclusive privileges, to make the rich richer and the potent more powerful, the humble members of society — the farmers, mechanics and laborers — who have neither the time nor means of securing favors to themselves, have a right to complain of the injustice of their government.

"*There are no necessary evils in government.* Its evils exist only in its abuses. If it could confine itself to equal protection, and, as Heaven does its rain, shower its favors alike on the high and the low, the rich and the poor, it would be an unqualified blessing. In the (Bank) Act before me there seems to be a wide and unnecessary departure from these principles.

"Nor is our Government to be maintained or our Union preserved by invasions of the rights and powers of the several States. In thus attempting to make our ... Government strong we make it weak. *Its true strength consists in leaving individuals and States as much as possible to themselves* — in making itself felt, not in its power but in its beneficence; not in its control but in its protection, not in binding the States more closely to the center, but in leaving each to move unobstructed in its proper orbit.

"*Experience should teach us wisdom.* Most of the difficulties our Government now encounters, and *most of the dangers which impend over our Union, have sprung from an abandonment of the legitimate objects of Government by our National Legislature and the adoption of such principles as are embodied in this (bank) act.*

"Many of our rich men have not been content with equal protection and equal benefits, but have besought us to make them richer by acts of Congress .... It is time to pause in our career to review our principles, *and, if possible, to revive that devoted patriotism ... which distinguished the sages of the revolution and the fathers of the union.*

"If we cannot at once, in justice to interests invested under improvident legislation, make our Government what it ought to be, we can, at least, *take a stand against all new grants of monopolies and exclusive privileges* [such as rechartering a private bank of issue] *against any prostitution of our government to the advancement of the few at the expense of the many,* and in favor of compromises and gradual reform in our code of laws and system of political economy.

"I have now done my duty to my country [in vetoing this measure ...]" (*Compilation of the Messages and Papers of the Presidents,* by James Richardson, a Representative from Tennessee. Published by authority of Congress, Vol. 2 pp. 576-591).

Under the dedicated leadership of President Andrew Jackson the National Debt was reduced to zero — the only time in our entire history when the United States Government was debt free.

In 1836 the Charter of the Second Bank of the United States expired.

During the years that followed the International Bankers strove mightily to undermine the sound, Constitutional money system established by the Jackson Administration. There is clear evidence that they engineered the Civil War on the "Divide and Conquer" principle, and placed their agents (or agentur) in strategic positions so as to be able to pick up the pieces afterwards. Their British representatives helped finance the North, while their "French Connection" backed the South!

LINCOLN'S CONSTITUTIONAL MONEY

When President Lincoln took office the National Debt amounted to $100,000,000 — and the Treasury was practically out of funds. Towards the end of 1861, in order to finance the war effort, the government floated a $150,000,000 bond issue which they demanded the banks pay for in specie (coin). The banks reluctantly complied with this request as they were opposed to the government's "hard money" policy. A panic (deliberately created?) at the end of 1861 caused the banks to suspend specie payment, and a reluctance developed on their part to cooperate in further bond issues.

When the banks refused to loan the government money, except at extremely high rates of interest, Lincoln was faced with a financial disaster. The army was already owed $100,000,000 in back pay, and was due to be paid another $250,000,000 within a few months. Money could not be borrowed except at great sacrifice; there was no money to buy bonds; gold and silver had ceased to circulate; and the banks were claiming that their capital had been exhausted in making previous loans. To meet this impending crisis, a bill was sent to Congress which resulted in the Act of February 25, 1862, one of the landmarks in the history of American finance. Its main provision authorized the issuance of $150,000,000 legal-tender United States Notes. These later became known as Lincoln Greenbacks. Two more issues of the same sum of these legal-tender notes, amounting to $300,000,000 were made on July 11, 1862 and on January 17, 1863 — making a grand total of $450,000,000 in all! Lincoln had met the monetary crisis, to the sore displeasure of the bankers who never received a cent of interest or taxes on this United States money. The bankers were soon to get their revenge!

During the time when Lincoln was struggling to defeat the vicious schemes of the International Bankers and maintain a constitutionally authorized money system, the English International Banker-controlled papers were expressing grave fear. The famous *Times of London* stated: "If that mischievous financial policy, which had its origin in the North American Republic ... should become indurated down to a fixture, then that government will furnish its own money without cost. *It will pay off its debts and be without a debt. It will have all the money necessary to carry on its commerce. It will become prosperous beyond precedent in the history of the civilized governments of the world. The brains and the wealth of all countries will go to North America. That government must be destroyed or it will destroy every monarchy on the globe."*

The reader should note the clever appeal made to the monarchs, who were deeply in debt to the bankers.!

Had a truly honest money system been allowed to become firmly established in the United States, no other nation would have been able to maintain a dishonest money system. Their peoples would have seen the tremendous blessing flowing from it, and one nation after another would have broken loose from the shackles of the private money manipulators!

Infuriated by Lincoln's courageous stand in favor of a constitutional money system, the infamous Hazard Circular was written by the Internationalists and distributed among American bankers. It stated: "Slavery is likely to be abolished by war power. This, I and my European friends are in favor of, because slavery is but the owning of labor, and carries with it the care of the laborers, while the European plan ... is that capital money lenders shall control labour by controlling wages.

"The great debt that Capitalists [the bankers] will see is made out of the war, must be used to control the value of money. To accomplish this, government bonds [with interest being paid to the bankers] must be used as a banking basis. We are now waiting for the secretary of the treasury [Salmon P. Chase] to make that recommendation. It will not allow Greenbacks, as they are called, to circulate as money for any length of time as we cannot control that. But we can control the bonds, and through them, the banking issues."

The campaign for the passage of the National Banking Act of 1863, which again delegated to a private corporation the all-powerful right to issue our money, was heavily financed by the International Bankers. It passed Congress and became law — in spite of loud protests from Lincoln.

The new Act gave the banks the power to issue currency (paper money) by simply depositing certain issues of government bonds with the United States Treasury and obtaining currency. These privately-owned banks collected (and still collect) interest on the bonds deposited with the Treasury, but they pay no interest for the currency which is released to them.

As Gertrude Coogan says in *Money Creators* (published in 1935): "Government bonds are tax payers' promises to pay, secured by a first lien on all physical property within the nation and a first lien on national income, because Congress has the power to tax. These fully secured interest-bearing tax payers' promises-to-pay are created by the government and exchanged for privately owned banks' promises-to-pay which are unsecured. These unsecured promises-to-pay of private individuals are borrowed by the United States Government. These private individuals' promises-to-pay are called money. Imagine a banking system which permits tax payers' promises-to-pay to be exchanged for private individuals' promises-to-pay!"

Horace Greeley, writing in 1872, recognized the true nature of the "National" Bank Act: *"We have stricken the shackles from four million human beings [the black slaves] and brought all laborers to a common level, not so much by the elevation of the former slaves as by practically reducing the whole working population, white and black, to a condition of serfdom. While boasting of our noble deeds, we are careful to conceal the ugly fact that by our iniquitous money system we have nationalized a system of oppression which, though more refined, is not less cruel than the old system of chattel slavery."*

When the new law was passed, Lincoln clearly saw the danger signals flashing. He said: "I see in the near future a crisis approaching that unnerves me, and causes me to tremble for the safety of our country; corporations have been enthroned, an era of corruption in high places will follow and the money power of the country will endeavor to prolong its reign by working upon the prejudices of the people, until the wealth is aggregated in a few hands and the republic is destroyed."

Secretary of the Treasury, Salmon P. Chase, deeply repented of having allowed himself to be used as a tool of the Internationalists. He stated publicly: "My agency in promoting the passage of the National Banking Act was the greatest financial mistake of my life. It has built up a monopoly which effects every interest in the country. It should be repealed, but before that can be accomplished the people will be arrayed on one side and the banks on the other, in a contest such as we have never seen before in this country."

Following his reelection, but before he could have legislation enacted to counter the new power of the bankers, Lincoln was assassinated by John Wilkes Booth who, it was discovered later,

This One
MAD ACT...

THE UNKNOWN STORY OF

JOHN WILKES BOOTH

AND HIS FAMILY

by

HIS GRANDDAUGHTER

IZOLA FORRESTER

HALE, CUSHMAN & FLINT

Boston, 1937

PLATE 28 — *This One Mad Act* (title page)

had ties to the International Bankers! (See, *This One Mad Act*, by Izola Forrester, Hale, Cushman and Flint, Boston, 1937).

THE FEDERAL RESERVE SYSTEM

In the years since, the fears of Lincoln and Greeley have proved to have been amply justified. The full treacherous story of how the International Money Barons created the depressions of 1890 and 1907 (and reaped a vast financial harvest as a result) and went on to establish the one thing they had schemed and plotted many years — a central bank in the United States (masquerading under the name of the "Federal" Reserve Bank) — is told in graphic detail in Eustace Mullins', *Secrets of the Federal Reserve*. This book is "must" reading for those who wish to truly understand the causes for our present financial woes!

In his book, Mullins strips aside all of the facades and smoke-screens erected by "the powers that be" to deceive the American people about the true nature of this horribly destructive organization. He provides his readers with thorough documentation that shows that the International Bankers have used the Fed to fleece the American nation, to plunder and pillage its wealth and turn us into a nation of slaves. "The American citizen is born owing interest to the private stockholders (of the Fed) ... and when he dies, his children take up his burden. The poet Ezra Pound stated to me that when he came to Washington in 1939, in an attempt to stave off World War II, he failed because he could find no one in Congress who knew the difference between interest-bearing and non-interest-bearing currency ... (War) Debt is slavery."

The supporters of the Federal Reserve Act of 1913 promised that it would stabilize the dollar, that never again would the dollar madly fluctuate and lose its purchasing power. Never again, we were promised, would Americans "lose their shirts" as the result of depressions or panics. All would now be well on the American scene — and the nation would grow and develop and enjoy unbounded wealth.

Americans chose to ignore the warnings issued by clear-headed, far-seeing and patriotic men who "cried aloud" that the Fed could only lead to financial catastrophe for the American Nation. Senator Henry Cabot Lodge, Sr. declared that "the powers vested in the Federal Reserve Board seem to me highly dangerous, especially where there is political control of the board .... It seems to me to contain features and to rest upon principles in the highest degree menacing to our prosperity ... and to the welfare of the people of the United States."

Senator Elihu denounced the Fed as an outrage on the liberties of the American people: "Long before we wake up from our dreams of prosperity through an inflated currency, our gold, which alone could have kept us from catastrophe, will have vanished and no rate of interest will tempt it to return."

President Wilson, in a 1916 speech, referred to the financial oligarchy that controls the Federal Reserve System: "A great industrial nation is controlled by its system of credit. The growth of the nation, therefore, and all our activities are in the hands of a few men. We have come to be one of the worst ruled, one of the most completely controlled governments in the civilized world — no longer a government of free opinion, no longer a government by conviction and the vote of the majority, but a government by the opinion and duress of a small group of dominant men" (*National Economy and the Banking System*, Senate Documents, Col. 3, No. 23, 75th Congress, 1st Session, 1939).

Mullins traces the activities of the Fed from its inception, and demonstrates from various authoritative documents and official minutes from Senate hearings, the terribly destructive influence which this private banking monopoly has had on the American nation! The money manipulators created the recession of 1920 and reaped vast fortunes when they foreclosed on tens of thousands of properties around the nation.

It is now clear that the recession of 1920 was just a dress rehearsal for a much greater coup ... the Wall Street crash of 1929. In this coup they gained a stranglehold on American industry. Having sold out of the market when it was at its peak early in 1929, they reinvested their vast fortunes in gold and silver. Shortly afterwards, under their direction, the price of both these precious metals practically doubled in value. Then, when the value of industrial stocks had reached bottom, they stepped in and purchased vast blocks of shares at five-ten cents on the dollar. In this way their fortunes were multiplied up to forty times in a remarkably short space of time!

One of the greatest fallacies ever perpetrated on the American public is the belief that "in the Stock Market crash of 1929 everyone lost." Not so! For everyone who lost money someone made money. Those "somebodies" were the people "in the know" — the elitist bankers and their friends (*FDR — My Exploited Father-In-Law*, by Curtis B. Dall, 1968, pp. 73, 74).

Let us now look at the clear, irrefutable and fully documented proof that the International Bankers have systematically raided our nation's coffers since they gained full control of our banking system in 1913.

It has been truly said that a picture is worth a thousand words. It is especially true when it comes to the way in which the real wealth of the American people has been plundered and looted, and the Treasury left threadbare!

The six photographs on the following pages graphically trace the history of the American dollar. Just a few years ago the dollar was truly "as good as gold." In recent years, however, it has to all intents and purposes been reduced (under the expert guidance of the Federal Reserve Board) to a worthless scrap of paper — an irredeemable, fiat currency!

Right now, we are paying the International Bankers hundreds of Billions of dollars each year in interest on our National Debt. This money (or credit) was created by the bankers out of nothing — and loaned to us at a high rate of interest.

If the reader is still not convinced that the "dollars" he carries around in his wallet have been reduced to a state of worthlessness, he should read the article by Jo Hindman (titled "$1,000 Bill Worth Less Than A 10-Cent Trading Stamp") that was published in the Central Valley (CA) *Valley Times*, May 15, 1969. It was inserted in the *Congressional Record* by Congressman John Rarick of Louisiana on May 22, 1969: "A recent court ruling that effects your money reveals that the Federal Reserve credit and currency — the same as you are earning and spending — has no lawful value.

"It came about this way: a bank foreclosed by advertisement on a borrower's note, bought the property (loan's collateral) at a Sherriff's sale, sued to acquire possession of the real estate in a case titled: *First National Bank of Montgomery (Minn.) vs. Jerome Daly*.

The Gold Certificate, representing actual gold coin on deposit in the Treasury was as sound as paper money could get. The integrity of the entire nation stood behind it, not with "fractional reserves" but with *gold coin* as stipulated. The United States has never been the same since!

The "United States Note" is commonly referred to as a "Lincoln Greenback." When Lincoln rebelled at paying the International Bankers high interest to borrow "money" with which to pursue war, these were issued as a general obligation against the United States. *Not one cent of interest has ever been paid to any International Banker or the "Fed" for their issuance.* It has been suggested that his assassination was linked to this.

The solemn pledge on the face of the Silver Certificate, that has now been repudiated by the government in Washington, D.C., shared with the Gold Certificate, the guarantee of being redeemable with a dollar in silver, which was on deposit. The government has now reneged on this.

PLATE 29 — United States Currency

When the "Federal" Reserve Note was first issued, it clearly stipulated that it was *redeemable in Gold,* on demand, at the U.S. Treasury or *in gold or "lawful money"* at any "Federal" Reserve Bank. By 1932 this was no longer the case, but the seed had been planted. Americans were accepting "Federal" Reserve Notes instead of the United States Notes (Lincoln Greenbacks) and Gold and Silver Certificates issued by the Treasury of the United States. We have never recovered from this infamous step!

For many years, the gullible public accepted the "Federal" Reserve Note as though it were real money, but only because of the fact that the Note clearly stated that it was *redeemable in lawful money* at the Treasury or any "Federal" Reserve Bank.

The United States has now reached the final step. We do not have a Gold Certificate, we do not have a Silver Certificate, and we do not have "Federal" Reserve paper that is redeemable in gold, silver or "lawful money." It simply states, "This *note* is legal tender for all debts, public and private." The citizen is given no alternative but to accept. While it is true that the "Lincoln Greenback" simply said that it was "legal tender," the credit of the nation stood behind it. Unlike the "Federal" Reserve Note, the Lincoln Greenback has *never* resulted in one cent of interest At the same time, the "Fed" has systematically looted the Treasury to the point that we are left with only unpayable debt!

PLATE 29A — United States Currency

THE 1970 REPUDIATION

On april 14, 1970, [C.V. Myers] sent Treasury Secretary Kennedy two $100 Federal Reserve Notes— bearing the signature of two U.S. Treasury Secretaries, **promising to redeem in LAWFUL MONEY.** The notes are in themselves a pronouncement that they were not at the time they were written—Lawful money. So whatever the Treasury meant by lawful money in 1934 and in 1950—it was obviously something more than these notes. To claim these notes are in themselves a fulfillment of those promises is to invoke nothing short of MAGIC. Here is the photographed promise:

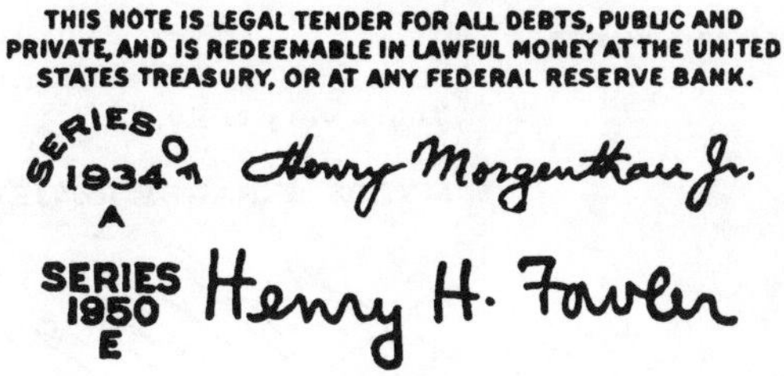

April 14, 1970

Mr. David Kennedy,
Secretary of the Treasury,
U.S. Treasury Department,
Washington, D.C. USA

Dear Sir:

I am enclosing two $100 Federal Reserve notes inscribed..."Redeemable in lawful money at the United States Treasury, or at any Federal Reserve Bank", one signed by Henry Morgenthau, Jr. (1934); and one signed by Henry H. Fowler (1950), both Secretaries of the Treasury.

Webster defines redeemable "to pay off (mortgage or note)..." "to convert (paper money) into coin" -- "to fulfill as a promise".

That is what I ask for here.

The reason I approach you directly is that Federal Reserve branches have in the past failed to make good on this pledge of the U.S. Treasury. Instead they have claimed that the note is in itself lawful money. This is unacceptable: For to make a promise and in the next breath to say that the promise is its own fulfillment is patently absurd.

To maintain that the promise can be fulfilled by repetition of the promise (another Federal Reserve note) is likewise patently absurd. To point to subsequent legislation nullifying the promise (as Fed branches have done) is patently a repudiation of the promise.

PLATE 30 — Letter from C. V. Myers to Mr. David Kennedy

I do not think that you will repudiate on the written pledge of a U.S. Secretary of the Treasury.

I confront you here with the solemn guarantee of the richest nation in the world, and I am asking that the promise be fulfilled. I do not know what you will send me as lawful money but you must know what the U.S. Treasurers called lawful money in 1934 and in 1950, when they wrote these promises. I do know you have silver dollars in the Treasury and I will be satisfied with them.

Thanking you in advance.

Yours very truly,

MYERS' FINANCE REVIEW

C. V. Myers.

CVM:ej.

P.S. Since I have several thousand dollars in these pledges, this is no academic exercise, but a matter of considerable material importance.

Here is the reply from the U.S. Treasury:

THE DEPARTMENT OF THE TREASURY
FISCAL SERVICE
WASHINGTON, D.C. 20220

OFFICE OF
TREASURER OF THE UNITED STATES
IN REPLYING PLEASE QUOTE
JPP:hbc

MAY 12 1970

Mr. C. V. Myers
Myers' Finance Review
903 Lancaster Building
Calgary 2, Alberta

Dear Mr. Myers:

Your letter of April 14, 1970, addressed to the Secretary, has been referred to me for reply.

As you have been informed, the two $100 Federal Reserve Notes which you forwarded with your letter are lawful money. United States notes and coin of the United States are also lawful money.

Silver dollars have not been issued since March 25, 1964, when the Secretary exercised the option granted him by section 2 of the Act of June 4, 1963 (31 U.S.C. 1964 ed., 405 a-1) and determined that silver certificates were thereafter exchangeable only for silver bullion. Prior to March 25, 1964, only the holders of silver certificates had an absolute right to exchange them for silver dollars.

PLATE 31 — Reply from U. S. Treasury to C. V. Myers letter (con't on next page)

Your two $100 Federal Reserve Notes are returned herewith.

Very truly yours,

Special Assistant Treasurer

Enclosures: 2

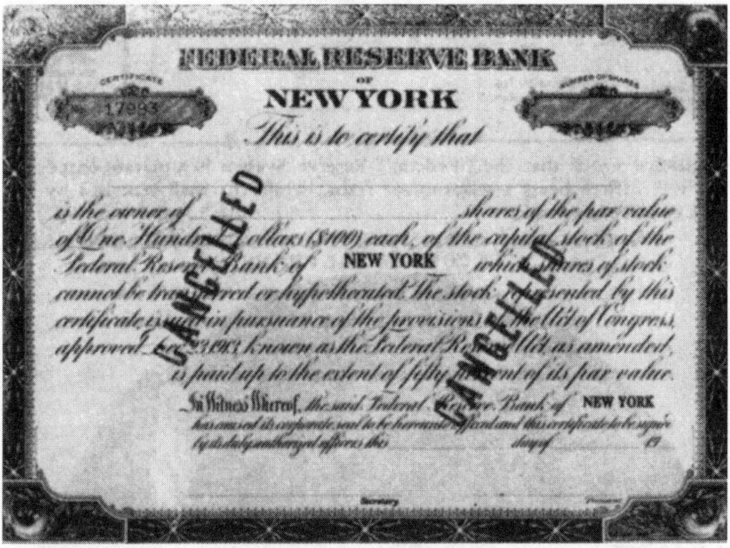

FEDERAL RESERVE BANK OF NEW YORK

Certificate No. 17993

This is to certify that

is the owner of shares of the par value of One Hundred Dollars ($100) each, of the capital stock of the Federal Reserve Bank of NEW YORK which shares of stock cannot be transferred or hypothecated. The stock represented by this certificate is issued in pursuance of the provisions of the Act of Congress approved 1913, known as the Federal Reserve Act as amended, is paid up to the extent of fifty per cent of its par value.

In Witness Whereof, the said Federal Reserve Bank of NEW YORK has caused its corporate seal to be hereunto affixed and this certificate to be signed by its duly authorized officers this day of 19

CANCELLED

CANCELLED

CERTIFICATE ISSUED TO STOCKHOLDERS OF FEDERAL RESERVE BANK OF NEW YORK

Private banks and persons, the owners of the "federal" Reserve, received certificates, as do the owners of other private corporations. The stock has the characteristics of cumulative perferred stock that bears a 6% rate of interest on the paid in capital. Only $50 dollars, half of the $100 per value has been called for and paid in, because the enormous "take," or profits, from the start have made further capital requirements unnecessary. If at any time there develops a need for further capital, the taxpayers are required to furnish it through purchase of stock in the 12 "F"R banks through the Treasury. The Treasury and the taxpayers are responsible for the liabilities of these private "Federal" Reserve banks under the terms fraudulently written into the "F"R Act by Pres. Woodrow Wilson, though they share in none of the profits and are systematically looted to provide them.

PLATE 32 — Certificate issued to stockholders of "Federal" Reserve Bank of New York

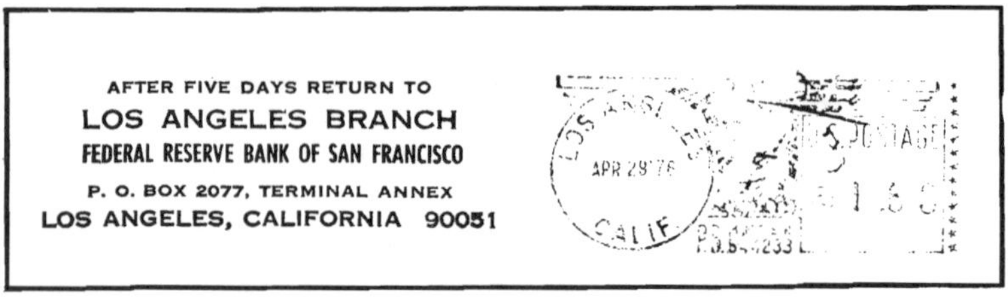
AFTER FIVE DAYS RETURN TO
LOS ANGELES BRANCH
FEDERAL RESERVE BANK OF SAN FRANCISCO
P. O. BOX 2077, TERMINAL ANNEX
LOS ANGELES, CALIFORNIA 90051

Internal Revenue Service

P.O. Box 2031, M.O. Los Angeles, CA 90053

Official Business

Penalty For Private Use, $300

Postage and Fees Paid
Department of the Treasury
554

U.S.MAIL

Additional proof that the "Federal" Reserve System is a private corporation. Mail leaving IRS offices bears a government frank, while the mail sent out by the "Fed" carries a commercial frank.

PLATE 33 — Envelopes showing Federal Reserve mail with commercial frank

PLATE 34 — Incorporation seal of the Federal Reserve Bank — Government agencies are never incorporated

"Martin V. Mahoney, Justice of the Peace, Credit River Township, Scott County (Minn.), presided at the jury trial on December 7, 1968. The jury found the note and mortgage to be void for failure of a lawful consideration: also the jury refused to give any validity to the Sherriff's sale. The bank lost. Jerome Daly, the defendant, won and kept his land.

"The president of the bank which is within the Federal Reserve System, admitted in testimony that the bank 'created' the money/credit by a bookkeeping entry, the so-called consideration for the note and mortgage deed; also that no U.S. law or statute existed that gave the bank the right to create money in that manner. Handing down the Judgment, Justice Mahoney said that 'only God can create something of value out of nothing.'

"The bank tried to appeal the case. The appeal fee of $2 was offered by the bank, using two Federal Reserve Notes. These were likewise declared unlawful and void. The bank agent failed to appear at a hearing on January 22, 1969, and the appeal was dropped.

"By comparison, a humble trading stamp is worth more than a $1 bill (Federal Reserve Note), or even a $1000 Federal Reserve Note. The two bills differ only in denomination and perhaps engraved design, each has paper-and-ink value of a fraction of a cent. On the other hand, basic trading stamps — the gold, the blue, the green — each has face value of one mill. Superior to paper money (FR notes), trading stamps have redemptive value in the merchandise offered in the stamp companies' catalog. The Fed's currency cannot be converted into the gold or silver it purports to represent, and can only be exchanged for more of the same — paper or cheap clad-copper coins.

"Fantastic? Remember the foregoing Daly case: A United States court prevented the bank's attempt to redeem its worthless note by seizing Daly's valuable land.

"The practice works if nobody objects. Do you object to working 23 hours (three days) to pay for a new suit? Or two weeks to buy an automatic washing machine? While a Federal Reserve banker needs only to uncap his pen to create and to multiply fiat dollars thousandfold? Fiat means money cannot be converted into metal coins — gold or silver, etc.

"Worse, the Federal Reserve System is a private corporation not a federal agency, despite its name and the 1913 Act that blessed it."

Within months Judge Mahoney was dead. He died from a heart attack brought on by what the coroner said were "unusual circumstances at the death scene and the controversy he was involved in at the time."

As *The Eagle* newspaper, Yakima, Washington, said in its issue of September 11, 1969: "Whether he was given a whiff of prussic acid or handed a fatal cigarette is not known at this time, but the possibility is certainly more than idle speculation. The international conspiracy which owns and controls our Federal Reserve System, and which has brought our nation to the brink of the most cataclysmic financial crash in history, is understandably unhappy with the earthy judge whose name is Mahoney. The case and its outcome has sent quivers and spasms up and down the entire trunklines and tentacles of the conspiracy as literally thousands of people across the nation have challenged the duplicity of the king-makers over the thievery of their hard-earned wealth."

Jerome Daly, the winner of the above case, was an attorney in Minnesota. He later went to court to defend three men who were accused of counterfeiting Federal Reserve Notes. Within minutes he had proved to the complete satisfaction of the jury that Fed notes have no more real value (legally and constitutionally) than those printed by his clients. Both were irredeemable scraps of paper. Case dismissed!

Shortly thereafter, Jerome Daly lost his license to practice law.

Truly the United States has come to a sorry state when a judge is "eliminated" for rendering a Constitutional verdict in a case involving money, and a lawyer is disbarred for proving that the International Bankers have stripped us of all our wealth and reduced our currency to worthless scraps of paper!

By now it should be abundantly clear to the unbiased reader that the International Bankers who control the Federal Reserve System are the enemies of the United States and our Constitution — that "that dark crew of financial pirates" have fleeced the American "sheeple" and reduced us to a state of bondage.

It is imperative that we understand that this disastrous situation has come about with the consent of Congress, and all the Presidents since 1912. It must also be noted that all of these men took a solemn oath of office to obey and defend the Constitution of these United States.

The Constitution clearly defines treason (in Article 3, Section 3) as: "Treason against the United States shall consist only in levying war against them, or in adhering to their enemies, giving them aid and comfort."

The U.S. Constitution is unassailable. It clearly states: "This Constitution and the laws of the United States which shall be made in pursuance thereof ... shall be the supreme law of the land, and judges in each state shall be bound thereby ... all executive and judicial officers ... shall be bound by oath or affirmation to support this constitution" —Article VI.

When the privately-owned Fed gained control of our money supply in 1914, our National Debt was one Billion dollars. Today, having spent almost a century under the Fed's "expert" guidance, we find ourselves floundering in red ink tens of Trillions of dollars deep. A huge percentage of our National Budget goes to pay interest on the credit (created out of thin air) loaned to us by this "dark crew of financial pirates."

Had interest-free currency been used, as advocated by President Jackson, and constitutionally used by President Lincoln, instead of borrowing at interest, the United States Treasury would have Trillions of dollars in hand — and no debt! Truly, we would be "prosperous beyond precedent in the history of the civilized governments of the world" instead of having to carry a greater burden of debt than all of the other nations of the world combined!

MOVES TO REPEAL THE FEDERAL RESERVE

Over the years various loyal men in Congress have introduced Bills to repeal the Federal Reserve Act of 1913, and to buy back control of our money system. Among these have been Louis T. McFadden's Impeachment Resolution of 1934, still in Committee in Judiciary; Congressman Goldborough's Bill HR9216 of 1935; Congressman Voorhis's HR2809 (1940) and HR373 (1943) and Congressman John Rarick's HR17140 (1970) and HR351 (1971). None of the above have been acted upon by our alleged representatives who are sworn to uphold our Constitution. They all lie buried in committee!

Can we honestly call this enormous crime against the people of these United States anything but treason —"adhering to our enemies, giving them aid and comfort"?

It may be conceded that a few of these men who were meant to be representing us in Congress, the Senate, and the White House have been ignorant of the facts that are so clearly documented in history — and that they have been swept along by carefully created and controlled "public opinion." The only comment this author wishes to make is that if they are *that* ignorant they are *too* ignorant to be your representatives!

The truth is best expressed by Sir John Harrington (1561-1612): "Treason doth never prosper; for if it prosper, none dare call it treason."

When the International Bankers bring about the next great crash they will be playing for total stakes — total control of the world! The stage is now all set for this planned catastrophe — only the timing is not known. The results will make the Crash of 1929 and resultant Great Depression look like a time of great prosperity.

It takes little effort to visualize the astounding fortunes that will be made when the banks (owned or controlled by the International Bankers, of course!) foreclose on the unpaid mortgages on multiple millions of properties around the nation. That one move alone will leave that "dark crew of financial pirates" in control of most of the property in the United States.

With this in mind, the reader should begin to grasp the tremendous insight and understanding possessed by Abraham Lincoln. Just prior to his assassination, Lincoln stated: "I see in the near future a crisis approaching that unnerves me, and causes me to tremble for the safety of our country. Corporations have been enthroned, an era of corruption in high places will follow, and the money power of the country will endeavor to prolong its reign by working upon the prejudices of the people, until the wealth is aggregated in a few hands and the Republic is destroyed."

Lincoln further stated that the credit dealers had, even at that early date, placed the American citizen in this situation: "They have him in his prison house. They have searched his person and have left no prying instrument with him. One after another, they have closed the heavy iron doors upon him and now they have him, as it were, bolted in with a lock of one hundred keys which can never be unlocked without the concurrence of every key; the keys in the hands of a hundred different men, and they scattered to a hundred different places; and they stand musing as to what invention in all the dominion of mind and matter can be produced to make the impossibility of his escape more complete than it is" (*Other People's Money*, Brandeis, p.1).

Clearly, the Federal Reserve Act of 1913 has proven to be the national disaster predicted by its critics at its inception. Their greatest fears have been realized. In 1962 **[please note the date]** a then honest and realistic Alan Greenspan exposed how the international bankers stole our nation blind:

"The abandonment of the gold standard **[i.e. constitutional or "lawful money"]** made it possible … to use the banking system as a means to an unlimited expansion of credit. They have created paper reserves in the form of government bonds which — through the use of a series of complex steps — the banks accept **in place of tangible assets** and treat **as if** they **were** an actual deposit…. The holder of a government bond or a bank deposit **created by paper reserves** believes [he has blind faith!] that he has a valid claim on a real asset. But the fact is there are now **[1962]** more claims outstanding than real assets.

"The law of supply and demand is not to be conned…. In the absence of the gold standard, there is no way to protect savings from confiscation through inflation. There is no safe store of value. If there were the government would have to make its holding illegal, as it has done in the case of gold…. The financial policy of the welfare state demands that there be no way for the owners of wealth to protect themselves.

"This is the shabby secret of the welfare statists' tirade against gold [Constitutional or "lawful money"]. Deficit spending is simply a scheme for the confiscation of wealth."

Read those words again, and again! They are factual dynamite — and one of the reasons our nation is doomed. Unless there is a political, monetary and, above all, **a spiritual** revolution to clear the way for a return to political and monetary sanity, national historians will shortly write America's none-too-complimentary obituary.

CHAPTER ELEVEN

THE MASTER PLAN

INTRODUCTION

Is there in existence a Blueprint — *a Master Plan* — for the systematic destruction of civilization, all governments and religions, and the establishment of a New World Order?

Yes, such *a Master Plan* does exist. It has been known and published in various forms since the Bavarian government circulated its famous report on the activities and plans of the Illuminati in the 1780s.

The leaders of the Illuminati, as we have seen, are a small but powerful group which includes international bankers, industrialists, scientists, military and political leaders, educationalists, economists, etc. At the very highest level, there are men who have accepted the Luciferian doctrine of Adam Weishaupt and Albert Pike. They worship Lucifer as required by Albert Pike in his book, Morals and Dogma. They acknowledge the authority of no mortal being except their leader. They give loyalty to no nation. They direct the continuing LUCIFERIAN CONSPIRACY to obtain absolute control of this world and everything in it.

They use all subversive movements to divide the masses of the people into opposing camps on political, social, racial, economic and religious issues. They arm and finance these groups and encourage them to fight with each other. They hope to make humanity follow this process of self-destruction until all existing political and religious institutions have been eliminated. They then plan to crown their King-despot of the entire world, and enforce their global dictatorship with Luciferian despotism.

In order to prove this contention, the document published as The Protocols of *the Learned Elders of Zion* must be studied carefully, bearing in mind that in spite of all the arguments regarding its source and origin, it is undoubtedly and indisputably the Master Plan by which this comparatively small group of immensely wealthy, diabolically crafty and extremely influential men have subverted and perverted the leadership in every strata of society in order to attain their goal. They use the promise of wealth, luxury, "self esteem" and sensual pleasures to lure these leaders into their trap from which there is no escape.

The men who conceived the diabolical conspiracy as laid out in the Protocols were not atheists: they were members of the Illuminati, followers of the original "light bearer," Lucifer. They were worshippers of Lucifer. This is the plan of Lucifer.

The Protocols, as we know them today, were first made public when they appeared in a Russian publication in 1905. A copy of the Protocols was purchased by the British Museum in London on August 10, 1906.

The Protocols — or the Master Plan to gain ultimate world domination — were broken up by British journalist Victor Marsden into Articles and Paragraphs for easy reference. Marsden said that he could not stand to work on the project more than an hour at a time in the British Museum. The diabolical spirit of the matter which he was obliged to turn into English made him positively ill. His translation was issued by the British Publishing Society, in London, in 1921.

In the first chapter of his book, *Red Fog Over America*, the late William Guy Carr, who had been a Commander in the Canadian Navy, gave details of his investigation into the origin of the Protocols. Through his many contacts in intelligence circles around the world, he ascertained that the Protocols are in fact genuine.

He states that the directors of the Illuminati became worried in the 1890s when historians began to study the plot leading up to the French Revolution which took place in 1789, and particularly that phase of it which indicated that the Illuminati were behind it. The papers found on the body of the courier of the Illuminati, who was killed by lightning in 1785, proved conclusively their connection with the plot. This gave the Illuminati considerable concern.

"Because the policy of the directors has always been to work behind the scenes, and never allow their identity or connections with the revolutionary forces to be known, it was decided that a new document should be made available to the historians. The new document was written in such a way that suspicion was turned away from the directors of the Illuminati and directed towards the leaders of the Jewish revolutionary movement in Russia. Those charged with preparing the hoax used the plan found on the courier's body, *but they changed certain words and phrases to make those who read the "new" document believe it was the Jewish plot to obtain world domination in accordance with the policy of political Zionism as advocated by Herzl in 1897* ....

"The conspirators decided that the altered plans should be placed in the hands of an outstanding Russian whose character and reputation were beyond reproach. The man they chose to be their unsuspecting accomplice was Professor S. Nilus. He checked and believed the documents placed in his hands [by a person who claimed he got them from a prostitute who stole them from a leading Jew] were genuine, as in actual fact they were. By publishing them as *The Jewish Peril* in 1905, Nilus played right into the hands of the Illuminati (*Red Fog Over America*, pp. 3,4).

Belief in their authenticity would be suppressed by charges of "rabid anti-semitism," "Jew baiting," "racism," and other slurs that would tend to draw people away from the facts as they really are.

To say that the whole affair is a "Jewish Conspiracy" is an oversimplification of the facts: it *is clearly a Luciferian conspiracy*. However, to deny that many Jews have been involved in the Plot would be ridiculous: Weishaupt, Marx, the Warburgs, the Rothschilds, Jacob Schiff, etc. were all Jews!

In an effort to divert public attention from the deadly seriousness of the message contained in this Satanically-inspired document, some people have claimed that it is a forgery or a plagiarism.

The famous *Times* of London ran articles on August 16, 17 and 18, 1921, in which they claimed to have made a "sensational discovery." The articles, supposedly written by their "correspondent in Constantinople," claimed that the Protocols were a "clumsy plagiarism" of a French book entitled *The Dialogues of Geneva* published in Brussels in 1865.

Had they been totally honest and objective in their "investigation" into the origin of the Protocols, the *Times* would no doubt have made another "sensational discovery," namely that a similar book, *Machiavelli Montesquieu and Rousseau,* written by Jacob Venedey and published by Franz Dannicker in Berlin, 1850, also contained passages out of the Protocols.

The simple truth is that both these books contained passages found in the Protocols. This fact proves nothing one way or the other. The Plan outlined in the Protocols is clearly embodied in the writings of the Illuminati as published by the Bavarian government. The authors of both books were obviously acquainted with these documents and quoted extensively from them.

Of course, the real proof of the authenticity or the falseness of the Protocols is not contained in what people say about them. The real proof of the Protocols is contained in what the Protocols, themselves, say — and in the deadly accuracy of their predictions of the future (as of 1901).

Henry Ford, the famed auto pioneer, in an interview published in the *New York World,* February 17, 1921, put the case for the veracity of the Protocols very convincingly: "The only statement I care to make about the Protocols is that they fit in with what is going on. They are [at least] sixteen years old, and they have fitted the world situation up to this time. They fit it now."

In a letter to the *Spectator,* August 27, 1921, Lord Sydenham stated: "The Protocols explain in almost laborious detail the objects of Bolshevism and the methods of carrying it into effect. These methods were in operation in 1901, when Nilus said that he received the documents, but Bolshevism was then Marxian Communism, and the time had not come for applying it by military force. Nothing that was written in 1865 can have any bearing on the deadly accuracy of the forecasts in the Protocols, most of which have since been fulfilled to the letter.

"What is the most striking characteristic of the Protocols? The answer is knowledge of a rare kind, embracing the widest field. The solution of the mystery, if it is one, is to be found by ascertaining where this uncanny knowledge, on which prophecies now literally fulfilled are based, can be shown to reside."

These statements were made in 1921 when the predictions contained in the Protocols were just beginning to be fulfilled. *How much more weight should they carry in the world today when they are virtually an accomplished fact?*

In the text of the Protocols, two words frequently recur. They are "Goyim" and "Agentur." The first word, meaning "human cattle," is used in a slurring manner to indicate all peoples of all races and creeds who are not members of the Illuminati apparatus. The word "Agentur" means the whole body of agents made use of by the Illuminati. In particular, it refers to Illuminists who act as "advisers" and "specialists" to governments and leading institutions.

Following are excerpts from the Victor Marsden translation of the Protocols:

-1-

...Putting aside fine phrases we shall speak of the significance of each thought: by comparisons and deductions we shall throw light upon surrounding facts.

What I am about to set forth, then, is our system from the two points of view, that of ourselves and that of the *goyim*.

It must be noted that men with bad instincts are more in number than the good, and therefore the best results in governing them are attained by violence and terrorization, and not by academic discussions. Every man aims at power, everyone would like to become a dictator if only he could, and rare indeed are the men who would not be willing to sacrifice the welfare of all for the sake of securing their own welfare ...

Political freedom is an idea but not a fact. This idea one must know how to apply whenever it appears necessary with this bait of an idea to attract the masses of the people to one's party for the purpose of crushing another who is in authority. This task is rendered easier if the opponent has himself been infected with the idea of freedom, *so-called liberalism*, and, for the sake of an idea, is willing to yield some of his power. It is precisely here that the triumph of our theory appears: the slackened reins of government are immediately, by the law of life, caught up and gathered together by a new hand, because the blind might of the nation cannot for one single day exist without guidance, and the new authority merely fits into the place of the old already weakened by liberalism.

In our day the power which has replaced that of the rulers who were liberal is the power of Gold. Time was when Faith ruled. The idea of freedom is impossible of realization because no one knows how to use it with moderation. It is enough to hand over a people to self-government for a certain length of time for that people to be turned into a disorganized mob ...

Whether a State exhausts itself in its own convulsions, whether its internal discord brings it under the power of external foes — in any case it can be accounted irretrievable lost: *it is in our power*. The despotism of Capital, which is entirely in our hands, reaches out to it a straw that the State, willy-nilly, must take hold of: if not — it goes to the bottom ...

Is it possible for any sound logical mind to hope with any success to guide crowds by the aid of reasonable counsels and arguments, when any objection or contradiction, senseless though it may be, can be made and when such objection may find more favour with the people, whose powers of reasoning are superficial? Men in masses and the men of the masses, being guided solely by petty passions, paltry beliefs, customs, traditions and sentimental theorism, fall a prey to party dissention, which hinders any kind of agreement even on the basis of a perfectly reasonable argument...

The political has nothing in common with the moral. The ruler who is governed by the moral is not a skilled politician, and is therefore unstable on his throne. He who wishes to rule must have recourse both to cunning ... and to make-believe. Great national qualities, like frankness and honesty, are vices in politics, for they bring down rulers from their thrones more effectively and more certainly than the most powerful enemy. Such qualities must be the attributes of the kingdoms of the *goyim* but we must in no wise be guided by them ...

Our power in the present tottering condition of all forms of power will be more invincible than any other, because it will remain invisible until the moment when it has gained such strength that no cunning can any longer undermine it.

Out of the temporary evil we are now compelled to commit will emerge the good of an unshakable rule, which will restore the regular course of the machinery of the national life, brought to naught by liberalism. The result justifies the means. Let us, however, in our plans, direct our attention not so much to what is good and moral as to what is necessary and useful.

Before us is a plan in which is laid down strategically the line from which we cannot deviate without running the risk of seeing the labour of many centuries brought to naught. In order to elaborate satisfactory forms of action it is necessary to have regard to the rascality, the slackness, the instability of the mob, its lack of capacity to understand and respect the conditions of its own life, or its own welfare. It must be understood that the might of a mob is blind, senseless and unreasoning force ever at the mercy of a suggestion from any side. The blind cannot lead the blind without bringing them into the abyss; consequently, members of the mob, upstarts from the people even though they should be as a genius for wisdom, yet having no understanding of the political, cannot come forward as leaders of the mob without bringing the whole nation to ruin ...

Our countersign is — force and Make-Believe. Only force conquers in political affairs, especially if it be concealed in the talents essential to statesmen. Violence must be the principle, and cunning and make-believe the rule for governments which do not want to lay down their crowns at the feet of agents of some new power. This evil is the one and only means to attain the end, the good. Therefore we must not stop at bribery, deceit and treachery when they should serve towards the attainment of our end. In politics one must know how to seize the property of others without hesitation if by it we secure submission and sovereignty.

Our State, marching along the path of peaceful conquest, has the right to replace the horrors of war by less noticeable and more satisfactory sentences of death, necessary to maintain the terror which tends to produce blind submission. Just but merciless severity is the greatest factor of strength in the State: not only for the sake of gain but also in the name of duty, for the sake of victory ...

Far back in ancient times we were the first to cry among the masses of the people the words "Liberty, Equality, Fraternity," words many times repeated since those days of stupid poll-parrots who from all sides round flew down upon these baits and with them carried away the well-being of the world, true freedom of the individual, formerly so well guarded against the pressure of the mob. The would-be wise men of the *goyim*, the intellectuals, could not make anything out of the uttered words in their abstractness; did not note the contradiction of their meaning and inter-relation; did not see that in nature there is no equality, cannot be freedom; that Nature herself has established inequality of minds, of characters, and capacities, just as immutably as she has established subordination to her laws; never stopped to think that the mob is a blind thing, that upstarts elected from among it to bear rule are in regard to the political, the same blind men as the mob itself ...

In all corners of the earth the words "Liberty, Equality, Fraternity" brought to our ranks, thanks to our blind agents, whole legions who bore our banners with enthusiasm. And all the time these words were canker-worms at work boring into the well-being of the *goyim*, putting an end everywhere to peace, quiet, solidarity and destroying all the foundations of the *goy* states. As you will see later, this helped us to our triumph; it gave us the possibility, among other things, of getting into our hands the master card — the destruction of the privileges, or in other words of the very existence of the aristocracy of the *goyim*, that class which was the only defense peoples and countries had against us...

Our triumph has been rendered easier by the fact that in our relations with the men whom we wanted we have always worked upon the most sensitive chords of the human mind, upon the cash account, upon the cupidity, upon the insatiability for material needs of man; and each one of these human weaknesses, taken alone, is sufficient to paralyze initiative, for it hands over the will of men to the disposition of him who has bought their activities.

-2-

Our international rights will then wipe out national rights, in the proper sense of right, and will rule the nations precisely as the civil law of States rules the relations of their subjects among themselves.

The administrators, whom we shall choose from among the public, with strict regard to their capacities for servile obedience, will not be persons trained in the arts of government, and will therefore easily become pawns in our game in the hands of men of learning and genius who will be their advisers, specialists bred and reared from early childhood to rule the affairs of the whole world. As is well known to you, these specialists of ours have been drawing, to fit them for rule, the information they need from our political plans from the lessons of history, from observations made of the events of every moment as it passes. The *goyim* are not guided by practical use of unprejudiced historical observation, but by theoretical routine without any critical regard for consequent results. We need not, therefore, take any account of them — let them amuse themselves until the hour strikes, or live on hopes of new forms of enterprising pastime, or on the memories of all they have enjoyed. For them, let that play the principal part which we have persuaded them to accept as the dictates of science (theory). It is with this object in view that we are constantly, by means of our press, arousing a blind confidence in these theories. The intellectuals of the *goyim* will puff themselves up with their knowledge and, without any logical verification of them, will put into effect all the information available from science, which our *agentur* specialists have cunningly pieced together for the purpose of educating their minds in the direction we want.

Do not suppose for a moment that these statements are empty words: think carefully of the successes we arranged for Darwinism, Marxism, Nietzsche-ism. To us [Illuminists], at any rate, it should be plain to see what a disintegrating importance these directives have had upon the minds of the *goyim* ...

In the hands of the States of today there is a great force that creates the movement of thought in the people, and that is the Press. The part played by the Press is to keep pointing out requirements supposed to be indispensable, to give voice to the complaints of the people, to express and create discontent. It is in the Press that the triumph of freedom of speech finds its force; and it has fallen into our hands. Through the Press we have gained the power to influence while remaining ourselves in the shade; thanks to the Press we have got the *gold* in our hands, notwithstanding that we have had to gather it out of oceans of blood and tears. But it has paid us, though we have sacrificed many of our people. Each victim on our side is worth in the sight of God a thousand *goyim*.

-3-

The constitution scales of these days will shortly break down, for we have established them with a certain lack of accurate balance in order that they may oscillate incessantly until they wear through the pivot on which they turn. The *goyim* are under the impression that they have welded them sufficiently strong and they have all along kept on expecting that the scales would come into equilibrium ...

In order to incite seekers after power to a misuse of power, we have set all forces in opposition one to another, breaking up their liberal tendencies towards independence. To this end we have stirred up every form of enterprise, we have armed all parties, we have set up authority as a target for every ambition. Of States we have made gladiatorial arenas where a host of confused issues contend ... A little more, and disorders and bankruptcy will be universal ...

Babblers inexhaustible have turned into oratorical contests the sittings of Parliament and Administrative Boards. Bold journalists and unscrupulous pamphleteers daily fall upon executive officials. Abuses of power will put the final touch in preparing all institutions for their overthrow and everything will fly skyward under the blows of the maddened mob.

All people are chained down to heavy toil by poverty more firmly than ever they were chained by slavery and serfdom; from these, one way and another, they might free themselves, these could be settled with, but from want they will never get away. We have included in the constitution such rights as to the masses appear fictitious and not actual rights. All these so-called "People's Rights" can exist only in idea, an idea which can never be realized in practical life. What is to the proletariat labourer, bowed double over his heavy toll, crushed by his lot in life, if talkers get the right to babble, if journalists get the right to scribble any nonsense side by side with good stuff, once the proletariat has no other profit out of the constitution save only those pitiful crumbs which we fling them from our table in return for their voting in favour of what we dictate, in favour of the men we place in power, the servants of our *agentur* ...

We appear on the scene as alleged saviours of the worker from this oppression when we propose to him to enter the ranks of our fighting forces — Socialists, Anarchists, Communists — to whom we always give support in accordance with an alleged brotherly rule (of the solidarity of all humanity) of our *social masonry*. The aristocracy, which enjoyed by law the labour of the workers, was interested in seeing that the workers were well fed, healthy and strong. We are interested in just the opposite — in the diminution, the *killing out of the GOYIM*. Our power is in the chronic shortness of food and physical weakness of the worker because by all that this implies he is made the slave of our will, and he will not find in his own authorities either strength or energy to set against our will. Hunger creates the right of capital to rule the worker more surely than it was given to the aristocracy by the legal authority of kings.

By want and the envy and hatred which it engenders we shall move the mobs and with their hands we shall wipe out all those who hinder us on our way.

When the hour strikes for our Sovereign Lord [SATAN, see p. 70-71] of all the World to be crowned, it is these same hands which will sweep away everything that might be a hindrance thereto.

The *goyim* have lost the habit of thinking unless prompted by the suggestions of our specialists. Therefore they do not see the urgent necessity of what we, when our kingdom comes, shall adopt at once, namely this, that *it is essential to teach in national schools one simple, true piece of knowledge, the basis of all knowledge — the knowledge of the structure of human life, of social existence, which requires division of labour, and consequently, the division of men into classes and conditions*. It is essential for all to know that *owing to differences in the objects of human activity there cannot be any equality,* that he who by any act of his, compromises a whole class cannot be equally responsible before the law with him who affects no one but only his own honour. The true knowledge of the structure of society, into the secrets of which we do not admit the *goyim,* would demonstrate to all men that the positions and work must be kept within a certain circle, that they may not become a source of human suffering, arising from an education which does not correspond with the work which individuals are called upon to do. After a thorough study of this knowledge the peoples will voluntarily submit to authority and accept such position as is appointed them in the State. In the present state of knowledge and the direction we have given to its development the people, blindly believing things in print, cherishes —thanks to promptings intended to mislead and to its own ignorance — a blind hatred towards all conditions which it considers above itself, for it has no understanding of the meaning of class and condition.

This hatred will be still further magnified by the effects of an *economic crisis,* which will stop dealings on the exchanges and bring industry to a stand-still. We shall create by all the secret subterranean methods open to us and with the aid of gold, which is all in our hands, *a universal economic crisis whereby we shall throw upon the streets whole mobs of workers simultaneously in all the countries of Europe*. These mobs will *rush delightedly* to shed the blood of those whom, in the simplicity of their ignorance, they have envied from their cradles, and whose property they will then be able to loot.

"Ours" they will not touch, because the moment of attack will be known to us and we shall take measures to protect our own.

We have demonstrated that progress will bring all the *goyim* to the sovereignty of reason. Our despotism will be precisely that; for it will know how, by wise severities, to pacificate all unrest, to cauterize liberalism out of all institutions.

When the populace has seen that all sorts of concessions and indulgences are yielded to it in the name of freedom, it has imagined itself to be sovereign lord and has stormed its way to power. But, naturally, like every other blind man it has come upon a host of stumbling blocks, *it has rushed to find a guide, it has never had the sense to return to the former state* and it has laid down its plenipotentiary powers at *our* feet. Remember the French Revolution, to which it was we who gave the name of "Great": the secrets of its preparations are well known to us for it was wholly the work of our hands...

And thus the people condemn the upright and acquit the guilty, persuaded ever more and more that it can do whatsoever it wishes. Thanks to this state of things, the people are destroying every kind of stability and creating disorders at every step.

-4-

... Who and what is in a position to overthrow an invisible force? And this is precisely what our force is. *Gentile* masonry blindly serves as a screen for us and our objectives, but the plan of action of our force, even its very abiding place, remains for the whole people an unknown mystery.

But even freedom might be harmless and have its place in the State economy, without injury to the well-being of the peoples, if it rested upon the foundation of faith in God, upon the brotherhood of humanity, unconnected with the conception of equality, which is negatived by the very laws of creation, for they have established subordination. With such a faith as this a people might be governed by a wardship of parishes, and would walk contentedly and humbly under the guiding hand of its spiritual pastor submitting to the dispositions of God upon earth. This is the reason why *it is indispensable for us to undermine all faith, to tear out of the minds of the GOYIM the very principle of Godhead and the spirit, and to put in its place arithmetical calculations and material needs.*

In order to give the *goyim* no time to think and take note, their minds must be diverted towards industry and trade. Thus, all the nations will be swallowed up in the pursuit of gain and in the race for it will not take note of their common foe. But again, in order that freedom may once for all disintegrate and ruin the communities of the *goyim*, we must put industry on a speculative basis: the result of this will be that what is withdrawn from the land by industry will slip through the hands and pass into speculation, that is to our classes.

-5-

We shall create an intensified centralization of government in order to grip in our hands all the forces of the community. We shall regulate mechanically all the actions of the political life of our subjects by new laws. These laws will withdraw one by one all the indulgences and liberties which have been permitted by the *goyim,* and our kingdom will be distinguished by a despotism of such magnificent proportions as to be at any moment and in every place in a position to wipe out any *goyim* who oppose us by deed or word. We shall be told that such a despotism as I speak of is not consistent with the progress of these days, but I will prove to you that it is.

In the times when the peoples looked upon kings on their thrones as on a pure manifestation of the will of God, they submitted without a murmur to the despotic power of the kings: but from the day when we insinuated into their minds the conception of their own rights they began to regard the occupants of thrones as mere ordinary mortals. The holy unction of the Lord's Anointed has fallen from the heads of kings in the eye of the people, and when we also robbed them of their faith in God the might of power was flung upon the streets into the place of public proprietorship and was seized by us.

Moreover, the art of directing masses and individuals by means of cleverly manipulated theory and verbiage, by regulations of life in common and all sorts of other quirks, in all which the *goyim* understand nothing, belongs likewise to the specialists of our administrative brain. Reared on analysis, observation, on delicacies of fine calculation, in this species of skill we have no rivals, any more than we have either in the drawing up of plans of political actions and solidarity ...

For a time perhaps we might be successfully dealt with by a coalition of the GOYIM of all the world: but from this danger we are secured by the discord existing among them whose roots are so deeply seated that they can never now be plucked up. We have set one against another the personal and national reckonings of the *goyim,* religious and race hatreds, which we have fostered into a huge growth in the course of the past twenty centuries. This is the reason why there is not one State which would anywhere receive support if it were to raise its arm, for everyone of them must bear in mind that any agreement against us would be unprofitable to itself. We are too strong — there is no evading our power. *The nations cannot come to even an inconsiderable private agreement without our secretly having a hand in it ...* Capital, if it is to co-operate untrammelled, must be free to establish a monopoly of industry and trade: this is already being put in execution by an unseen hand in all quarters of the world. This freedom will give political force to those engaged in industry, and that will help to oppress the people. Nowadays it is more important to disarm the peoples than to lead them into war; more important to use for our advantage the passions which have burst into flames than to quench their fire; more important to catch up and interpret the ideas of others to suit ourselves than to eradicate them. *The principal object of our directorate consists in this: to debilitate the public mind by criticism; to lead it away from serious reflections calculated to arouse resistance; to distract the forces of the mind towards a sham fight of empty eloquence.*

In all ages the peoples of the world, equally with individuals, have accepted words for deeds, for *they are content with a show* and rarely pause to note, in the public arena, whether promises are followed by performance. Therefore we shall establish show institutions which will give eloquent proof of their benefit to progress.

We shall assume to ourselves the liberal physiognomy of all parties, of all directions, and we shall give that physiognomy a voice *in orators who will speak so much that they will exhaust the patience of their hearers and produce an abhorrence of oratory.*

In order to put public opinion into our hands we must bring it into a state of bewilderment by giving expression from all sides to so many contradictory opinions and for such length of time as will suffice to make the GOYIM lose their heads in the labyrinth and come to see that the best thing is to have no opinion of any kind in matters political, they are understood only by him who guides the public. This is the first secret.

The second secret requisite for the success of our government is comprised in the following: To multiply to such an extent national failings, habits, passions, conditions of civil life, that it will be impossible for anyone to know where he is in the resulting chaos, so that the people in consequence will fail to understand one another. This measure will also serve us in another way, namely, to sow discord in all parties, to dislocate all collective forces which are still unwilling to submit to us, and to discourage any kind of personal initiative which might in any degree hinder our affair. *There is nothing more dangerous than personal initiative;* if it has genius behind it, such initiative can do more than can be done by millions of people among whom we have sown discord. We must so direct the education of the *goyim* communities that whenever they come upon a matter requiring initiative they may drop their hands in despairing impotence. The strain which results from freedom of action saps the forces when it meets with the freedom of another. From this collision arise grave moral shocks, disenchantments, failures. *By all these means we shall so wear down the GOYIM that they will be compelled to offer us international power of a nature that by its position will enable us without any violence gradually to absorb all the State forces of the world and to form a Super-Government.* In place of the rulers of today we shall set up a bogey which will be called the Super-Government Administration. Its hands will reach out in all directions like nippers and its organization will be of such colossal dimensions that it cannot fail to subdue all the nations of the world.

-6-

What we want is that industry should drain off from the land both labour and capital and by means of speculation transfer into our hands all the money of the world, and thereby throw all the *goyim* into the ranks of the proletariat. Then the *goyim* will bow down before us, if for no other reason but to get the right to exist ... *We shall raise the rate of wages which, however, will not bring any advantage to the workers, for at the same time, we shall produce a rise in prices of the first necessaries of life, alleging that it arises from the decline of agriculture and cattle-breeding; we shall further undermine artfully and deeply sources of production, by accustoming the workers to anarchy and to drunkenness and side by side therewith taking all measure to extirpate from the face of the earth all the educated forces of the GOYIM.*

In order that the true meaning of things may not strike the GOYIM before the proper time we shall mask it under an alleged ardent desire to serve the working classes and the great principles of political economy about which our economic theories are carrying on an energetic propaganda.

-7-

The intensification of armaments, the increase of police forces — are all essential for the completion of the aforementioned plans. What we have to get at is that there should be in all the States of the world, besides ourselves, only the masses of the proletariat, a few millionaires devoted to our interests, police and soldiers.

We must be in a position to respond to every act of opposition by war with the neighbors of that country which dares to oppose us; but if these neighbors should also venture to stand collectively together against us, then we must offer resistance by a universal war.

The principal factor of success in the political is the secrecy of its undertakings; the word should not agree with the deeds of the diplomat.

We must compel the governments of the *goyim* to take action in the direction favored by our widely-conceived plan, already approaching the desired consummation, by what we shall represent as public opinion, secretly prompted by us through the means of that so-called "Great Power" — *the Press, which, with a few exceptions that may be disregarded, is already entirely in our hands.*

In a word, to sum up our system of keeping the governments of the *goyim* in Europe in check, we shall show our strength to one of them by terrorist attempts and to all, if we allow the possibility of a general rising against us, we shall respond with the guns of America or China or Japan.

-8-

We must arm ourselves with all the weapons which our opponents might employ against us. We must search out in the very finest shades of expression and the knotty points of the lexicon of law justification for those cases where we shall have to pronounce judgments that might appear abnormally audacious and unjust, for it is important that these resolutions should be set forth in expressions that shall seem to be the most exalted moral principles cast into legal form. Our directorate must surround itself with all these forces of civilization among which it will have to work. It will surround itself with publicists, practical jurists, administrators, diplomats and, finally, with persons prepared by a special super-educational training *in our special schools [Gordonstoun, Scotland, etc.]*. These persons will have cognizance of all the secrets of the social structure, they will know all the languages that can be made up by political alphabets and words; they will be made acquainted with the whole underside of human nature, with all its sensitive chords on which they will have to play.

These chords are the cast of mind of the *goyim*, their tendencies, shortcomings, vices and qualities, the particularities of classes and conditions. Needless to say that the talented assistants of authority, of whom I speak, will be taken not from among the *goyim*, who are accustomed to perform their administrative work without giving themselves the trouble to think what its aim is, and never consider what it is needed for. The administrators of the *goyim* sign papers without reading the, and they serve either for mercenary reasons or from ambition ...

For a time, until there will no longer be any risk in entrusting responsible posts in our States to our brother-[Illuminists] we shall put them in the hands of persons whose past and reputation are such that between them and the people lies an abyss, persons who, in case of disobedience to our instructions, must face criminal charges or disappear — this in order to make them defend our interests to their last gasp.

-9-

For us there are no checks to limit the range of our activity. Our Super-Government subsists in extra-legal conditions which are described in the accepted terminology by the energetic and forcible word —Dictatorship. I am in a position to tell you with a clear conscience that at the proper time we, the lawgivers, shall execute judgment and sentence, we shall slay and we shall spare, we, as head of all our troops, are mounted on the steed of the leader. We rule by force of will, because in our hands are the fragments of a once powerful party, now vanquished by us. *And the weapons in our hands are limitless ambitions, burning greediness, merciless vengeance, hatreds and malice.*

It is from us that the all-engulfing terror proceeds. We have in our service persons of all opinions, of all doctrines, restorating monarchists, demagogues, socialists, communists, and utopian dreamers of every kind. We have harnessed them all to the task: *each one of them on his own account is boring away at the last remnants of authority, is striving to overthrow all established form of order.* By these acts all States are in torture; they exhort to tranquility, are ready to sacrifice everything for peace; *but we will not give them peace until they openly acknowledge our international Super-Government,* and with submissiveness.

The people have raised a howl about the necessity of settling the question of Socialism by way of an international agreement. *Division into fractional parties has given them into our hands, for, in order to carry on a contested struggle one must have money, and the money is all in our hands ...*

In this way the blind force of the people remains our support and we, and we only, shall provide them with a leader and, of course, direct them along the road that leads to our goal ...

In order not to annihilate the institutions of the *goyim* before it is time we have touched them with craft and delicacy, and have taken hold of the ends of the springs which move their mechanism. These springs lay in a strict but just sense of order; we have replaced them by the chaotic license of liberalism. We have got our hands into the administration of the law, into the conduct of elections, into the press, into liberty of the person, *but principally into education and training as being the corner-stones of a free existence.*

We have fooled, bemused and corrupted the youth of the goyim by rearing them in principles and theories which are known to us to be false although it is by us that they have been inculcated.

Above the existing laws without substantially altering them, and by merely twisting them into contradictions of interpretations, we have erected something grandiose in the way of results. These results found expression first in the fact that the *interpretations masked the laws:* afterwards they entirely hid them from the eyes of the governments owing to the impossibility of making anything out of the tangled web of legislation.

This is the origin of the theory, of course, of arbitration.

You may say that the *goyim* will rise upon us, arms in hand, if they guess what is going on before the time comes; but in the West we have against this a manoeuvre of such appalling terror that the very stoutest hearts quail — the undergrounds, metropolitans, those subterranean corridors which, before the time comes, will be driven under all the capitals and from whence those capitals will be blown into the air with all their organizations and archives.

-10-

When we have accomplished our coup d'etat we shall say then to the various peoples: "Everything has gone terribly badly, all have been worn out with sufferings. We are destroying the causes of your torment — nationalities, frontiers, differences of coinages. Your are at liberty, of course, to pronounce sentence upon us, but can it possibly be a just one if it is confirmed by you before you make any trial of what we are offering you." ... Then will the mob exalt us and bear us up in their hands in a unanimous triumph of hopes and expectations. Voting, which we have made the instrument which will set us on the throne of the world by teaching even the very smallest units of members of the human race to vote by means of meetings and agreements by groups, will then have served its purposes and will play its part then for the last time by a unanimity of desire to make close acquaintance with us before condemning us.

To secure this we must have everybody vote without distinction of classes and qualifications, in order to establish an absolute majority, which cannot be got from the educated propertied classes. In this way, by inculcating in all a sense of self-importance, we shall destroy among the *goyim* the importance of the family and its educational value and remove the possibility of individual minds splitting off, for the mob, handled by us, will not let them come to the front nor even give them a hearing; it is accustomed to listen to us only who pay it for obedience and attention. In this way we shall create a blind, mighty force which will never be in a position to move in any direction without the guidance of our agents set at its head by us as leaders of the mob ...

When we introduced into the State organism the poison of Liberalism its whole political complexion underwent a change. States have been seized with a mortal illness — blood-poisoning. All that remains is to await the end of their death agony ...

In order that our scheme may produce this result we shall arrange elections in favour of such presidents as have in their past some dark, undiscovered stain, some "Panama" or other — then they will be trustworthy agents for the accomplishment of our plans out of fear of revelations and from the natural desire of everyone who has attained power, namely, the retention of the privileges, advantages and honour connected with the office of president. The chamber of deputies will provide cover for, will protect, will elect presidents, but we shall take from it the right to propose new, or make changes in existing laws, for this right will be given by us to the responsible president, a puppet in our hands. Naturally, the authority of the president will then become a target for every possible form of attack, but we shall provide him with a means of self-defense in the right of an appeal to the people, for the decision of the people over the heads of their representatives, that is to say, an appeal to that same blind slave of ours — the majority of the mob. Independently of this we shall invest the president with the right of declaring a state of war. We shall justify this last right on the ground that the president, as chief of the whole army of the country, must have it at his disposal, in case of need for the defense of the new republican constitution, the right to defend which will belong to him as the responsible representative of this constitution.

It is easy to understand that in these conditions the key of the shrine will lie in our hands, and no one outside ourselves will any longer direct the force of legislation ...

But you yourselves perfectly well know that *to produce the possibility of the expression of such wishes by all the nations it is indispensable to trouble in all countries the people's relations with their governments so as to utterly exhaust humanity with dissension, hatred, struggle, envy and even by the use of torture, by starvation. By the inoculation of diseases [AIDS?], by want, so that the GOYIM see no other issue than to take refuge in our complete sovereignty in money and in all else.*

But if we give the nations of the world a breathing space the moment we long for is hardly likely ever to arrive.

-11-

This, then, is the program of the new constitution. We shall make Law, Right and Justice (1) in the guise of proposals to the Legislative Corps, (2) by decrees of the president under the guise of general regulations, of orders of the Senate and of resolutions of the State Council in the guise of ministerial orders, (3) and in case a suitable occasion should arise — in the form of a revolution in the State ... What we want is that from the first moment of its promulgation, while the peoples of the world are still stunned by the accomplished fact of the revolution, still in a condition of terror and uncertainty, they should recognize once for all that we are so strong, so inexpugnable, so superabundantly filled with power, that in no case shall we take any account of them, and so far from paying any attention to their opinions or wishes, we are ready and able to crush with irresistible power all expression or manifestation thereof at every moment and in every place, that we have seized at once everything we wanted and shall in no case divide our power with them ... Then in fear and trembling they will close their eyes to everything, and be content to await what will be the end of it all.

The *goyim* are a flock of sheep, and we are their wolves. And you know what happens when the wolves get hold of the flock? ...

There is another reason also why they will close their eyes: for we shall keep promising them to give back all the liberties we have taken away as soon as we have quelled the enemies of peace and tamed all parties ...

It is not worth while to say anything about how long a time they will be kept waiting for this return of their liberties ...

-12-

The word "freedom," which can be interpreted in various ways, is defined by us as follows: —

Freedom is the right to do that which the law allows. This interpretation of the word will at the proper time be of service to us, because all freedom will thus be in our hands, since the laws will abolish or create only that which is desirable for us according to the aforesaid program.

We shall deal with the press in the following way: What is the part played by the press today? It serves to excite and inflame those passions which are needed for our purpose or else it serves selfish ends of parties. It is often vapid, unjust, mendacious, and the majority of the public have not the slightest idea what ends the press really serves. We shall saddle and bridle it with a tight curb; we shall do the same also with all productions of the printing press, for where would be the sense of getting rid of the attacks of the press if we remain targets for pamphlets and books? ...

Not a single announcement will reach the public without our control. Even now this is already attained by us inasmuch as all news items are received by a few agencies, in whose offices they are focused from all parts of the world. These agencies will then be already entirely ours and will give publicity only to what we dictate to them.

If already now we have contrived to possess ourselves of the minds of the *goy* communities to such an extent that they all come near looking upon the events of the world through the coloured glasses of those spectacles we are setting astride their noses: if already now there is not a single State where there exist for us any barriers to admittance into what *goy* stupidity calls State secrets; what will our position be then, when we shall be acknowledged supreme lords of the world in the person of our king of all the world ...

All the so-called liberals are anarchists, if not in fact, at any rate in thought. Every one of them is hunting after phantoms of freedom, and falling exclusively into license, that is, into the anarchy of protest for the sake of protest ...

In the third rank we shall set up our own, to all appearance, opposition, which, in at least one of its organs, will present what looks like the very antipodes to us. Our real opponents at heart will accept this simulated opposition as their own and will show us their cards.

All our newspapers will be of all possible complexions — aristocratic, republican, revolutionary, even anarchical — for so long, of course, as the constitution exists ... Like the Indian idol Vishnu they will have a hundred hands, and every one of them will have a finger on any one of the public opinions as required. When a pulse quickens these hands will lead opinion in the direction of our aims, for an excited patient loses all power of judgment and easily yields to suggestion. Those fools who will think they are repeating the opinion of a newspaper of their own camp will be repeating our opinion or any opinion that seems desirable for us. In the vain belief that they are following the organ of their party they will in fact follow the flag which we hang out for them ...

These attacks upon us will also serve another purpose, namely, that our subjects will be convinced of the existence of full freedom of speech and so give our agents an occasion to affirm that all organs which oppose us are empty babblers, since they are incapable of finding any substantial objections to our orders.

Methods of organization like these, imperceptible to the public eye but absolutely sure, are the best calculated to succeed in bringing the attention and the confidence of the public to the side of our government. Thanks to such methods we shall be in a position as from time to time may be required, to excite or to tranquilize the public mind on political questions, to persuade or to confuse, printing now truth, now lies, facts or their contradictions, according as they may be well or ill received, always very cautiously feeling our ground before stepping upon it ... *We shall have a sure triumph over our opponents since they will not have at their disposition organs of the press in which they can give full and final expression to their views* owing to the aforesaid methods of dealing with the press. We shall not even need to refute them except very superficially.

Trial shots like these, fired by us in the third rank of our press, in case of need, will be energetically refuted by us in our semi-official organs ...

When we are in the period of the new regime transitional to that of our assumption of full sovereignty we must not admit any revelations by the press of any form of public dishonesty; it is necessary that the new regime should be thought to have so perfectly contented everybody that even criminality has disappeared ... Cases of the manifestation of criminality should remain known only to their victims and to chance witnesses — no more.

The need for daily bread forces the *goyim* to keep silence and be our humble servants. Agents taken on to our press from among the *goyim* will at our orders discuss anything which it is inconvenient for us to issue directly in official documents, and we meanwhile, quietly amid the din of the discussion so raised, shall simply take and carry through such measures as we wish and then offer them to the public as an accomplished fact. No one will dare to demand the abrogation of a matter once settled, all the more so as it will be represented as an improvement ... And immediately the press will distract the current of thought towards new questions (have we not trained people always to be seeking something new?) ...

In order to distract people who may be too troublesome from discussions of questions of the political we are now putting forward what we allege to be new questions of the political, namely, questions of industry. In this sphere let them discuss themselves silly! The masses are agreed to remain inactive, to take a rest from what they suppose to be political activity (which we trained them to in order to use them as a means of combating the *goy* governments) only on condition of being found new employments, in which we are prescribing them something that looks like the same political object.

In order that the masses themselves may not guess what they are about *we further distract them with amusements, games pastimes, passions, people's palaces ... Soon we shall begin through the press to propose competitions in art, in sport of all kinds; these interests will finally distract their minds from questions in which we should find ourselves compelled to oppose them. Growing more and more disaccustomed to reflect and form any opinions of their own, people will begin to talk in the same tone as we, because we alone shall be offering them new directions for thought ... of course through such persons as will not be suspected of solidarity with us.*

The part played by the liberals, utopian dreamers, will be finally played out when our government is acknowledge. Till such time they will continue to do us good service. Therefore we shall continue to direct their minds to all sorts of vain conceptions of fantastic theories, new and apparently progressive; for have we not with complete success turned the brainless heads of the *goyim* with progress, till there is not among the *goyim* one mind able to perceive that under this word lies a departure from truth in all cases where it is not a question of material inventions, for truth is one, and in it there is no place for progress. Progress, like a fallacious idea, serves to obscure truth so that none may know it except us, the Chosen of God, its guardians.

When we come into our kingdom our orators will expound great problems which have turned humanity upside down in order to bring it at the end under our beneficent rule.

Who will ever suspect then that *all these peoples were stage-managed by us according to political plan which no one has so much as guessed at in the course of many centuries? ...*

-14-

...Useless changes of forms of government to which we instigated the *GOYIM when we were undermining their state structures, will have so wearied the peoples by that time that they will prefer to suffer anything under us rather than run the risk of enduring again all the agitations and miseries they have gone through.*

At the same time we shall not omit to emphasize the historical mistakes of the *goy* governments which have tormented humanity for so many centuries by their lack of understanding of everything that constitutes the true good of humanity in their chase after fantastic schemes of social blessings, and have never noticed that these schemes kept on producing a worse and never a better state of the universal relations which are the basis of human life...

The whole force of our principles and methods will lie in the fact that we shall present them and expound them as a splendid contrast to the dead and decomposed old order of things in social life.

Our philosophers will discuss all the shortcomings of the various beliefs of the *GOYIM, but no one will ever bring under discussion our faith from its true point of view since this will be fully learned by none save ours, who will never dare to betray its secrets.*

In countries known as progressive and enlightened, we have created a senseless, filthy abominable literature. For some time after our entrance to power we shall continue to encourage its existence in order to provide a telling relief by contrast to the speeches, party program, which will be distributed from exalted quarters of ours ... Our wise men, trained to become leaders of the *goyim,* will compose speeches, projects, memoirs, articles, which will be used by us to influence the minds of the *goyim,* directing them towards such understanding and forms of knowledge as have been determined by us.

-15-

When we at last definitely come into our kingdom by the aid of *coups d'etat* prepared everywhere for one and the same day, after the worthlessness of all existing forms of government has been definitely acknowledged (and not a little time will pass before that comes about, perhaps even a whole century) we shall make it our task to see that against us such things as plots shall no longer exist. With this purpose we shall slay without mercy all who take arms (in hand) to oppose our coming into our kingdom. Every kind of new institution of anything like a secret society will also be punished with death; those of them which are now in existence, are known to us, serve us and have served us, we shall disband and send into exile to continents far removed from Europe. *In this way we shall proceed with those GOY masons* who know too much; such of these as we may for some reason spare will be kept in constant fear of exile. We shall promulgate a law making all former members of secret societies liable to exile from Europe as the centre of our rule.

Resolutions of our government will be final, without appeal.

In the *goy* societies, in which we have planted and deeply rooted discord and protestantism, the only possible way of restoring order is to employ merciless measures that prove the direct force of authority: no regard must be paid to the victims who fall, they suffer for the well-being of the future. The attainment of that well-being, even at the expense of sacrifices, is the duty of any kind of government that acknowledges, as justification for its existence, not only its privileges but its obligations. The principal guarantee of stability of rule is to confirm the aureole of power, and this aureole is attained only by such a majestic inflexibility of might as shall carry on its face the emblems of inviolability from mystical causes — from the choice of God. *Such was, until recent times, the Russian autocracy, the one and only serious foe we had in the world without counting the Papacy...*

The class of people who most willingly enter into secret societies are those who live by their wits, careerists, and in general people, mostly light-minded, with whom we shall have no difficulty in dealing and in using to wind up the mechanism of the machine devised by us. If this world grows agitated the meaning of that will be that we have had to stir it up in order to break up its too great solidarity. *But if there should arise in its midst a plot, then at the head of that plot will be no other than one of our most trusted servants.* It is natural that we and no other should lead *masonic* activities, for we know whither we are leading, we know the final goal of every form of activity whereas the *goyim* have knowledge of nothing, not even of the immediate effect of action.

When it comes the time of our overt rule, the time to manifest its blessings, we shall remake all legislatures, all our laws will be brief, plain, stable, without any kind of interpretations, so that anyone will be in a position to know them perfectly. The main feature which will run right through them is submission to orders, and this principle will be carried to a grandiose height. Every abuse will then disappear in consequence of the responsibility of all down to the lowest unit before the higher authority of the representative of power. Abuses of power subordinate to this last instance will be so mercilessly punished that none will be found anxious to try experiments with their own powers. We shall follow up jealously every action of the administration on which depends the smooth running of the machinery of the State, for slackness in this produces slackness everywhere; not a single case of illegality or abuse of power will be left without exemplary punishment.

Concealment of guilt, connivance between those in the service of the administration — all this kind of evil will disappear after the very first examples of severe punishment. The sufferer, though his punishment may exceed his fault, will count as a soldier falling on the administrative field of battle in the interest of authority, principle and law, which do not permit that any of those who hold the reins of the public coach should turn aside from the public highway to their own private paths. *For example: our judges will know that whenever they feel disposed to plume themselves on foolish clemency they are violating the law of justice which is instituted for the exemplary edification of men by penalties for lapses and not for display of the spiritual qualities of the judge...*

We shall root out liberalism from all the important strategic posts of our government on which depends the training of subordinates for our State structure. Such posts will fall exclusively to those who have been trained by us for administrative rule. To the possible objection that the retirement of old servants will cost the Treasury heavily, I reply, firstly they will be provided with some private service in place of what they lose, and, secondly, I have to remark that all the money in the world will be concentrated in our hands, consequently it is not our government that has to fear expense.

Our government will have the appearance of a patriarchal paternal guardianship on the part of our ruler. Our own nation and our subjects will discern in his person a father caring for their every need, their every act, their every inter-relation as subjects one with another, as well as their relations to the ruler. They will then be so thoroughly imbued with the thought that it is impossible for them to dispense with this wardship and guidance, if they wish to live in peace and quiet, *that they will acknowledge the autocracy of our ruler with a devotion bordering on Apotheosis,* especially when they are convinced that those whom we set up do not put their own in place of his authority, but only blindly execute his dictates. They will be rejoiced that we have regulated everything in their lives as is done by wise parents who desire to train their children in the cause of duty and submission.

We are obliged without hesitation to sacrifice individuals, who commit a breach of established order, for in the exemplary punishment of evil lies a great educational problem.

-16-

In order to effect the destruction of all collective forces except ours, we shall emasculate the first stage of collectivism — the *universities,* by reeducating them in a new direction. *Their officials and professors will be prepared for their business by detailed secret programs of action from which they will not with immunity diverge, not by one iota. They will be appointed with especial precaution, and will be so placed as to be wholly dependent upon the Government ...*

We shall erase from the memory of men all facts of previous centuries which are undesirable to us, and leave only those which depict all the errors of the governments of the *goyim.* The study of practical life, of the obligations of order, of the relations of people one to another, of avoiding bad and selfish examples which spread the infection of evil, and similar questions of an educative nature, will stand in the forefront of the teaching program, which will be drawn up on a separate plan for each calling or state of life, in no wise generalizing the teaching. This treatment of the question has special importance.

Each state of life must be trained within strict limits corresponding to its destination and work in life. The *occasional genius has always managed and always will manage to slip through into other states of life, but it is the most perfect folly for the sake of this rare occasional genius to let through into ranks foreign to them the untalented who thus rob of their places those who belong to those ranks by birth or employment. You know yourselves in what all this has ended for the goyim who allowed this crying absurdity.*

In a word, knowing by the experience of many centuries that people live and are guided by ideas, that these ideas are imbibed by people only by the aid of education provided with equal success for all ages of growth, but of course by varying methods, we shall swallow up and confiscate to our own use the last scintilla of independence of thought, which we have for long past been directing towards subjects and ideas useful for us. The system of bridling thought is already at work in the so-called system of teaching by *object lessons,* the purpose of which is to turn the *goyim* into unthinking submissive brutes waiting for things to be presented before their eyes in order to form an idea of them...

-17-

They do not usually decline to undertake any defense whatever, they strive for an acquittal at all costs, cavilling over every petty crux of jurisprudence and thereby they demoralize justice. For this reason we shall set this profession into narrow frames which will keep it inside this sphere of executive public service. Advocates, equally with judges, will be deprived of the right of communication with litigants; they will receive business only from the court and will study it by notes of report and documents, defending their clients after they have been interrogated in court on facts that have appeared. They will receive an honorarium without regard to the quality of the defense. This will render them mere reporters on law-business in the interests of justice and as counterpoise to the proctor who will be the reporter in the interests of prosecution; this will shorten business before the courts. In this way will be established a practice of honest unprejudiced defense conducted not from personal interest but by conviction. This will also, by the way, remove the present practice of corrupt bargain between advocates to agree only to let that side win which pays most...

Day by day its influence on the peoples of the world is falling lower. *Freedom of conscience* has been declared everywhere, *so that now only years divide us from the moment of the complete wrecking of that Christian religion,* as to other religions we shall have still less difficulty in dealing with them, but it would be premature to speak of this now...

In our program *one-third of our subjects will keep the rest under observation* from a sense of duty, on the principle of volunteer service to the State. It will then be no disgrace to be a spy and informer, but a merit: unfounded denunciations, however, will be cruelly punished that there may be no development of abuses of this right.

This body, having no rights and not being empowered to take any action on their own account, and consequently a police without any power, will only witness and report: verification of their reports and arrests will depend upon a responsible group of controllers of police affairs, while the actual act of arrest will be performed by the gendarmerie and the municipal police. Any person not denouncing anything seen or heard concerning questions of polity will also be charged with and made responsible for concealment, if it be proved that he is guilty of this crime.

Just as nowadays our brethren are obliged at their own risk to denounce to the kabal apostates of their own family or members who have been noticed doing anything in opposition to the *kabal, so in our kingdom over all the world it will be obligatory for all our subjects to observe the duty of service to the State in this direction.*

-18-

We have compelled the rulers to acknowledge their weakness in advertising over measures of secret defense and thereby we shall bring the promise of authority to destruction.

Our ruler will be secretly protected only by the most insignificant guard, because we shall not admit so much as a thought that there could exist against him any sedition with which he is not strong enough to contend and is compelled to hide from it.

Criminals with us will be arrested at the first more or less well-grounded *suspicion*; it cannot be allowed that out of fear of a possible mistake an opportunity should be given of escape to persons suspected of a political lapse or crime, for in these matters we shall be literally merciless. If it is still possible, by stretching a point, to admit a reconsideration of the motive causes in simple crimes, there is no possibility of excuse for persons occupying themselves with questions in which nobody except the government can understand anything ... And it is not all governments that understand true policy.

-19-

Sedition-mongering is nothing more than the yapping of a lap-dog at an elephant. For a government well organized, not from the police but from the public point of view, the lap-dog yaps at the elephant in entire unconsciousness of its strenght and importance. It needs no more than to take a good example to show the relative importance of both and the lap-dogs will cease to yap and will wag their tails the moment they set eyes on an elephant.

-20-

Economic crises have been produced by us for the *goyim* by no other means than the withdrawal of money from circulation. Huge capitals have stagnated, withdrawing money from States, which were constantly obliged to apply to those same stagnant capitals for loans. These loans burdened the finances of the state with the payment of interest, and made them the bond slaves of these capitals ... The concentration of industry in the hands of capitalists out of the hands of small masters has drained away all the juices of the peoples and with them also of the States ...

The present issue of money in general does not correspond with the requirements per head, and cannot therefore satisfy all the needs of the workers. The issue of money ought to correspond with the growth of population and thereby children also must absolutely be reckoned as consumers of currency from the day of their birth. The revision of issue is a material question for the whole world.

You are aware that the gold standard has been the ruin of the States which adopted it, for it has not been able to satisfy the demands for money, the more so that we have removed gold from circulation as far as possible.

With us the standard that must be introduced is the cost of working-man power, whether it be reckoned in paper or in wood. We shall make the issue of money in accordance with the normal requirements of each subject, adding to the quantity with every birth and subtracting with every death.

The reform projected by us in the financial institutions and principles of the *goyim* will be clothed by us in such forms as will alarm nobody. We shall point out the necessity of reforms in consequence of the disorderly darkness into which the *goyim* by their irregularities have plunged the finances. The first irregularity, as we shall point out, consists in their beginning with drawing up a single budget which year after year grows owing to the following cause: this budget is dragged out to half the year, then they demand a budget to put things right, and this they expend in three months, after which they ask for a supplementary budget, and all this ends with a liquidation budget. But, as the budget of the following year is drawn up in accordance with the sum of the total addition, the annual departure from the normal reaches as much as 50 percent in a year, and so the annual budget is trebled in ten years. Thanks to such methods, allowed by the carelessness of the *goy* States, their treasuries are empty. The period of loans supervenes, and that has swallowed up remainders and brought all the *goy* States to bankruptcy.

You understand perfectly that economic arrangements of this kind, which have been suggested to the *goyim* by us, cannot be carried on by us...

What also indeed is, in substance, a loan, especially a foreign loan? A loan is — an issue of government bills of exchange containing a percentage obligation commensurate to the sum of the loan capital. If the loan bears a charge of 5 percent, then in twenty years the State vainly pay away in interest a sum equal to the loan borrowed, in forty years it is paying a double sum, in sixty — treble, and all the while the debt remains an unpaid debt.

From this calculation it is obvious that with any form of taxation per head the State is baling out the last coppers of the poor taxpayers in order to settle accounts with wealthy foreigners, from who it has borrowed money instead of collecting these coppers for its own needs without the additional interest.

So long as loans were internal the *goyim* only shuffled money from the pockets of the poor to those of the rich, but when we bought up the necessary person in order to transfer loans into the external sphere all the wealth of States flowed into our cash-boxes and all the *goyim* began to pay us the tribute of subjects ...

How clear is the undeveloped power of thought of the purely brute brains of the *goyim,* as expressed in the fact that they have been borrowing from us with payment of interest without ever thinking that all the same these very moneys plus an addition for payment of interest must be got by them from their own State pockets in order to settle up with us. What could have been simpler than to take the money they wanted from their own people?

But it is a proof of the genius of our chosen mind that we have contrived to present the matter of loans to them in such a light that they have even seen in them an advantage for themselves.

Our accounts, which we shall present when the time comes, in the light of centuries of experience gained by experiments made by us on the *goy* States, will be distinguished by clearness and definiteness, and will show at a glance to all men the advantage of our innovations. They will put an end to those abuses to which we owe our mastery over the *goyim,* but which cannot be allowed in our kingdom...

You know to what they have been brought by this carelessness, to what a pitch of financial disorder they have arrived, notwithstanding the astonishing industry of their peoples ...

-21-

If everybody expressed his unwillingness and demanded his money back, the government would be hooked on their own flies and would be found insolvent and unable to pay the proposed sums. By good luck the subjects of the *goy* governments, knowing nothing about financial affairs, have always preferred losses on exchange and diminution of interest to the risk of new investments of their moneys, and thereby many a time enabled these governments to throw off their shoulders a debit of several millions.

Nowadays, with external loans, these tricks cannot be played by the *goyim* for they know that we shall demand all our moneys back.

In this way an acknowledged bankruptcy will best prove to the various countries the absence of any means between the interests of the people and of those who rule them.

I beg you to concentrate your particular attention upon this point and upon the following: nowadays all internal loans are consolidated by so-called flying loans, that is, such as have terms of payment more or less near. These debts consist of moneys paid into the savings banks and reserve funds. If left for long at the disposition of a government, these funds evaporate in the payment of interest on foreign loans, and are replaced by the deposit of equivalent amount of *rentes*.

-22-

We shall contrive to prove that we are benefactors who have restored to the rent and mangled earth the true good and also freedom of the person, and therewith we shall enable it to be enjoyed in peace and quiet, with proper dignity of relations, on the condition, of course, of strict observance of the laws established by us ...

Our authority will be glorious because it will be all-powerful, will rule and guide, and not muddle along after leaders and orators shrieking themselves hoarse with senseless words which they call great principles and which are nothing else, to speak honestly, but utopian ... Our authority will be the crown of order, and in that is included the whole happiness of man. The aureole of this authority will inspire a mystical bowing of the knee before it and a reverent fear before it of all the peoples. True force makes no terms with any right, not even with that of God: none dare come near to it so as o take so much as a span from it away.

-23-

That the peoples may become accustomed to obedience it is necessary to inculcate lessons of humility and therefore to reduce the production of articles of luxury. By this we shall improve morals which have been debased by emulation in the sphere of luxury. We shall re-establish small master production which will mean laying a mine under the private capital of manufacturers. This is indispensable also for the reason that manufacturers on the grand scale often move, though not always consciously, the thoughts of the masses in directions against the government. A people of small masters knows nothing of unemployment, and this binds him closely with existing order, and consequently with the firmness of authority. Unemployment is a most perilous thing for a government. For us its part will have been played out the moment authority is transferred into our hands. Drunkenness also will be prohibited by law and punishable as a crime against the humanness of man who is turned into a brute under the influence of alcohol.

Subjects, I repeat once more, give blind obedience only to the strong hand which is absolutely independent of them, for in it they feel the sword for defense and support against social scourges ... What do they want with an angelic spirit in a king? What they have to see in him is the personification of force and power.

CHAPTER TWELVE

TRAGEDY . . . AND HOPE

In the preceding chapters, we have traced the Luciferian (or Satanic) Conspiracy from its earliest beginnings.

As we continue our journey into our third century as a nation, we have almost reached the point of total degeneration and disintegration. Everywhere we see clear evidence of the success enjoyed by the Weishauptian Conspiracy in its quest for total world power.

The United States Constitution has been emasculated to the point of non-existence. Treason is lauded and praised by most "authorities" and "experts." Patriotism is scoffed at on every hand. The nation is drowning in an ocean of red ink. Crime abounds. Evil is called good. Good is called foolishness.

Truly, we are living in perilous times. Most of the great, cherished pillars of society seem ready to cave in and come crashing down around our ears.

The Tragedy is that Satan (or Lucifer, "the god of this world," II Corinthians 4:4) has seduced most people into breaking away from reality. As a nation, we have become lost in a maze of foolish reasoning and vain speculation. Through following the scheme outlined in the Master Plan (chapter 11), the writings of Adam Weishaupt, and the Rockefeller-controlled General Education Board's *Occasional Letter, Number 1* (see chapter 6), the conspirators have come remarkably close to the fulfillment of their diabolical purpose.

IS THERE ANY HOPE?

The reader may ask: "Do we have any hope of stopping this diabolical conspiracy? Can our nation be brought back to basic sanity and moral soundness?"

In the long term, there is no reason why we should be thrown into a state of despair by an acknowledgment of the Tragedy that is hanging over our nation. There is no need to adopt an attitude of hopelessness. *The Satanic Plot is doomed to failure!*

To grasp the Big Picture, it is necessary for us to understand some basic truths regarding the nature of the Conspiracy now threatening to enslave the United States in a totalitarian One World Government, or New World Order: "We wrestle not against flesh and blood, but against principalities, against powers, against the rulers of the darkness of this world, against spiritual wickedness [or, wicked spirits] in high places" (*Ephesians* 6:11).

The vast majority of the authors who write on the International Conspiracy make the basic mistake of not recognizing the true nature of the enemy. Most of them believe that we are only engaged in a battle against "flesh and blood" (mortal, human beings who may be defeated by conventional means). They reject the concept that our real enemy is Satan and his demons, "the rulers of the darkness of this world ... spiritual wickedness in high places."

As a result of this basic misunderstanding, they believe the conspiracy can be successfully combated by patriotic Americans regaining control of Congress, and by the emergence of a "whole new breed of articulate, well-informed, tough-minded political leaders who have done their homework and are capable of taking on this gigantic international network of global power."

Such a "solution" sounds great. Only one problem: it won't work. Why? We are not fighting a physical or political enemy. Our real enemy is Satan (or Lucifer), a spiritual being of superior intelligence and incredible subtlety. He is the god of the Illuminati: Albert Pike tells us to "doubt it not!" (*Morals and Dogma*, p. 321). He stands clearly revealed as the one directing the conspiracy. This spiritual force of pure evil and diabolical ingenuity can only be thwarted in his purpose and totally defeated by another spiritual force *of even greater authority and power*.

The Lost Keys of Freemasonry

or

The Secret of Hiram Abiff

BY

MANLY P. HALL, 33°. K.T.

AUTHOR OF

Masonic, Hermetic, Qabbalistic and Rosicrucian Symbolical Philosophy; Lectures on Ancient Philosophy; etc., etc.

Foreword by Reynold E. Blight, 33°, K. T.

Illustrations by J. Augustus Knapp, 32°

[48]

When the Mason learns that the key to the warrior on the block is the proper application of the dynamo of living power, he has learned the mystery of his Craft. The seething energies of Lucifer are in his hands and before he may step onward and upward, he must prove his ability to properly apply energy. He must follow in the footsteps of his forefather, Tubal-Cain, who with the mighty strength of the war god hammered his sword into a plowshare. Incessant vigilance over thought, action, and desire is indispensable to those who wish to make progress in the unfolding of their own being, and the Fellow Craft's degree is the degree of transmutation.

MACOY PUBLISHING AND MASONIC SUPPLY COMPANY, INC.

RICHMOND, VIRGINIA

PLATE 35 — *The Lost Keys of Freemasonry*

At the very highest level, the leaders of the Luciferian Conspiracy are undoubtedly in direct contact with Lucifer. These are the individuals who, having come up through the ranks of the secret societies, are now the "real initiates [who] are called the 'Illuminati', (Sons of Light), — those who are illumined, and who in turn illuminate...."

"The concepts of the human mind are everywhere undergoing refinement, as man rises in the scale of human evolution....

"To all those profound secrets, the concept of 'the Grand Architect of the Universe' stands, and will forever remain the 'Rock of Ages', the acme and epitome of human wisdom as a concept of Divinity" (*The Genius of Freemasonry*, by J.D. Buck, Indio American Book Co., Chicago, 1907, p.36,37).

Notice that the true "Rock of Ages" (Jesus Christ) has been replaced by Lucifer, "the Great Architect of the Universe."

How does one reach the upper ranks of the Luciferian Conspiracy, the Illuminati? The answer, we believe, is found in Manley Hall's book, *The Lost Keys of Freemasonry*: "When the Mason learns that the key to the warrior on the block is the proper application of the dynamo of living power, he has learned the mystery of his craft. *The seething energies of Lucifer are in his hands and before he may step onward and upward, he must prove his ability to properly apply energy*.... Incessant vigilance over thought, action, and desire is indispensable for those who wish to make progress in the unfolding of their being, and the Fellow Craft's desire is the degree of transmutation (p.48).

The word transmutation, according to Webster's *Dictionary of the English Language*, 1828, means: "The change of anything into another substance, or into something of a different nature." The goal or purpose, then, is to be changed into "another substance," and thus have a "different nature"! Put in plain English, *the goal and purpose is to attain the position of deity, Lucifer's way*! This is perfectly in line with Satan's promise in the Garden of Eden, to those who follow his way, that "your eyes shall be opened, and you shall be as gods...." (*Genesis* 3:5).

Many students of Masonry believe that the ceremony of "the warrior on the block" (after which one receives "the seething energies of Lucifer") involves the sacrifice of a male child of perfect innocence and high intelligence (*Occult Theocrasy*, by Lady

Queenborough, p. 576). If this is correct, they would be bonded to Lucifer through a blood covenant, in somewhat the same manner as Christians are bonded to Jesus Christ through the shedding of His blood on the cross.

Again, a diabolical Luciferian counterfeit!

However, with most of the leaders Satan doesn't operate that way! A quick review of chapter four will reveal the fact that Satan appears as "an angel of light," one who can supply apparently logical answers to all the problems facing the human race. However, as history all too frequently demonstrates, following that way inevitably ends in disaster for those involved!

Satan, as ruler of this world or society, can spiritually transmit or make his wishes known in such a subtle manner as to give the recipients the honest impression that they have come up with a totally "fabulous idea" all on their own! Especially with those who have natural "smarts," he appeals to their vanity, jealousy, lust, and greed — their innate, Satan-inspired desire to be "as God." He appeals to their yearning for "authority" and "power" — their desire to be "somebody" and thus be "looked up to" and honored by those who are the Movers and Shakers in society. For unregenerate opportunists, it is naturally much easier — and much more financially and politically rewarding — to go along with the ways of the world (Satan's Babylonian System) than to make a stand for what is right, just and true!

Satan's unholy spirit is a counterfeit of God's Holy Spirit. Whereas God's Holy Spirit (which is the spirit of truth and of a sound mind, *II Timothy* 1:7) *leads* or guides people "into all truth" (*John* 16:13), Satan's unholy spirit guides or directs people along an unending path of error, vanity, self-deception, wilfulness and rebellion. Yes, "There is a way that seems right to a man, but the end thereof are the ways of death" (*Proverbs* 14:12). Or, as scripture says in another place, the "way of a fool is right in his *own* eyes..." (*Proverbs* 12:15).

SOCIALISM

Socialism is one modern example of this basic truth. During the first seventy years of the twentieth century, socialism (in its many forms and guises) was touted as the "answer" to all our problems: it was proclaimed to be the "savior" of mankind. The implementation of socialist principles worldwide, would, we were told, result in an Utopian society. Peace on earth, and good will among men!

Not only has the dream-world predicted by the purveyors of socialistic theories failed to materialize, it has degenerated into a hellish nightmare of hideous proportions. Hundreds of millions of human beings have lost their lives along the road to the Socialists' promised land. Around the globe, nation after nation lies in shambles. This is a result of their mindless implementation of a philosophy based upon the belief that man is god, and is thus capable of creating his own paradise.

Worldwide, chaos and confusion reign. Every man "does that which is right in his own eyes" (*Judges* 17:6). Globally, lawlessness, rebellion, violence, corruption, and the resultant moral, financial and spiritual bankruptcy is the order of the day.

THE FUTURE?

What about the present and immediate future? Should we all clothe ourselves with a mantle of defeatism, creep out into the desert, and await "the coming of the Lord"? The late Dr. Carroll Quigley would have us believe (*Tragedy and Hope*, pp. 979-980) that it is now too late to rescue the United States from the clutches of the Conspirators. Any resistance, he assured us as long ago as 1966, would be a *"revolt of the ignorant against the informed and educated* ... of the Midwest of Tom Sawyer against the cosmopolitan East of J. P. Morgan and Co., of old Siwash against Harvard." According to the learned doctor, any resistance would constitute a Tragedy. The only Hope for America lies in the hands of the Conspirators. Hence the title of his book!

Was Quigley correct in his analysis of our national predicament? Is it all over for America? Is national slavery a foregone conclusion?

No! All is not lost! Ultimately, the conspirators will not prevail! Their diabolical plot will collapse in ignominious ruins!

WHAT IS HAPPENING?

What we are witnessing in the United States, as well as around the world, is Satan's last ditch effort to "put it all together" and create a One World Government. It's his last desperate fling of spiritual insanity.

Satan is working through vain, lust-ridden human beings who reflect his attitude. They have sold out to him in a desperate effort to satisfy their craving for power. Arch-Illuminist, Albert Pike, head of Scottish Rite Masonry, openly acknowledged that Lucifer was his god. He tells us to "doubt it not" (*Morals And Dogma*, p.321).

BABYLON IS FALLEN

Being based on greed, pride, and avarice, Satan's plan for total world conquest is fatally flawed. It's in total violation of all the spiritual laws and principles set in motion, and sustained by, the Creator God. As a result, it's doomed!

Take a closer look at any phase or facet of Satan's Babylonian System, now dominant on the national or international scenes. Outwardly, it may have the appearance of vitality and strength. But appearances are deceptive. All is not well with Satan's governmental system on planet earth. It's striving desperately to hold itself together, but to no avail.

Massive flaws, huge cracks are everywhere evident in the superstructure of the Babylonian System. It's crumbling and falling apart at the seams. No wonder! It's built on lies and deceit. Being morally and spiritually depraved, it panders to the basest instincts of human nature. Ultimately, it can produce only corruption and confusion. The system is being held together by a massive, interlocking web of hate, fear, terror, manipulation, coercion, harassment and intimidation. Without these Satanic ingredients, and their ruthless enforcement by agents of the Conspiracy, the whole system would instantly collapse in ignominy.

The handwriting is on the wall. The Babylonian System — embodying, as it does, all the institutions which the world holds dear — has been weighed in the balance and found wanting. Its fate is sealed. Its days are numbered.

In the mind of the Almighty, Creator God, "Babylon the Great is fallen, is fallen" (*Revelation* 18:2). *To God, it is an accomplished fact!*

Satan's Babylonian System has been worshiped, honored and obeyed by the overwhelming majority of mankind from time immemorial. Its imminent collapse and destruction will come as a devastating blow to all who worship (wittingly or unwittingly) the diabolical religious/political/financial system which pollutes and corrupts the earth. In fact, the leaders of the nations, who have committed spiritual fornication with the Babylonian System, "shall bewail her, and lament for her, when they see the smoke of her burning.... And the merchants of the earth shall weep and mourn over her, for no man buys their merchandise any more; ... For in one hour [or, a very short space of time!] so great riches are brought to nought. And every shipmaster, and all the company in ships, and sailors, and as many as trade by sea, stood afar off, and cried when they saw saw the smoke of her burning...." (*Revelation* 18:9,11, 17, 18).

And what is God's message to Christians in these perilous days leading up to the demise of the Babylonian System, and its much-vaunted New World Order? It couldn't be clearer and more precise: "Come out of her, my people, that you be not partakers of her sins, and that you receive not of her plagues" (*Revelation* 18:4).

Satan's government is in disarray. It is toppling under the gigantic weight of its own spiritual depravity. It has violated and trampled underfoot every physical and spiritual law set in motion by a Loving God. God's laws are going to crush it into total submission. All the praise, honor and glory due for Babylon's fall will go to the One who brought it about!

Puny mortals play no part in that defeat. That job belongs to the Creator God, and He alone! Praise God! Yes, "every knee shall bow and every tongue confess to God" that Jesus Christ is Lord, to the glory of God the Father (*Romans* 14:11; *Philippians* 2:10).

Scripture clearly reveals that all power was given to the risen, Lord Jesus Christ following His resurrection from the dead (*Matthew* 28: 21). As the triumphant Christ now has *all* power, obviously Satan only has whatever power has been granted him. Notice another vital scripture. Christ overcomes Satan and his cohorts "because he **is** the King of kings, and the Lord of lords" (*Revelation* 17:14). It does *not* say that Christ defeats Satan and *becomes* King of kings and Lord of lords. *He is already Lord of all*!

SPIRITUAL REVOLUTION

As we enter the third millennium, what needs to happen to bring the United States back to sanity, prosperity and peace?

Another American Revolution — a SPIRITUAL REVOLUTION — is desperately needed in the hearts and minds of the American people.

Such a spiritual awakening — triggered by the dynamic preaching of George Whitefield — was largely responsible for saving early America from the clutches of the Illuminati. His basic teaching was centered on the Sovereignty of God and the Lordship of Jesus Christ. You may read about the "wonderful" and "extraordinary influence" Whitefield's preaching had on the American public in Benjamin Franklin's book, *Nation Under God.*

Is a similar miracle possible at this time? Yes, it is! BUT, first, we must understand one vital fact. American society is in near total rebellion against its Creator. We thumb our collective noses at the laws of God. We embrace the humanistic philosophy espoused by our enemies. Our national lawlessness grows daily. Our rebellion knows no bounds.

There is no indication of repentance on a national scale. In fact, as a nation, we are becoming increasingly hardened in our rebellion against our Creator and His Truth!

As the late General Douglas MacArthur once stated, "History fails to record a single precedent in which nations subject to moral decay have not passed into economic and political decline. There has either been a spiritual awakening to overcome the moral lapse, or a progressive deterioration leading to ultimate national disaster."

NATIONAL JUDGMENT

If the United States, as a nation, was not judged for its wilful rebellion and its violation of His laws, God would not be God! That judgment (spiritually, financially, socially, politically etc.) is as certain as the rising of tomorrow's sun. It's not a matter of if that judgment comes, it's only a matter of when! God is not mocked. What we have sown we will also reap!

At the same time as judgment day is closing in on the United States, a spiritual awakening is also taking place. Wonderful and extraordinary changes are taking place in the hearts and minds of multiple thousands of individuals nationwide. Individual lives are being revolutionized. Many whose lives were shattered and in turmoil are regaining their emotional and spiritual sanity. They are recapturing true values!

For more than one hundred years the American body politic has been infected with the deadly virus of humanism. In recent decades that virus has run rampant, destroying untold millions of "cells" in that body. The result? A chronically sick society. In those who are part of the spiritual awakening, the process is slowly being reversed. Many individual "cells" in the American body are now being healed spiritually and restored to vibrant health. Yes, a spiritual renewal movement is under way nationwide!

Just as their counterparts on the other side are hardening their hearts in their rebellion against their Creator, so these newly born again Christians are becoming increasingly bold in their proclamation of the Sovereignty of God and the Lordship of Jesus Christ. America is being warned of pending judgment.

What America needs in the new millennium is millions more "salty" Christians (*Matthew* 5:13) who both see and "tell it like it is" — without fear or favor. What America needs is millions of these dedicated *witnesses* who are willing to stand up and be counted — and tell the truth, letting the chips fall where they may!

A true witness is just that — a witness. He is not the jury or the judge. His sole job is to bear witness, telling others the facts as he sees them. It is up to others to render a judgment on the evidence he presents!

ALL ALONE IN THE STRUGGLE?

To the honest, dedicated individual who is earnestly striving to serve and obey the true God, it may well seem at times as if they are all alone in their struggle. Like Elijah of old, they may be tempted to say, "I, even I alone, am left; and they seek my life to take it away" (*I Kings* 19:10). But they may be assured that such is not the case. What is God's answer ? "I have reserved seven thousand men who have not bowed the knee to Baal [Satan]."

"Even so then at this present time also there is a *remnant* according to the election of grace" *(Romans* 11:5).

Appearances are deceptive. The victory is God's, not man's!

In the final analysis, it all boils down to one basic question: Which God are you, personally and individually, going to worship and serve? Is it going to be the "god of this world," and all that he stands for? Or is it going to be the one true, living God of the Bible, the God of Jesus Christ and the Apostles?

"How long halt you between two opinions? if the Lord be God, follow him; but if Baal [or Satan, be your god], then follow him" (*I Kings* 18:21).

APPENDIX I

WANTED A MAN — A MAN WHO WILL STAND

By Senator Frank Carlson, U.S. Senator from Kansas (1951-1957)

The subject of the text I am using is, "Wanted A Man — A Man Who Will Stand." We have had men in both ancient and modern history who have had the courage to take a stand and stand firm.

In *Ezekiel* 22:30, the prophet says: "And I sought a man among them who would build up a wall, and stand in the breach before me for the land, that I should not destroy it."

God is searching for men who are unique, thoroughly saved, and filled to running over with His spirit. God and the world need men who will stand in the gap.

Modern Americans have accepted and are tolerating conditions never before permitted by any generation of our ancestors.

Never have so many hated on such flimsy cause. Never have so many denounced so many with so little knowledge. Never has the dollar been as important as it is today. Never has wild pleasure or physical abandonment been considered fitting human behavior as it is today.

Never have public officials been so brazen and open in seeking the vote of the people through promises of things that are morally and spiritually wrong. Never have ministers of the gospel turned their pulpits and their pastoral duties towards direction of the social order as abounds in our time.

RELIGIOUS LEADERS

In the 22nd chapter of Ezekiel, the prophet speaks of Israel's religious leaders in these words: "Her priests have done violence to my law and have profaned my holy things; they have made no distinction between the holy and the common, neither have they taught the difference between the unclean and the clean, and they disregard my Sabbaths, so that I am profaned among them."

Israel's religious leaders of that earlier time would be appalled to observe what is transpiring in the churches today. Even the daily press — notoriously indifferent to religious news — reports a few lines on the inner and back pages that tell us clearly how growing numbers of Americans treat holy things with irreverence and sacred things with contempt.

Not only have vast numbers of Americans lost all sense of the sacred, the moral, and the ethical, but the spiritual leaders from both the laity and the priesthood are often found in the forefront of this irreligious pursuit of comfort rather than conviction — of accommodation rather than truth — of the pleasant life rather than the meaningful life.

If God is to have men who will stand in the gap and hold back the flood of destructive, emotional and spiritual forces, we must first understand the nature of the problem and why things are the way they are.

THREE DESTRUCTIVE FORCES

There are major forces that have brought about the chaos, frustration and anti-Christian era in which we live. They touch both the philosophical and religious bases, were first voiced by few in number whose intensity deceived millions, and have been permitted to flourish by both the unwary and the fearful.

First, we live in the age of uncertainty because we have either accepted or endured the doctrine of universal conformity.

The forces that reduce the power of an influence of God and Christ in the lives of our people are seeking to become levelers of men. It is their conviction that only by lowering mankind to a dependence upon the ideas, ideals, and material judgments of superior people can we live together in harmony and peace.

Evidence is rampant that this kind of meddling and interference with God's natural law brings fearful conflict, death, destruction, riots, crime, and disregard for decency and principle among our people.

DOCTRINE OF UNIVERSAL CHANGE

Today there is widespread devotion to the idea that nothing, absolutely nothing, can be allowed to remain the same. All things must change, and there is practically no consideration given as to whether the change is good or bad — right or wrong — easy or difficult — necessary or unnecessary.

The doctrine of change stands on just the precise idea that change is inevitable. That is absolutely true. Changes of various types and sorts take place every day everywhere. But irresponsible, erratic, violent change only for the sake of making things different is as illogical and as unreasonable as it is unspiritual.

No intelligent person argues against the necessity of using question marks after many of our inherited ideas and practices of the past. But when the question mark is turned into a totem pole or a marble altar on which the people are meant to lay their sacrificial offerings, such people have escaped the general limits of common sense and sound judgment, and have launched off into material idolatry and are rushing toward a degree of spiritual insanity.

If human reason has so completely lost its respectability, and no one is allowed to go from a major or minor premise to some sort of orderly conclusion, then the welfare of our people is entrusted to the care of strange and weird people.

Great changes had to take place during these recent years, and even greater changes will take place in the future. But no safe and proper change seen in recent time — and certainly none of the irrational changes that outnumber the sane ones — can justify the wholesale abandonment of the sure and safe principles of God and this country which have brought us safely this far. *In the face of great changes, we Christians have to remember that we have a firm point of view and that we operate from certain unchanging foundations.*

We believe in a God who does not change — in a human nature which does not change except for its accommodation with and acceptance of God — in standards of right and wrong that do not change — in death and judgment that are inescapable — and we believe in a truth that is absolute, not relative, and which is forever settled in heaven and can never pass away.

The Christian today — even in the midst of the erratic and erotic commitments of irreligious leaders — does not follow the failing steps of the priests of Israel. Christians make a clear distinction between the holy and the common. They teach the difference between the clean and the unclean. They observe and keep the Sabbath, and they do not profane either the name, the spirit, nor the power of God.

DOCTRINE OF UNIVERSAL CRITICISM

The third cause of uncertainties in this time is the doctrine of universal criticism. Today, man is taught not to accept anything until he has first put it under strong and critical examination. Trust nobody — believe nobody — have faith in nothing — and accept no truth until it has been proved to you with mathematical exactness and material demonstration. That is the agony of the hour when the doctrine of criticism has taken over our people.

You cannot pick up a paper, a magazine, or a book that is not in and of itself critical of something or somebody, even including among its victims Almighty God Himself! In truth, the criticisms of God rank well above all other criticisms. Most people — in more ways and on more occasions — cast doubt, hurl darts, and throw charges against God such as this country has never seen in all of its history.

To accept the doctrine of universal criticism leaves us with almost nothing that is sacred — almost nothing that is absolute — and nothing that is eternal. So real has our acceptance of the doctrine of criticism become that even the word "indoctrination" has been turned into an evil word that must be shunned like "discipline," "disciple," or "patriotism."

These three doctrines — universal conformity, universal change, and universal criticism — have left our nation without moorings and anchors. We are being tossed about in a sea of doubt and uncertainty that is about to sink the ship of God before our very eyes.

The world today is looking for:

Men who are not for sale;
Men who are honest, sound from center to circumference, true to the heart's core;
Men with consciences as steady as the needle to the pole;
Men who will stand for the right if the heavens totter and the earth reels;
Men who tell the truth and look the world right in the eye;
Men who will neither brag nor run;
Men who neither flag nor flinch;
Men who have courage without shouting it;
Men in whom the courage of everlasting life runs deep, still and strong;
Men who know their message and tell it;
Men who know their place and fill it;
Men who know their business and attend to it;
Men who will not lie, shirk or dodge;
Men who are not too lazy to work, or too proud to be poor;
Men who are not ashamed to say "No" with emphasis, and who are not ashamed to say, "I can't afford it."

God is looking for men. He wants those who can unite together around a common faith — who can join hands in a common task — and who can come to the kingdom for such a time as this.

GOD GIVE US MEN

(*U.S. News and World Report*, June 8, 1968. Senator Frank Carlson was Governor of Kansas, 1947-50, and Senator from Kansas, 1950-1957).

[Such Christian "soldiers" as those described by Senator Carlson are certainly few and far between. It seems that at present close to half of the would-be Christian soldiers are on R and R, while most of the rest have gone AWOL].

Appendix II

Red Symphony (X-Ray of Revolution)

INTRODUCTION

When the book you are now reading was first written, the author was unaware of the existence of the immensely important historical document you are about to read.

In chapters 5 and 6, we presented the fully documented story of the rise and development of the top-secret Illuminati organization, the aim of which is to enslave all mankind in a worldwide concentration camp euphemistically described as the New World Order.

We also presented evidence that the real power behind this diabolical plot is an elite, nefarious coterie — International Bankers and "intellectuals" — which fancies itself as being the only group capable of ruling mankind. One of their agents, James Warburg, son of Paul M. Warburg, organizer and one of the original board members of the Federal Reserve System, had the audacity and arrogance to proclaim before the U.S. Senate on February 17, 1950 : "We shall have world government whether or not we like it. *The only question is whether world government will be achieved by conquest or consent."*

Although there is positive *proof* that the international money monarchy financed the Bolshevik Revolution in Russia in 1917, and has kept Communism afloat ever since with huge infusions of capital, this writer was unaware of any conclusive proof — *from within Russia* — that the Communist leaders were dancing to the tune called by the International Bankers and that communism is, in fact, a latter-day manifestation of Adam Weishaupt's Illuminati.

These facts come to the fore — direct from Russia — in a remarkable document known as *Red Symphony*. It was first published as chapter XL of a book, *Sinfonia en Rojo Mayor,* by the well-known Spanish publisher, Señor Don Mauricio Carlavilla.

C. G. RAKOVSKY

In this work, we see the Communist-International Banker connection brilliantly described by one of the major exponents of the subversive takeover of the world, Christian G. Rakovsky. Rakovsky, one of the founders of Soviet Bolshevism, was also a victim of the show trials under Stalin just before World War II.

Red Symphony is of tremendous historical significance and nobody who wishes to be well-informed should fail to read it. In the Spanish book, Señor Carlavilla explains the origin of the document: "This [book] is the result of a painstaking translation of several copy books found on the body of Dr. Landowsky in a hut on the Petrograd front by a Spanish volunteer.

"He brought them to us. In view of the condition of the manuscripts, their restoration was a long and tiring job, lasting several years. For a long time we were not sure if they could be published. So *extraordinary and unbelievable were his final conclusions that we would never have dared to publish these memoirs if the persons and events mentioned had not accorded fully with the facts.*

"Before these reminiscences saw the light of day we prepared ourselves for proofs and polemics. We answer fully and personally for the veracity of the basic facts.

"Let us see if anyone will be able to disprove them..."

DR. LANDOWSKY

Dr. Landowsky was a Russianized Pole who lived in Russia. His father, a Colonel of the Russian Imperial Army, was shot by the Bolsheviks during the 1917 revolution. The life story of Dr. Landowsky is astonishing. He finished the Faculty of Medicine in Russia before the revolution, and then studied for two years at the Sorbonne in Paris. He spoke fluent French. He was interested in the effects of drugs on the human organism, to help surgeons in operations. Being a talented doctor, Landowsky carried out experiments in this field; he achieved considerable results.

However, after the revolution all roads were closed to him. He lived with his family in poverty, eking out a meager living by chance jobs. Not being able to publish learned papers in his own name, Landowsky permitted a more fortunate colleague to publish them in his own name.

The all-seeing NKVD (secret police) became interested in these works and easily discovered the real author. His specialty was very valuable to them. One day in 1936, there was a knock at the doctor's door. Landowsky was invited to follow, and he was never again allowed to rejoin his family.

Dr. Landowsky was placed in the building of the chemical laboratory of the NKVD near Moscow. He lived there, and was forced to carry out various jobs given him by his masters. He was a witness at questionings, tortures and the most terrible crimes. *He had the courage to keep notes of what he had seen and heard, and he kept whenever possible such documents and letters as passed through his hands, hiding all this in the hollow legs of his table in the chemical laboratory.* So he lived until the Second World War. How he came to Petrograd, and how he was killed is not known.

The document that follows is an exact recorded report of the questioning of the former Ambassador in France, C. G. Rakovsky, during the period of the trials of the Trotzkyists, in the USSR in 1938, when he was tried together with Bukharin, Rykoff, Yagoda, Karakhan and others.

In an effort to save his own life, the accused Rakovsky made it clear that he could supply information about matters of very great interest. Stalin gave orders to his foreign agent to carry out the questioning.

It is known that Rakovsky was sentenced to be shot, like the others, but was reprieved and given 20 years in prison.

GABRIEL — STALIN'S FOREIGN AGENT

The background of the above mentioned agent is of great interest. This was a certain Rene Duval (also known as Gavriil Gavriilovitch Kus'min or "Gabriel"). Gabriel was the son of a millionaire, very good looking and talented. He studied in France. His widowed mother adored him. But the young man was carried away with Communist propaganda and fell into the hands of their agency. They suggested that he should study in Moscow, and he gladly accepted the proposal. He passed through the severe school of the NKVD, and became a foreign agent. When he wanted to change his mind it was too late: they do not let people out of their grip. By the exercise of willpower he reached the "heights of evil," as he called it, and enjoyed the full confidence of Stalin himself.

The questioning took place in French by this agent. Dr. Landowsky was present in order to put drug pills unnoticed into the glass of Rakovsky, to induce energy and a good mood. Behind the wall the conversation was registered on apparatus, and the technician who operated it did not understand French. Then Dr. Landowsky had to translate into Russian, with two copies, for Stalin and Gabriel. Secretly, he dared to make a third carbon copy, which he hid away.

The author acknowledges with thanks the wholehearted cooperation given by Mr. George Knupffer of *The Plain Speaker Publishing Company*, 43 Bath Road, London, England, in the production of this chapter.

Mr. Knupffer translated *Red Symphony* from a Russian edition as well as from the Spanish.

Born in Russia early in the century, Mr. Knupffer was a witness of the Russian Civil War against the Bolsheviks. He speaks fluent Russian, English, German and French.

The translator's own book *The Struggle For World Power* also deals with the whole problem of super power and global enslavement through the masters of both usury-Capitalism and terroristic Communism which are both the tools of the same forces and serving the same purpose.

* * *

XL
X-RAY OF REVOLUTION

I returned to the laboratory. My nervous system bothered me and I prescribed myself complete rest. I am in bed almost the whole day. Here I am quite alone for already four days. Gabriel enquired about me every day. He has to reckon with my condition. At the mere thought that they could again send me to the Lubianka (Moscow HQ of the secret police) to be present at a new scene of terror I become excited and tremble. I am ashamed of belonging to the human race. How low have people fallen! How low have I fallen!

* * *

These lines are all I was able to write after five days following my return from the Lubianka, when trying to describe on paper the horror, and thereby interrupting the chronological order of my notes. I could not write. Only after several months, when Summer began, I was able calmly and simply to set out all that I had seen, disgusting, vicious, evil. . .

During these past months I asked myself a thousand times the same question: "Who were the people who were anonymously present at the torture?" I strained all my intuitive and deductive capabilities. Was it Ezhov? It is possible, but I see no reason why he should have concealed himself. Officially he is responsible and the fear which made him hide does not lead to a logical explanation. Even more: if I have any reason for describing myself as a psychologist, then this fanatic, the chief of the NKVD, with signs of abnormality, would be certain to enjoy a criminal display. Such things as the expression of haughtiness in front of a humbled enemy, who had been converted into a wreck psychologically and physically, should have given him an unhealthy pleasure. I analyzed still further. The absence of prior preparation was obvious; evidently the decision to call this satanic session had been taken in a hurry. The circumstance that I had been appointed to be present was the result of a sudden agreement. If Ezhov had been able to chose the time freely, then timely preparations would have been made. And then I would not have been called; that general of the NKVD who was hardly able to come in time, for the purpose of being present at the torture, would have known about this beforehand. If this was not Ezhov, then who had decided on the time? Which other chief was able to arrange it all? However poor are my informations about the Soviet hierarchy, but above Ezhov in affairs along the line of the NKVD there is only one man—Stalin. Therefore it was he?. . .

Asking myself these questions, which arose from my deductions, I remembered yet other facts in support of my opinion. I remembered that when I looked from the window over the square a few minutes before we went down to the "spectacle" I saw how there drove across it four large identical cars; all we Soviet people know that Stalin travels in a caravan of identical machines, so that nobody would know in which he is sitting, to make attack more difficult. Was he there?. . .

But here I came across another mystery: according to the details which Gabriel gave me, the hidden observers were to sit behind our back. But there I could only see a long mirror, through which nothing could be seen. Perhaps it was transparent? I was puzzled.

* * *

Only seven days passed when one morning Gabriel appeared in the house. I found that he had an energetic and enthusiastic appearance and was in an optimistic mood. Yet these flashes of happiness which lit up his face at first, did not return later. It seemed as if he wanted to chase away the shadows which passed over his face by increased activity and mental exertion.

After lunch he told me:

"We have a guest here."

"Who is it" I asked.

"Rakovsky, the former Ambassador in Paris."

"I do not know him."

"He is one of those whom I pointed out to you on that night; the former Ambassador in London and Paris. . . Of course a big friend of your acquaintance Navachin. . . Yes, this man is at my disposal. He is here with us; he is being well treated and looked after. You shall see him."

"I, why? You know well that I am not curious about matters of this kind. . . I would ask you to spare me this sight; I am still not quite well after what you had forced me to see. I cannot guarantee my nervous system and heart."

"Oh, do not worry. Now we are not concerned with force. This man has already been broken. No blood, no force. It is only necessary to give him moderate doses of drugs. Here I have brought you details: they are from Levin*, who still serves us with his knowledge. Apparently there is a certain drug somewhere in the laboratory, which can work wonders."

"You believe all this?"

"I am speaking in symbolic form. Rakovsky is inclined to confess to everything he knows about the matter. We have already had a preliminary talk with him, and the results are not bad."

"In that case why is there a need for a miraculous drug?"

"You will see, doctor, you will see. This is a small safety measure, dictated by the professional experience of Levin. It will help to achieve that our man being questioned would feel optimistic and would not lose hope and faith. He can already see a chance of saving his life as a long shot. This is the first effect which we must attain. Then we must make sure that he would all the time remain in a state of the experience of the decisive happy moment, but without losing his mental capacities; more exactly, it will be necessary to stimulate and sharpen them. He must have induced in him a quite special feeling. How can one express it? More exactly a condition of enlightened stimulation."

"Something like hypnosis?"

"Yes, but without sleepiness."

"And I must invent a drug for all this? I think you exaggerate my scientific talents. I cannot achieve it."

* Former NKVD doctor, was a co-defendant with Rakovsky at the trial.

"Yes, but it is unnecessary to invent anything, doctor. As for Levin, he asserts that the problem has already been solved."

"He always left me with the impression of being something of a charlatan. . ."

"Probably yes, but I think that the drug he has mentioned, even if it is not as effective as he claims, will still help us to achieve the necessary; after all, we need not expect a miracle. Alcohol, against our will, makes us speak nonsense. Why cannot another substance encourage us to say the reasonable truth? Apart from that, Levin had told me of previous cases, which seem to be genuine."

"Why do you not want to force him to take part in this affair once more? Or will he refuse to obey?"

"Oh no, he would like to. It is enough to want to save or to extend your life with the help of this or another service, for not refusing. But it is I myself who does not want to use his services. He must not hear anything of that which Rakovsky will tell me. Not he, not anyone. . ."

"Therefore I. . ."

"You—that is another matter, doctor. You are a deeply decent person. But I am not Diogenes, to rush to look for another over the snowy distances of the USSR."

"Thank you, but I think that my honesty. . ."

"Yes, doctor, yes; you say that we take advantage of your honesty for various depravities. Yes, doctor, that is so. . . ; but it is only so from your absurd point of view. And who is attracted to-day by absurdities? For example such an absurdity as your honesty? You always manage to lead one away towards conversation about most attractive things. But what, in fact, will take place? You must only help me to give the correct doses of Levin's drug. It would appear that in the dosage there is an invisible line which divides sleep from a state of activity, a clear condition from a befogged one, good sense from nonsense . . . ; there can come an artificial excessive enthusiasm."

"If that is all. . ."

"And yet something else. Now we shall speak seriously. Study the instructions of Levin, weigh them, adapt them reasonably to the condition and strength of the prisoner. You have time for study until nightfall; you can examine Rakovsky as often as you wish. And that is all for the moment. You would not believe how terribly I want to sleep. I shall sleep a few hours. If by evening nothing extraordinary happens then I have given instructions that I am not to be called. I would advise you to have a good rest after dinner, because after that it will not be possible to sleep for a long time."

We entered the vestibule. Having taken his leave from me he quickly ran up the stairs, but in the middle he halted.

"Ah, doctor—he exclaimed—I had forgotten. Many thanks from Comrade Ezhov. Expect a present, perhaps even a decoration."

He waved me goodbye and rapidly disappeared on the staircase landing of the top floor.

* * *

The notes of Levin were short, but clear and exact. I had no difficulty in finding the medicine. It was in doses of a milligram in tiny tablets. I made a test and, in accordance with his explanation, they dissolved very easily in water and better still in alcohol. The formula was not indicated there, and I decided later to make a detailed analysis, when I shall have the time.

Undoubtedly it was some substance of the specialist Lümenstadt, that scientist of whom Levin had spoken to me during the first meeting. I did not think I would discover during analysis something unexpected or new. Probably again some base with a considerable amount of opium of a more active kind than tebain. I was well acquainted with 19 main types and some more besides. In those practical conditions in which my experiments were conducted I was satisfied with those facts which my investigations had yielded.

Although my work had an altogether different direction, yet I was quite at home in the realm of hallucinatory substances. I remembered that Levin had told me of the distillation of rare types of Indian Hemp. I was bound to be dealing with opium or hashish, in order to penetrate the secret of this much praised drug. I would have been glad to have had the opportunity of coming across one or more new bases which gave rise to his "miraculous" qualities. In principle I was prepared to assume such a possibility. After all the work of investigation in conditions of unlimited time and means, while not having to reckon with economic limitations, which was possible in conditions of the NKVD, provided unlimited scientific possibilities. I flattered myself with the illusion of being able to find, as the result of these investigations, a new weapon in my scientific fight against pain.

I could not give much time to the diversion of such pleasant illusions. I concentrated my thoughts in order to think how and in what proportion I shall have to give Rakovsky this drug. According to the instructions of Levin, one tablet would have to produce the desired result. He warned that if the patient had any heart weakness there could follow sleepiness and even complete lethargy, with a consequent dimming of the mind. While bearing all this in mind, I had first of all to examine Rakovsky. I did not expect to find the internal condition of his heart to be normal. If there were no damage, then surely there would be a lowering of tone as the result of the nervous experiences, as his system could not have remained unchanged after a long and terrifying torture.

I put off the examination until after lunch. I wanted to consider everything, both for the case that Gabriel would want to give the drug with the knowledge of Rakovsky, as also without his knowledge. In both cases I would have to busy myself with him, insofar as I myself would have to give him the drug, of which I had been told concretely. There was no need for the participation of a professional, as the drug was given by mouth.

After lunch I went to visit Rakovsky. He was kept locked up in one room of the ground floor and was guarded by one man, who did not take his eyes off him. Of furniture there was only one small table, a narrow bed without ends and another small, rough table. When I entered Rakovsky was sitting. He immediately got up. He looked at me closely and I read in his face doubt and, it seemed, also fright. I think he must have recognized me, having seen me when he sat that memorable night at the side of the generals.

I ordered the guard to leave and told him to bring me a chair.

I sat down and asked the prisoner to sit. He was about 50 years old. He was a man of medium height, bald in front, with a large, fleshy nose. In youth his face was probably pleasant. His facial outlines were not typically semitic, but his origin was nevertheless clear. Once upon a time he was probably quite fat, but not now, and his skin hung everywhere, while his face and neck were like a burst balloon, with the air let out. The usual dinner at the Lubianka was apparently too strict a diet for the former Ambassador in Paris. At that moment I made no further observations.

"You smoke?" I asked, opening the cigarette case, with the intention of establishing somewhat more intimate relations with him.

"I gave up smoking in order to preserve my health" he replied with a very pleasant tone of voice, "but I thank you; I think I have now recovered from my stomach troubles."

He smoked quietly, with restraint and not without some elegance.

"I am a doctor" I introduced myself.

"Yes I know that; I saw how you acted 'there' " he said with trembling voice.

"I came to enquire about the state of your health. How are you? Do you suffer from any illness?"

"No, nothing."

"Are you sure? What about your heart?"

"Thanks to the results of enforced dieting I do not observe in myself any abnormal symptoms."

"There are some which cannot be noticed by the patient himself, but only by a doctor."

"I am a doctor" he interrupted me.

"A doctor?" I repeated in surprise.

"Yes, didn't you know?"

"Nobody had told me of it. I congratulate you. I shall be very glad to be of use to a colleague and, possibly, a fellow student. Where did you study? In Moscow or Petrograd?"

"Oh no! At that time I was not a Russian subject. I studied in Nancy and Montpellier; in the latter I received my doctorate."

"This means that we may have studied at the same time; I did several courses in Paris. Were you French?"

"I intended to become French. I was born a Bulgarian, but without asking my permission I was converted into a Rumanian. My province was Dobrudga, where I was born, and after the peace treaty it went to Rumania."

"Permit me to listen to your chest"—and I put the stethoscope in my ears.

He took off his torn jacket and stood up. I listened. The examination shewed nothing abnormal; as I had assumed, weakness, but without defects.

"I suppose one must give food for the heart."

"Only the heart, comrade?" he asked ironically.

"I think so" I said, pretending not to have noticed the irony, "I think your diet, too, should be strengthened."

"Permit me to listen to myself."

"With pleasure"—and I gave him the stethoscope.

He quickly listened to himself.

"I had expected that my condition would be much worse. Many thanks. May I put my jacket on?"

"Of course. Let us agree, then, that it is necessary to take a few drops of digitalis, don't you think?"

"You consider that absolutely essential? I think that my old heart will survive the few days or months which remain to me quite well."

"I think otherwise; I think that you will live much longer."

"Do not upset me, colleague. . . To live more! To live still longer! . . . There must be instructions about the end; the court case cannot last longer. . . And then, then rest."

And when he said this, having in mind the final rest, it seemed that his face had the expression of happiness almost. I shuddered. This wish to die, to die soon which I read in his eyes, made me faint. I wanted to cheer him up from a feeling of compassion.

"You have not understood me, comrade. I wanted to say that in your case it may be decided to continue your life, but life without suffering. For what have you been brought here? Does one not treat you well now?"

"The latter, yes, of course, Concerning the rest I have heard hints, but. . ."

I gave him another cigarette and then added:

"Have hope. For my part and to the extent which my chief will allow, I shall do everything that can depend on me, to make sure that you come to no harm. I shall begin immediately by feeding you, but not excessively, bearing in mind the state of your stomach. We shall begin with a milk diet and some more substantial additions. I shall give instructions at once. You may smoke . . . take some . . ." and I left him everything that remained in the packet.

I called the guard and ordered him to light the prisoner's cigarette whenever he wants to smoke. Then I left and before having a couple of hours rest I gave instructions that Rakovsky was to have half a litre of milk with sugar.

* * *

We prepared for the meeting with Rakovsky at midnight. Its "friendly" character was stressed in all the details. The room was well warmed, there was a fire in the fire-place, soft lighting, a small and well-chosen supper, good wines; all had been scientifically improvised. "As for a lovers meeting," observed Gabriel. I was to assist. My chief responsibility was to give the prisoner the drug in such a manner that he would not notice it. For this purpose the drinks had been placed as if by chance near me, and I shall have to pour out the wine. Also I would have to observe the weakening of the drug's effect, so as to give a new dose at the right moment. This was my most important job. Gabriel wants, if the experiment succeeds, to get already at the first meeting real progress towards the essence of the matter. He is hopeful of success. He has had a good rest and is in good condition. I am interested to know how he will struggle with Rakovsky who, it seems to me, is an opponent worthy of him.

Three large arm-chairs were placed before the fire. The one nearest the door is for me, Rakovsky will sit in the middle, and in the third will be Gabriel, who had shewn his optimistic mood even in his clothes, as he was wearing a white Russian shirt.

It had already struck midnight when they brought the prisoner to us. He had been given decent clothes and had been well shaved. I looked at him professionally and found him to be livelier.

He asks to be excused for not being able to drink more than one glass, mentioning the weakness of his stomach. I did not put the drug into this glass and regretted it.

The conversation began with banalities . . . Gabriel knows that Rakovsky speaks much better French than Russian and begins in that language. There are hints about the past. It is clear that Rakovsky is an expert conversationalist. His speech is exact, elegant and even decorative. He is apparently very erudite; at times he quotes easily and always accurately. Sometimes he hints at his many escapes, at exile, about Lenin, Plekhanov, Luxemburg, and he even said that when he was a boy he had shaken the hand of the old Engels.

We drink whisky. After Gabriel had given him the opportunity of speaking for about half an hour, I asked as if by chance: "Should I add more soda water?" "Yes, add enough" he replied absentmindedly. I manipulated the drink and dropped a tablet into it, which I had been holding from the very beginning. First I gave Gabriel some whisky, letting him know by a sign that the job had been done. I gave Rakovsky his glass and then began to drink mine. He sipped it with pleasure. "I am a small cad" I told myself. But this was a passing thought and it dissolved in the pleasant fire in the fire-place.

Before Gabriel came to the main theme, the talk had been long and interesting.

I had been fortunate in obtaining a document which reproduces better than a shorthand note all that had been discussed between Gabriel and Rakovsky. Here it is:

INFORMATION

THE QUESTIONING OF THE ACCUSED CHRISTIAN GEORGIEVITCH RAKOVSKY BY GAVRIIL GAVRIILOVITCH KUS'MIN ON THE 26th JANUARY, 1938.

Gavriil G. Kus'min. In accordance with our agreement at the Lubianka, I had appealed for a last chance for you; your presence in this house indicates that I had succeeded in this. Let us see if you will not deceive us.

Christian G. Rakovsky. I do not wish and shall not do that.

G.—But first of all: a well-meant warning. Now we are concerned with the real truth. Not the "official" truth, that which is to figure at the trial in the light of the confessions of the accused. . . This is something which, as you know, is fully subject to practical considerations, or "considerations of State" as they would say in the West. The demands of international politics will force us to hide the whole truth, the "real truth" . . . Whatever may be the course of the trial, but governments and peoples will only be told that which they should know. But he who must know everything, Stalin, must also know all this. Therefore, whatever may be your words here they cannot make your position worse. You must know that they will not worsen your crime but, on the contrary, they can give the desired results in your favour. You will be able to save your life, which at this moment is already lost. So now I have told you this, but now let us see: you will all admit that you are Hitler's spies and receive wages from the Gestapo and OKW*.

Is that not so?

R.—Yes.

G.—And you are Hitler's spies?

R.—Yes.

G.—No, Rakovsky, no. Tell the real truth, but not the court proceedings one.

R.—We are not spies of Hitler, we hate Hitler as you can hate him, as Stalin can hate him; perhaps even more so, but this is a very complex question. . .

G.—I shall help you. . . By chance I also know one or two things. You, the Trotzkyists, had contacts with the German Staff. Is that not so?

R.—Yes.

G.—From which period?

R.—I do not know the exact date, but soon after the fall of Trotzky. Of course before Hitler's coming to power.

G.—Therefore let us be exact: you were neither personal spies of Hitler, nor of his regime.

R.—Exactly. We were such already earlier.

G.—And for what purpose? With the aim of giving Germany victory and some Russian territories?

R.—No, in no case.

G.—Therefore as ordinary spies, for money?

R.—For money? Nobody received a single Mark from Germany. Hitler has not enough money to buy, for example, the Commissar for Foreign Affairs of the USSR, who has at his disposal freely a budget which is greater than the total wealth of Morgan and Vanderbilt, and who does not have to account for his use of the money.

G.—Well, then for what reason?

R.—May I speak quite freely?

G.—Yes, I ask you to do so; for that reason you have been invited.

R.—Did not Lenin have higher aims when he received help from Germany in order to enter Russia? And is it necessary to accept as true those libellous inventions which had been circulated to accuse him? Was he not also called a spy of the Kaiser? His relations with the Emperor and the German intervention in the affair of the sending to Russia of the Bolshevik destroyers—are quite clear.

* OKW—Oberkommando der Wehrmacht, Supreme Command of the German Army—Transl.

G.—Whether it is true or not does not have any bearing on the present question.

R.—No, permit me to finish. Is it not a fact that the activity of Lenin was in the beginning advantageous to the German troops? Permit me. . . There was the separate peace of Brest-Litovsk, at which huge territories of the USSR were ceded to Germany. Who had declared defeatism as a weapon of the Bolsheviks in 1913? Lenin. I know by heart his words from his letter to Gorky: "War between Austria and Russia would be a most useful thing for the revolution, but it is hardly possible that Francis-Joseph and Nicholas would present us with this opportunity." As you see, we, the so-called Trotzkyists, the inventors of the defeat in 1905, continue at the present stage the same line, the line of Lenin.

G.—With a small difference, Rakovsky; at present there is Socialism in the USSR, not the Tsar.

R.—You believe that?

G.—What?

R.—In the existence of Socialism in the USSR?

G.—Is the Soviet Union not Socialist?

R.—For me only in name. It is just here that we find the true reason for the opposition. Agree with me, and by the force of pure logic you must agree, that theoretically, rationally, we have the same right to say—no, as Stalin can say—yes. And if for the triumph of Communism defeatism can be justified, then he who considers that Communism has been destroyed by the bonapartism of Stalin and that he betrayed it, has the same right as Lenin to become a defeatist.

G.—I think, Rakovsky, that you are theorizing thanks to your manner of making wide use of dialectics. It is clear that if many people were present here, I would prove this; all right, I accept your argument as the only one possible in your position, but nevertheless I think that I could prove to you that this is nothing other than a sophism. But let us postpone this for another occasion; some day it will come. And I hope that you will give me the chance to reply. But at the present moment I shall only say this: if your defeatism and the defeat of the USSR has as its object the restoration of Socialism in the USSR, real Socialism, according to you— Trotzkyism, then, insofar as we have destroyed their leaders and cadres, defeatism and the defeat of the USSR has neither an objective nor any sense. As a result of defeat now there would come the enthronement of some Führer or fascist Tsar. Is that not so?

R.—It is true. Without flattery on my part—your deduction is splendid.

G.—Well, if, as I assume, you assert this sincerely, then we have achieved a great deal: I am a Stalinist and you a Trotzkyist; we have achieved the impossible. We have reached the point at which our views coincide. The coincidence lies in that at the present moment the USSR must not be destroyed.

R.—I must confess that I had not expected to face such a clever person. In fact at the present stage and for some years we cannot think of the defeat of the USSR and to provoke it, as it is known that we are at present in such a position, that we can not seize power. We, the Communists, would derive no profit from it. This is exact and coincides with your view. We can not be interested now in the collapse of the Stalinist State; I say this and at the same time I assert that this State, apart from all that has been said, is anti-Communistic. You see that I am sincere.

G.—I see that. This is the only way in which we can come to terms. I would ask you, before you continue, to explain to me that which seems to me a contradiction: if the Soviet State is anti-Communistic to you, then why should you not wish its destruction at the given moment? Someone else might be less anti-Communistic and then there would be fewer obstacles to the restoration of your pure Communism.

R.—No, no, this deduction is too simple. Although the Stalinist bonapartism also opposes Communism as the napoleonic one opposed the revolution, but the circumstance is clear that, nevertheless, the USSR continues to preserve its Communistic form and dogma; this is formal and not real Communism. And thus, like the disappearance of Trotzky gave Stalin the possibility automatically to transform real Communism into the formal one, so also the disappearance of Stalin will allow us to transform his formal Communism into a real one. One hour would suffice for us. Have you understood me?

G.—Yes, of course; you have told us the classical truth that nobody destroys that which he wants to inherit. Well, all right; all else is sophistical agility. You rely on the assumption which can be easily disproved: the assumption of Stalin's anti-Communism. Is there private property in the USSR? Is there personal profit? Classes? I shall not continue to base myself on facts—for what?

R.—I have already agreed that there exists formal Communism. All that you enumerate are merely forms.

G.—Yes? For what purpose? From mere obstinacy?

R.—Of course not. This is a necessity. It is impossible to eliminate the materialistic evolution of history. The most that can be done is to hold it up. And at what a price? At the cost of its theoretical acceptance, in order to destroy it in practice. The force which draws humanity towards Communism is so unconquerable that that same force, but distorted, opposed to itself, can only achieve a slowing down of development; more accurately—to slow down the progress of the permanent revolution.

G.—An example?

R.—The most obvious—with Hitler. He needed Socialism for victory over Socialism: it is this his very anti-Socialist Socialism which is National-Socialism. Stalin needs Communism in order to defeat Communism. The parallel is obvious. But, notwithstanding Hitler's anti-Socialism and Stalin's anti-Communism, both, to their regret and against their will, transcendentally create Socialism and Communism. . . ; they and many others. Whether they want it or not, whether they know it or not, but they create formal Socialism and Communism, which we, the Communist-Marxists, must inevitably inherit.

G.—Inheritance? Who inherits? Trotzkyism is completely liquidated.

R.—Although you say so, you do not believe it. However great may be the liquidations, we Communists will survive them. The long arm of

Stalin and his police cannot reach all Communists.

G.—Rakovsky, I ask you, and if necessary command, to refrain from offensive hints. Do not go too far in taking advantage of your "diplomatic immunity."

R.—Do I have credentials? Whose ambassador am I?

G.—Precisely of that unreachable Trotzkyism, if we agree to call him so.

R.—I cannot be a diplomat of Trotzkyism, of which you hint. I have not been given that right to represent it, and I have not taken this role on myself. You have given it to me.

G.—I begin to trust you. I take note in your favour that at my hint about this Trotzkyism you did not deny it. This is already a good beginning.

R.—But how can I deny it? After all, I myself mentioned it.

G.—Insofar as we have recognized the existence of this special Trotzkyism by our mutual arrangement, I want you to give definite facts, which are necessary for the investigation of the given coincidence.

R.—Yes, I shall be able to mention that which you consider necessary to know and I shall do it on my own initiative, but I shall not be able to assert that this is always the thinking also of "Them."

G.—Yes, I shall look on it like that.

R.—We agreed that at the present moment the opposition cannot be interested in defeatism and the fall of Stalin, insofar as we do not have the physical possibility of taking his place. This is what we both agree. At present this is an incontrovertible fact. However, there is in existence a possible aggressor. There he is, that great nihilist Hitler, who is aiming with his terrible weapon of the Wehrmacht at the whole horizon. Whether we want it or not, but he will use it against the USSR? Let us agree that for us this is the decisive unknown factor. Do you consider that the problem has been correctly stated?

G.—It has been well put. But I can say that for me there is no unknown factor. I consider the attack of Hitler on the USSR to be inevitable.

R.—Why?

G.—Very simple; because he who controls it is inclined towards attack. Hitler is only the condottiere of international Capitalism.

R.—I agree that there is a danger, but from that to the assumption on this ground of the inevitability of his attack on the USSR—there is a whole abyss.

G.—The attack on the USSR is determined by the very essence of Fascism. In addition he is impelled towards it by all those Capitalist States which had allowed him to re-arm and to take all the necessary economic and strategical bases. This is quite obvious.

R.—You forget something very important. The re-armament of Hitler and the assistance he received at the present time from the Versailles nations (take good note of this)—were received by him during a special period, when we could still have become the heirs of Stalin in the case of his defeat, when the opposition still existed. . . Do you consider this fact to be a matter of chance or only a coincidence in time?

G.—I do not see any connexion between the permission of the Versailles Powers of German re-armament and the existence of the opposition. . . The trajectory of Hitlerism is in itself clear and logical. The attack on the USSR was part of his programme already a long time ago. The destruction of Communism and expansion in the East—these are dogmas from the book "Mein Kampf," that Talmud of National-Socialism . . . , but that your defeatists wanted to take advantage of this threat to the USSR—that is, of course, in accordance with your train of thought.

R.—Yes, at a first glance this appears to be natural and logical, too logical and natural for the truth.

G.—To prevent this happening, so that Hitler would not attack us, we would have to entrust ourselves to an alliance with France . . . , but that would be a naivete. It would mean that we believe that Capitalism would be willing to make sacrifices for the sake of saving Communism.

R.—If we shall continue the discussion only on the foundation of those conceptions which apply for use at mass meetings, then you are quite right. But if you are sincere in saying this then, forgive me, I am disappointed; I had thought that the politics of the famous Stalinist police stand on a higher level.

G.—The Hitlerist attack on the USSR is, in addition, a dialectical necessity; it is the same as the inevitable struggle of the classes in the international plane. At the side of Hitler, inevitably, there will stand the whole global Capitalism.

R.—And so, believe me, that in the light of your scholastic dialectics, I have formed a very negative opinion about the political culture of Stalinism. I listen to your words as Einstein could listen to a schoolboy talking about physics in four dimensions. I see that you are only acquainted with elementary Marxism, i.e. with the demagogic, popular one.

G.—If your explanation will not be too long and involved, I should be grateful to you for some explanation of this "relativity" or "quantum" of Marxism.

R.—Here there is no irony; I am speaking with the best intentions. . . In this same elementary Marxism, which is taught even in your Stalinist University, you can find the statement which contradicts the whole of your thesis about the inevitability of the Hitlerist attack on the USSR. You are also taught that the cornerstone of Marxism is the assertion that, supposedly, contradictions are the incurable and fatal illness of Capitalism. . . Is that not so?

G.—Yes, of course.

R.—But if things are in fact such that we accuse Capitalism of being imbued with continuous Capitalistic contradictions in the sphere of economics, then why should it necessarily suffer from them also in politics? The political and economic is of no importance in itself; this is a condition or measurement of the social essence, but contradictions arise in the social sphere, and are reflected simultaneously in the economic or political ones, or in both at the same time. It would be absurd to assume fallibility in economics and simultaneously infallibility in politics—which is something essential in order that an attack on the USSR should become inevitable—according to your postulate—absolutely essential.

G.—This means that you rely in everything on the contradictions, fatality and inevitability of the errors which must be committed by the bourgeoisie, which will hinder Hitler from attacking the USSR. I am a Marxist, Rakovsky, but here, between ourselves, in order not to provide the pretext for anger to a single activist, I say to you that with all my faith in Marx I would not believe that the USSR exists thanks to the mistakes of its enemies. . . And I think that Stalin shares the same view.

R.—But I do think so. . . Do not look at me like that, as I am not joking and am not mad.

G.—Permit me at least to doubt it, until you will have proved your assertions.

R.—Do you now see that I had reasons for qualifying your Marxist culture as being doubtful? Your arguments and reactions are the same as any rank and file activist.

G.—And they are wrong?

R.—Yes, they are correct for a small administrator, for a bureaucrat and for the mass. They suit the average fighter. . . They must believe this and repeat everything as it has been written. Listen to me by way of the completely confidential. With Marxism you get the same results as with the ancient esoteric religions. Their adherents had to know only that which was the most elementary and crude, insofar as by this one provoked their faith, i.e. that which is absolutely essential, both in religion and in the work of revolution.

G.—Do you not now want to open up to me the mystical Marxism, something like yet another freemasonry?

R.—No, no esoterics. On the contrary, I shall explain it with the maximal clarity. Marxism, before being a philosophical, economic and political system, is a conspiracy for the revolution. And as for us the revolution is the only absolute reality, it follows that philosophy, economics and politics are true only insofar as they lead to revolution. The fundamental truth (let us call it subjective) does not exist in economics, politics or even morals; in the light of scientific abstraction it is either truth or error, but for us, who are subject to revolutionary dialectic, it is only truth. And insofar as to us, who are subject to revolutionary dialectic, it is only truth, and therefore the sole truth, then it must be such for all that is revolutionary, and such it was to Marx. In accordance with this we must act. Remember the phrase of Lenin, in reply to someone who demonstrated by way of argument that, supposedly, his intention contradicted reality: "I feel it to be real" was his answer. Do you not think that Lenin spoke nonsense? No, for him every reality, every truth was relative in the face of the sole and absolute one: the revolution. Marx was a genius. If his works had amounted to only the deep criticism of Capitalism, then even that would have been an unsurpassed scientific work; but in those places where his writing reaches the level of mastery, there comes the effect of an apparently ironical work. "Communism" he says "must win because Capital will give it that victory, though its enemy." Such is the magisterial thesis of Marx. . .

Can there be a greater irony? And then, in order that he should be believed, it was enough for him to depersonalize Capitalism and Communism, having transformed the human individual into a consciously thinking individual, which he did with the extraordinary talent of a juggler. Such was his sly method, in order to demonstrate to the Capitalists that they are a reality of Capitalism and that Communism can triumph as the result of inborn idiocy; since without the presence of immortal idiocy in *homo economico* there could not appear in him continuous contradictions as proclaimed by Marx. To be able to achieve the transformation of *homo sapiens* into *homo stultum* is to possess magical force, capable of bringing man down to the first stage of the zoological ladder, i.e. to the level of the animal. Only if there is *homo stultum* in the epoch of the apogee of Capitalism could Marx formulate his axiomatic proposition: contradictions plus time equal Communism. Believe me, when we who are initiated into this, contemplate the representation of Marx, for example the one which is placed above the main entrance to the Lubianka, then we cannot prevent the inner explosion of laughter by which Marx had infected us; we see how he laughs into his beard at all humanity.

G.—And you are still capable of laughing at the most revered scientist of the epoch?

R.—Ridicule, me? . . . This is the highest admiration! In order that Marx should be able to deceive so many people of science, it was essential that he should tower above them all. Well: in order to have judgements about Marx in all his greatness, we must consider the real Marx, Marx the revolutionary, Marx, judged by his manifesto. This means Marx the conspirator, as during his life the revolution was in a condition of conspiracy. It is not for nothing that the revolution is indebted for its development and its recent victories to these conspirators.

G.—Therefore you deny the existence of the dialectical process of contradictions in Capitalism, which lead to the final triumph of Communism?

R.—You can be sure that if Marx believed that Communism will achieve victory only thanks to the contradictions in Capitalism, then he would not have once, never, mentioned the contradictions on the thousands of pages of his scientific revolutionary work. Such was the categorical imperative of the realistic nature of Marx: not the scientific, but the revolutionary one. The revolutionary and conspirator will never disclose to his opponent the secret of his triumph. . . He would never give the information; he would give him disinformation which you use in counter-conspiracy. Is that not so?

G.—However, in the end we have reached the conclusion (according to you) that there are no contradictions in Capitalism, and if Marx speaks of them then it is only a revolutionary-strategical method. That is so? But the colossal and ever-growing contradictions in Capitalism are there to see. And so we get the conclusion that Marx, having lied, spoke the truth.

R.—You are dangerous as a dilectician, when you destroy the brakes of scholastic dogmatism and give free rein to your own inventiveness. So it is, that Marx spoke the truth when he lied. He lied when he led into error, having defined the contradictions as being "continuous" in the history of the economics of capital and called them "natural and inevitable," but at the same time he stated the truth because he knew that the contradictions would be created and would grow in an increasing progression until they reach their apogee.

G.—This means that with you there is an antithesis?

R.—There is no antithesis here. Marx deceives for tactical reasons about the origin of the contradictions in Capitalism, but not about their obvious reality. Marx knew how they were created, how they became more acute and how things went towards general anarchy in Capitalistic production, which came before the triumph of the Communist revolution. . . He knew it would happen because he knew those who created the contradictions.

G.—It is a very strange revelation and piece of news, this assertion and exposal of the circumstance that that which leads Capitalism to its "suicide," by the well-chosen expression of the bourgeois economist Schmalenbach, in support of Marx, is not the essence and inborn law of Capitalism. But I am interested to know if we will reach the personal by this path?

R.—Have you not felt this intuitively? Have you not noticed how in Marx words contradict deeds? He declares the necessity and inevitability of Capitalist contradictions, proving the existence of surplus value and accumulation, i.e. he proves that which really exists. He nimbly invents the proposition that to a greater concentration of the means of production corresponds a greater mass of the proletariat, a greater force for the building of Communism, is that not so? Now go on: at the same time as this assertion he founds the International. Yet the International is, in the work of the daily struggle of the classes, a "reformist," i.e. an organization whose purpose is the limitation of the surplus value and, where possible, its elimination. For this reason, objectively, the International is a counter-revolutionary organization and anti-Communist, in accordance with Marx's theory.

G.—Now we get that Marx is a counter-revolutionary and an anti-Communist.

R.—Well, now you see how one can make use of the original Marxist culture. It is only possible to describe the International as being counter-revolutionary and anti-Communist, with logical and scientific exactness, if one does not see in the facts anything more than the directly visible result, and in the texts only the letter. One comes to such absurd conclusions, while they seem to be obvious, when one forgets that words and facts in Marxism are subject to strict rules of the higher science: the rules of conspiracy and revolution.

G.—Will we ever reach the final conclusions?

R.—In a moment. If the class struggle, in the economic sphere. turns out to be reformist in the light of its first results, and for that reason contradicts the theoretical presuppositions, which determine the establishment of Communism, then it is, in its real and true meaning, purely revolutionary. But I repeat again: it is subject to the rules of conspiracy; that means to masking and the hiding of its true aims. . . The limitation of the surplus value and thus also of accumulations as the consequence of the class struggle—that is only a matter of appearances, an illusion, in order to stimulate the basic revolutionary movement in the masses. A strike is already an attempt at revolutionary mobilization. Independently of whether it wins or not, its economic effect is anarchical. As a result this method for the improvement of the economic position of one class brings about the impoverishment of the economy in general; whatever may be the scale and results of the strike, it will always bring about a reduction of production. The general result: more poverty, which the working class cannot shake off. That is already something. But that is not the only result and not the most important one. As we know, the only aim of any struggle in the economic sphere is to earn more and work less. Such is the economic absurdity, but according to our terminology, such is the contradiction, which has not been noticed by the masses, which are blinded at any given moment by a rise in wages, which is at once annulled by a rise in prices. And if prices are limited by governmental action, then the same thing happens, i.e. a contradiction between the wish to spend more, produce less, is qualified here by monetary inflation. And so one gets a vicious circle: a strike, hunger, inflation, hunger.

G.—With the exception when the strike takes place at the expense of the surplus value of Capitalism.

R.—Theory, pure theory. Speaking between ourselves, take any annual handbook concerning the economics of any country and divide rents and the total income by all those receiving wages or salaries, and you will see what an extraordinary result emerges. This result is the most counter-revolutionary fact, and we must keep it a complete secret. This is because if you deduct from the theoretical dividend the salaries and expenses of the directors, which would be the consequence on the abolition of ownership, then almost always there remains a dividend which is a debit for the proletariat. In reality always a debit, if we also consider the reduction in the volume and quality of production. As you will now see, a call to strike, as a means for achieving a quick improvement of the well-being of the proletariat—is only an excuse; an excuse required in order to force it to commit sabotage of Capitalistic production. Thus to the contradictions in the bourgeois system are added contradictions within the proletariat; this is the double weapon of the revolution, and it—which is obvious—does not arise of itself: there exists an organization, chiefs, discipline, and above that there exists stupidity. Don't you suspect that the much-mentioned contradictions of Capitalism, and in particular the financial ones, are also organized by someone? . . . By way of basis for these deductions I shall remind you that in its economic struggle the proletarian International coincides with the financial International, since both produce inflation, and wherever there is coincidence there, one should assume, is also agreement. Those are his own words.

G.—I suspect here such an enormous absurdity, or the intention of spinning a new paradox, that I do not want to imagine this. It looks as if you want to hint at the existence of something like a Capitalistic second Communist International, of course an enemy one.

R.—Exactly so. When I spoke of the financial International, I thought of it as of a Comintern, but having admitted the existence of the "Comintern," I would not say that they are enemies.

G.—If you want to make us lose time on inventions and phantasies, I must tell you that you have chosen the wrong moment.

R.—By the way, are you assuming that I am like the courtesan from the "Arabian Nights," who used her imagination at night to save her life. . . No. If you think that I am departing from the theme, then you are wrong. In order to reach that which we have taken as our aim I, if I am not to fail, must first of all enlighten you about the most important matters, while bearing in mind your general lack of acquaintance with that which I would call the "Higher Marxism." I dare not evade these explanations as I know well that such lack of knowledge exists in the Kremlin. . . Permit me to continue.

G.—You may continue. But it is true that if all this were to be seen to be only a loss of time to excite the imagination, then this amusement will have a very sad epilogue. I have warned you.

R.—I continue as if I have heard nothing. Insofar as you are a scholastic with relation to Capital, and I want to awaken your inductive talents, I shall remind you of some very curious things. Notice with what penetration Marx comes to conclusions given the then existence of early British industry, concerning its consequences, i.e. the contemporary colossal industry; how he analyzes it and criticises; what a repulsive picture he gives of the manufacturer. In your imagination and that of the masses there arises the terrible picture of Capitalism in its human concretization: a fat-bellied manufacturer with a cigar in his mouth, as described by Marx, with self-satisfaction and anger throwing the wife and daughter of the worker onto the street. Is that not so? At the same time remember the moderation of Marx and his bourgeois orthodoxy when studying the question of money. In the problem of money there do not appear with him his famous contradictions. Finances do not exist for him as a thing of importance in itself; trade and the circulation of moneys are the results of the cursed system of Capitalistic production, which subjects them to itself and fully determines them. In the question of money Marx is a reactionary; to ones immense surprise he was one; bear in mind the "five-pointed star" like the Soviet one, which shines all over Europe, the star composed of the five Rothschild brothers with their banks, who possess colossal accumulations of wealth, the greatest ever known. . . And so this fact, so colossal that it misled the imagination of the people of that epoch, passes unnoticed with Marx. Something strange. . . Is that not so? It is possible that from this strange blindness of Marx there arises a phenomenon which is common to all future social revolutions. It is this: we can all confirm that when the masses take possession of a city or a country, then they always seem struck by a sort of superstitious fear of the banks and bankers. One had killed Kings, generals, bishops, policemen, priests and other representatives of the hated privileged classes; one robbed and burnt palaces, churches and even centres of science, but though the revolutions were economic-social, the lives of the bankers were respected, and as a result the magnificent buildings of the banks remained untouched. . . According to my information, before I had been arrested, this continues even now. . .

G.—Where?

R.—In Spain. . . Don't you know it? As you ask me, so tell me now: Do you not find all this very strange? Think, the police. . . I do not know, have you paid attention to the strange similarity which exists between the financial International and the proletarian International. I would say that one is the other side of the other, and the back side is the proletarian one as being more modern than the financial.

G.—Where do you see similarity in things so opposed?

R.—Objectively they are identical. As I had proved, the Comintern, paralleled, doubled by the reformist movement and the whole of syndicalism, calls forth the anarchy of production, inflation, poverty and hopelessness in the masses. Finances, chiefly the financial international, doubled, consciously or unconsciously by private finances, create the same contradictions, but in still greater numbers. . . Now we can already guess the reasons why Marx concealed the financial contradictions, which could not have remained hidden from his penetrating gaze, if finances had not had an ally, the influence of which—objectively revolutionary—was already then extraordinarily important.

G.—An unconscious coincidence, but not an alliance which presupposes intelligence, will and agreement. . .

R.—Let us leave this point of view if you like. Now let us better go over to the subjective analysis of finances and even more: let us see what sort of people personally are at work there. The international essence of money is well known. From this fact emerges that the organization which owns them and accumulates them is a cosmopolitan organization. Finances in their apogee—as an aim in themselves, the financial International—deny and do not recognise anything national, they do not recognize the State; and therefore it is anarchical and would be absolutely anarchical if it—the denyer of any national State—were not itself, by necessity, a State in its own basic essence. The State as such is only power. And money is exclusively power.

This communistic super-state, which we are creating already during a whole century, and the scheme of which is the International of Marx. Analyse it and you will see its essence. The scheme of the International and its prototype of the USSR—that is also pure power. The basic similarity between the two creations is absolute. It is something fatalistic, inevitable, since the personalities of the authors of both was identical. The financier is just as international as the Communist. Both, with the help of differing pretexts and differing means, struggle with the national bourgeois State and deny it. Marxism in order to change it into a Communist State; from this comes that the Marxist must be an internationalist; the financier denies the bourgeois national State and his denial ends in itself; in fact he does not manifest himself as an internationalist, but as a cosmopolitan anarchist. . . That is his appearance at the given stage, but let us see what he really is and what he wants to be. As you see, in rejection there is a clear similarity individually between Communist-internationalists and financial-cosmopolitans; as a natural result there is the same similarity between the Communist International and the financial International. . .

G.—This is a chance similarity subjectively and objective in contradictions, but one easily eroded and having little significance and that which is most radical and existing in reality.

R.—Allow me not to reply just now, so as not to interrupt the logical sequence. . . I only want to decipher the basic axiom: money is power. Money is to-day the centre of global gravity. I hope you agree with me?

G.—Continue, Rakovsky, I beg of you.

R.—The understanding of how the financial International has gradually, right up to our epoch, become the master of money, this magical talisman, which has become for people that which God and the nation had been formerly, is something which exceeds in scientific interest even the art of revolutionary strategy, since this is also an art and also a revolution. I shall explain it to you. Historiographers and the masses, blinded by the shouts and the pomp of the French revolution, the people, intoxicated by the fact that it had succeeded in taking all power from the King and the privileged classes, did not notice how a small group of mysterious, careful and insignificant people had taken possession of the real Royal power, the magical power, almost divine, which it obtained almost without knowing it. The masses did not notice that the power had been seized by others and that soon they had subjected them to a slavery more cruel than the King, since the latter, in view of his religious and moral prejudices, was incapable of taking advantage of such a power. So it came about that the supreme Royal power was taken over by persons, whose moral, intellectual and cosmopolitan qualities did allow them to use it. It is clear that this were people who had never been Christians, but cosmopolitans.

G.—What is that for a mythical power which they had obtained?

R.—They had acquired for themselves the real privilege of coining money. . . Do not smile, otherwise I shall have to believe that you do not know what moneys are. . . I ask you to put yourself in my place. My position in relation to you is that of the assistant of a doctor, who would have to explain bacteriology to a resurrected medical man of the epoch before Pasteur. But I can explain your lack of knowledge to myself and can forgive it. Our language makes use of words which provoke incorrect thoughts about things and actions, thanks to the power of the inertia of thoughts, and which do not correspond to real and exact conceptions. I say: money. It is clear that in your imagination there immediately appeared pictures of real money of metal and paper. But that is not so. Money is now not that; real circulating coin is a true anachronism. If it still exists and circulates, then it is only thanks to atavism, only because it is convenient to maintain the illusion, a purely imaginary fiction for the present day.

G.—This is a brilliant paradox, risky and even poetical. . .

R.—If you like, this is perhaps brilliant, but it is not a paradox. I know—and that is why you smiled—that States still coin money on pieces of metal or paper with Royal busts or national crests; well, so what? A great part of the money circulating, money for big affairs, as representative of all national wealth, money, yes money—it was being issued by those few people about whom I had hinted. Titles, figures, cheques, promissory notes, indorsements, discount, quotations, figures without end flooded States like a waterfall. What are in comparison with these the metallic and paper moneys? . . . Something devoid of influence, some kind of minimum in the face of the growing flood of the all-flooding financial money. They, being the most subtle psychologists, were able to gain even more without trouble, thanks to a lack of understanding. In addition to the immensely varied different forms of financial moneys, they created credit-money with a view to making its volume close to infinite. And to give it the speed of sound . . . it is an abstraction, a being of thought, a figure, number; credit, faith. . .

Do you understand already? . . . Fraud; false moneys, given a legal standing . . . , using other terminology, so that you should understand me. Banks, the stock exchanges and the whole world financial system —is a gigantic machine for the purpose of bringing about unnatural scandals, according to Aristotle's expression; to force money to produce moneys—that is something that if it is a crime in economics, then in relations to finances it is a crime against the criminal code, since it is usury. I do not know by what arguments all this is justified: by the proposition that they receive legal interest. . . Even accepting that, and even that admission is more than is necessary, we see that usury still exists, since even if the interest received is legal, then it invents and falsifies the non-existent capital. Banks have always by way of deposits or moneys in productive movement a certain quantity of money which is five or perhaps even a hundred times greater than there are physically coined moneys of metal or paper. I shall say nothing of those cases when the credit-moneys, i.e. false, fabricated ones, are greater than the quantity of moneys paid out as capital. Bearing in mind that lawful interest is fixed not on real capital but on non-existing capital, the interest is illegal by so many times as the fictional capital is greater than the real one.

Bear in mind that this system, which I am describing in detail, is one of the most innocent among those used for the fabrication of false money. Imagine to yourself, if you can, a small number of people, having unlimited power through the possession of real wealth, and you will see that they are the absolute dictators of the stock-exchange; and as a result of this also the dictators of production and distribution and also of work and consumption. If you have enough imagination then multiply this by the global factor and you will see its anarchical, moral and social influence, i.e. a revolutionary one. . . Do you now understand?

G.—No, not yet.

R.—Obviously it is very difficult to understand miracles.

G.—Miracle?

R.—Yes, miracle. Is it not a miracle that a wooden bench has been transformed into a temple? And yet such a miracle has been seen by people a thousand times, and they did not bat an eyelid, during a whole century. Since this was an extraordinary miracle that the benches on which sat the greasy usurers to trade in their moneys, have now been converted into temples, which stand magnificently at every corner of contemporary big towns with their heathen colonnades, and crowds go there with a faith which they are already not given by heavenly gods, in order to bring assiduously their deposits of all their possessions to the god of money, who, they imagine, lives in the steel safes of the bankers, and who is preordained, thanks to his divine mission to increase the wealth to a metaphysical infinity.

G.—This is the new religion of the decayed bourgeoisie?

R.—Religion, yes, the religion of power.

G.—You appear to be the poet of economics.

R.—If you like, then in order to give a picture of finance, as of a work of art which is most obviously a work of genius and the most revolutionary of all times, poetry is required.

G.—This is a faulty view. Finances, as defined by Marx, and more especially Engels, are determined by the system of Capitalistic production.

R.—Exactly, but just the reverse: the Capitalistic system of production is determined by finance. The fact that Engels states the opposite and even tries to prove this, is the most obvious proof that finances rule bourgeois production. So it is and so it was even before Marx and Engels, that finances were the most powerful instrument of revolution and the Comintern was nothing but a toy in their hands. But neither Marx nor Engels will disclose or explain this. On the contrary, making use of their talent as scientists, they had to camouflage truth for a second time in the interests of the revolution. And that both of them did.

G.—This story is not new. All this somewhat reminds me of what Trotzky had written some ten years ago.

R.—Tell me. . .

G.—When he says that the Comintern is a conservative organization in comparison with the stock-exchange in New York; he points at the big bankers as being the inventors of the revolution.

R.—Yes, he said this in a small book in which he foretold the fall of England. . . Yes, he said this and added: "Who pushes England along the path of revolution?" . . . and replied: "Not Moscow, but New York."

G.—But remember also his assertion that if the financiers of New York had forged the revolution, then it was done unconsciously.

R.—The explanation which I had already given in order to help to understand why Engels and Marx camouflaged the truth, is equally applicable also to Leo Trotzky.

G.—I value in Trotzky only that he in a sort of literary form interpreted an opinion of a fact which as such was too well known, with which one had already reckoned previously. Trotzky himself states quite correctly that these bankers "carry out irresistibly and unconsciously their revolutionary mission."

R.—And they carry out their mission despite the fact that Trotzky has declared it? What a strange thing! Why do they not improve their actions?

G.—The financiers are unconscious revolutionaries since they are such only objectively, as the result of their intellectual incapacity of seeing the final consequences.

R.—You believe this sincerely? You think that among these real geniuses there are some who are unconscious? You consider to be idiots people to whom to-day the whole world is subjected? This would really be a very stupid contradiction!

G.—What do you pretend to?

R.—I simply assert that they are revolutionaries objectively and subjectively, quite consciously.

G.—The bankers! You must be mad?

R.—I, no . . . But you? Think a little. These people are just like you and me. The circumstance that they control moneys in unlimited amounts, insofar as they themselves create them, does not give us the opportunity of determining the limits of all their ambitions. . . If there is something which provides a man with full satisfaction then it is the satisfaction of his ambition. And most of all the satisfaction of his will to power. Why should not these people, the bankers, have the impulse towards power, towards full power? Just as it happens to you and to me.

G.—But if, according to you—and I think the same—they already have global political power, then what other power do they want to possess?

R.—I have already told you: Full power. Such power as Stalin has in the USSR, but world-wide.

G.—Such power as Stalin's, but with the opposite aim.

R.—Power, if in reality it is absolute, can be only one. The idea of the absolute excludes multiplicity. For that reason the power sought by the Comintern and "Comintern," which are things of the same order, being absolute, must also in politics be unique and identical: Absolute power has a purpose in itself, otherwise it is not absolute. And until the present day there has not yet been invented another machine of total power except the Communist State. Capitalistic bourgeois power, even on its highest rung of the ladder, the power of Caesar, is limited power since if, in theory, it was the personification of the deity in the Pharaohs and Caesars in ancient times, then nevertheless, thanks to the economic character of life in those primitive States and owing to the technical under-development of the State apparatus, there was always room for individual freedom. Do you understand that those who already partially rule over nations and worldly governments have pretensions to absolute domination? Understand that that is the only thing which they have not yet reached. . .

G.—This is interesting; at least as an example of insanity.

R.—Certainly, insanity in a lesser degree than in the case of Lenin, who dreamt of power over the whole world in his attic in Switzerland or the insanity of Stalin, dreaming of the same thing during his exile in a Siberian hut. I think that dreams of such ambitions are much more natural for the moneyed people, living in the skyscrapers of New York.

G.—Let us conclude: Who are they?

R.—You are so naive that you think that if I knew who "They" are, I would be here as a prisoner?

G.—Why?

R.—For a very simple reason, since he who is acquainted with them would not be put into a position in which he would be obliged to report on them. . . This is an elementary rule of every intelligent conspiracy, which you must well understand.

G.—But you said that they are the bankers?

R.—Not I; remember that I always spoke of the financial International, and when mentioning persons I said "They" and nothing more. If you want that I should inform you openly then I shall only give facts, but not names, since I do not know them. I think I shall not be wrong if I tell you that not one of "Them" is a person who occupies a political position or a position in the World Bank. As I understood after the murder of Rathenau in Rapallo, they give political or financial positions only to intermediaries. Obviously to persons who are trustworthy and loyal, which can be guaranteed a thousand ways; thus one can assert that bankers and politicians—are only men of straw . . . even though they occupy very high places and are made to appear to be the authors of the plans which are carried out.

G.—Although all this can be understood and is also logical, but is not your declaration of not knowing only an evasion? As it seems to me, and according to the information I have, you occupied a sufficiently high place in this conspiracy to have known much more. You do not even know a single one of them personally?

R.—Yes, but of course you do not believe me. I have come to that moment where I had explained that I am talking about a person and persons with a personality . . . how should one say? . . . a mystical one, like Ghandi or something like that, but without any external display. Mystics of pure power, who have become free from all vulgar trifles. I do not know if you understand me? Well, as to their place of residence and names, I do not know them. . . Imagine Stalin just now, in reality ruling the USSR, but not surrounded by stone walls, not having any personnel around him, and having the same guarantees for his life as any other citizen. By which means could he guard against attempts on his life? He is first of all a conspirator, however great his power: he is anonymous.

G.—What you are saying is logical, but I do not believe you.

R.—But still believe me; I know nothing; if I knew then how happy I would be! I would not be here, defending my life. I well understand your doubts and that, in view of your police education, you feel the need for some knowledge about persons. To honour you and also because this is essential for the aim which we both have set ourselves, I shall do all I can in order to inform you. You know that according to the unwritten history known only to us, the founder of the First Communist International is indicated, of course secretly, as being Weishaupt. You remember his name? He was the head of the masonry which is known by the name of the Illuminati; this name he borrowed from the second anti-Christian conspiracy of that era—gnosticism. This important revolutionary, Semite and former Jesuit, foreseeing the triumph of the French revolution decided, or perhaps he was ordered (some mention as his chief the important philosopher Mendelssohn) to found a secret organization which was to provoke and push the French revolution to go further than its political objectives, with the aim of transforming it into a social revolution for the establishment of Communism. In those heroic times it was colossally dangerous to mention Communism as an aim; from this derive the various precautions and secrets, which had to surround the Illuminati. More than a hundred years were required before a man could confess to being a Communist without danger of going to prison or being executed. This is more or less known. What is not known are the relations between Weishaupt and his followers with the first of the Rothschilds. The secret of the acquisition of wealth of the best known bankers could have been explained by the fact that they were the treasurers of this first Comintern. There is evidence that when the five brothers spread out to the five provinces of the financial empire of Europe, they had some secret help for the accumulation of these enormous sums; it is possible that they were those first Communists from the Bavarian catacombs who were already spread all over Europe. But others say, and I think with better reason, that the Rothschilds were not the treasurers, but the chiefs of that first secret Communism. This opinion is based on that well-known fact that Marx and the highest chiefs of the First International—already the open one—and among them Herzen and Heine, were controlled by Baron Lionel Rothschild, whose revolutionary portrait was done by Disraeli (in Coningsby—Transl.) the English Premier, who was his creature, and has been left to us. He described him in the character of Sidonia, a man, who, according to the story, was a multi-millionaire, knew and controlled spies, carbonari, freemasons, secret Jews, gypsies, revolutionaries etc., etc. All this seems phantastic. But it has been proved that Sidonia is an idealized portrait of the son of Nathan Rothschild, which can also be deduced from that campaign which he raised against Tsar Nicholas in favour of Herzen. He won this campaign. If all that which we can guess in the light of these facts is true, then, I think, we could even determine who invented this terrible machine of accumulation and anarchy, which is the financial International. At the same time, I think, he would be the same person who also created the revolutionary International. It is an act of genius: to create with the help of Capitalism accumulation of the highest degree, to push the proletariat towards strikes, to sow hopelessness, and at the same time to create an organization which must unite the proletarians with the purpose of driving them into revolution. This is to write the most majestic chapter of history. Even more: remember the phrase of the mother of the five Rothschild brothers: "If my sons want it, then there will be no war." This means that they were the arbiters, the masters of peace and war, but not emperors. Are you capable of visualizing the fact of such a cosmic importance? Is not war already a revolutionary function? War—the Commune. Since that time every war was a giant step towards Communism. As if some mysterious force satisfied the passionate wish of Lenin, which he had expressed to Gorky. Remember: 1905-1914. Do admit at least that two of the three levers of power which lead to Communism are not controlled and cannot be controlled by the proletariat. Wars were not brought about and were not controlled by either the Third International or the USSR, which did not yet exist at that time. Equally they cannot be provoked and still less controlled by those small groups of Bolsheviks who plod along in the emigration, although they want war. This is quite obvious. The International and the USSR have even fewer possibilities for such immense accumulations of capital and the creation of national or international anarchy in Capitalistic production. Such an anarchy which is capable of forcing people to burn huge quantities of foodstuffs, rather than give them to starving people, and is capable of that which Rathenau described in one of his phrases, i.e.: "To bring about that half the world will fabricate dung, and the other half will use it." And, after all, can the proletariat believe that it is the cause of this inflation, growing in geometric progression, this devaluation, the constant acquisition of surplus values and the accumulation of financial capital, but not usury capital, and that as the result of the fact that it cannot prevent the constant lowering of its purchasing power, there takes place the proletarization of the middle classes, who are the true opponents of revolution. The proletariat does not control the lever of economics or the lever of war. But it is itself the third lever, the only visible and demonstrable lever, which carries out the final blow at the power of the Capitalistic State and takes it over. Yes, they seize it, if "They" yield it to them. . .

G.—I again repeat to you that all this, which you have set out in such a literate form, has a name which we have already repeated to excess in this endless conversation: the natural contradictions of Capitalism and if, as you claim, there is yet someone else's will and activity apart from the proletariat, then I want you to indicate to me concretely a personal case.

R.—You require only one? Well, then listen to a small story: "They" isolated the Tsar diplomatically for the Russo-Japanese War, and the United States financed Japan; speaking precisely, this was done by Jacob Schiff, the head of the bank of Kuhn, Loeb & Co., which is the successor of the House of Rothschild, whence Schiff originated. He had such power that he achieved that States which had colonial possessions in Asia supported the creation of the Japanese Empire, which was inclined towards xenophobia; and Europe already feels the effects of this xenophobia. From the prisoner-of-war camps there came to Petrograd the best fighters, trained as revolutionary agents; they were sent there from America with the permission of Japan, obtained through the persons who had financed it. The Russo-Japanese War, thanks to the organized defeat of the Tsar's army, called forth the revolution of 1905, which, though it was premature, but was very nearly successful; even if it did not win, it still created the required political conditions for the victory of 1917. I shall say even more. Have you read the biography of Trotzky? Recall its first revolutionary period. He is still quite a young man; after his flight from Siberia he lived some time among the emigres in London, Paris, and Switzerland; Lenin, Plekhanov, Martov and other chiefs look on him only as a promising newcomer. But he already dares during the first split to behave independently, trying to become the arbiter of the reunion. In 1905 he is 25 years old and he returns to Russia alone, without a party and without his own organization. Read the reports of the revolution of 1905 which have not been "pruned" by Stalin; for example that of Lunatcharsky, who was not a Trotzkyite. Trotzky is the chief figure during the revolution in Petrograd. This is how it really was. Only he emerges from it with increased popularity and influence. Neither Lenin, nor Martov, nor Plekhanov acquire popularity. They only keep it and even lose a little. How and why there rises the unknown Trotzky, gaining power by one move greater than that which the oldest and most influential revolutionaries had? Very simple: he marries. Together with him there arrives in Russia his wife—Sedova. Do you know who she is? She is associated with Zhivotovsky, linked with the bankers Warburg, partners and relatives of Jacob Schiff, i.e. of that financial group which, as I had said, had also financed the revolution of 1905. Here is the reason why Trotzky, in one move, moves to the top of the revolutionary list. And here, too, you have the key to his real personality. Let us jump to 1914. Behind the back of the people who made the attempt on the Archduke there stands Trotzky, and that attempt provoked the European War. Do you really believe that the murder and the war—are simple coincidences? . . . , as had been said at one of the Zionist congresses by Lord Melchett. Analyze in the light of "non-coincidence" the development of the military actions in Russia. "Defeatism" is an exemplary word. The help of the Allies for the Tsar was regulated and controlled with such skill that it gave the Allied ambassadors the right to make an argument of this and to get from Nicholas, thanks to his stupidity, suicidal advances, one after another. The mass of the Russian cannon fodder was immense, but not inexhaustible. A series of organized defeats led to the revolution. When the threat came from all sides, then a cure was found in the form of the establishment of a democratic republic—an "ambassadorial republic" as Lenin called it, i.e. this meant the elimination of any threat to the revolutionaries. But that is not yet all. Kerensky was to provoke the future advance at the cost of a very great deal of blood. He brings it about so that the democratic revolution should spread beyond its bounds. And even still more: Kerensky was to surrender the State fully to Communism, and he does it. Trotzky has the chance in an "unnoticed manner" to occupy the whole State apparatus. What a strange blindness! Well that is the reality of the much praised October revolution. The Bolsheviks took that which "They" gave them.

G.—You dare to say that Kerensky was a collaborator of Lenin?

R.—Of Lenin—no. Of Trotzky—yes; it is more correct to say—a collaborator of "Them."

G.—An absurdity!

R.—You cannot understand . . . precisely you? It surprises me. If you were to be a spy and, while hiding your identity, you were to attain the position of commander of the enemy fortress, then would you not open the gates to the attacking forces in whose service you actually were? You would not have become a prisoner who had experienced defeat? Would you not have been in danger of death during the attack on the fortress if one of the attackers, not knowing that your uniform is only a mask, would have taken you for an enemy? Believe me: despite the statues and mausoleum—Communism is indebted to Kerensky much more than to Lenin.

G.—You want to say that Kerensky was a conscious and voluntary defeatist?

R.—Yes to me that is quite clear. Understand that I personally took part in all this. I shall tell you even more: Do you know who financed the October revolution? "They" financed it, in particular through those same bankers who had financed Japan in 1905, i.e. Jacob Schiff, and the brothers Warburg; that means through the great banking constellation, through one of the five banks who are members of the Federal Reserve, through the bank of Kuhn, Loeb & Co.; here there took part also other American and European bankers, such as Guggenheim, Hanauer, Breitung, Aschberg, the "Nya Banken" of Stockholm. I was there "by chance," there in Stockholm, and participated in the transmission of funds. Until Trotzky arrived I was the only person who was an intermediary from the revolutionary side. But at last Trotzky came; I must underline that the Allies had expelled him from France for being a defeatist. And the same Allies released him so that he could be a defeatist in allied Russia. . . "Another chance." Who arranged it? The same people who had succeeded that Lenin passed through Germany. Yes, "They" were able to get the defeatist Trotzky out of a Canadian camp to England and send him on to Russia, giving him the chance to pass freely through all the Allied controls; others of "Them"—a certain Rathenau—accomplishes the journey of Lenin through enemy Germany. If you will undertake the study of the history of the revolution and civil war without prejudices, and will use all your enquiring capabilities, which you know how to apply to things much less important and less obvious, then when you study informations in their totality, and also study separate details right up to anecdotal happenings, you will meet with a whole series of "amazing chances."

G.—Alright, let us accept the hypothesis that not everything was simply a matter of luck. What deductions to you make here for practical results?

R.—Let me finish this little story, and then we shall both arrive at conclusions. From the time of his arrival in Petrograd Trotzky was openly received by Lenin. As you know sufficiently well, during the interval between the two revolutions there had been deep differences between them. All is forgotten and Trotzky emerges as the master of his trade in the matter of the triumph of the revolution, whether Stalin wants this or not. Why? This secret is known to the wife of Lenin—Krupskaya. She knows who Trotzky is in fact; it is she who persuaded Lenin to receive Trotzky. If he had not received him, then Lenin would have remained blocked up in Switzerland; this alone had been for him a serious reason, and in addition he knew that Trotzky provided money and helped to get a colossal international assistance; a proof of this was the sealed train. Furthermore it was the result of Trotzky's work, and not of the iron determination of Lenin that there was the unification round the insignificant party of the Bolsheviks of the whole Left-wing revolutionary camp, the social-revolutionaries and the anarchists. It was not for nothing that the real party of the "non-party" Trotzky was the ancient "Bund" of the Jewish proletariat, from which emerged all the Moscow revolutionary branches, and to whom it gave 90% of its leaders; not the official and well-known Bund, but the secret Bund, which had been infiltrated into all the Socialist parties, the leaders of which were almost all under its control.

G.—And Kerensky too?

R.—Kerensky too. . . , and also some other leaders who were not Socialists, the leaders of the bourgeois political fractions.

G.—How is that?

R.—You forget about the role of freemasonry in the first phase of the democratic-bourgeois revolution?

G.—Were they also controlled by the Bund?

R.—Naturally, as the nearest step, but in fact subject to "Them."

G.—Despite the rising tide of Marxism which also threatened their lives and privileges?

R.—Despite all that; obviously they did not see that danger. Bear in mind that every mason saw and hoped to see in his imagination more that there was in reality, because he imagined that which was profitable for him. As a proof of the political power of their association they saw that masons were in governments and at the pinnacle of the States of the bourgeois nations, while their numbers were growing all the time. Bear in mind that at that time the rulers of all the Allied nations were freemasons, with very few exceptions. This was to them an argument of great force. They fully believed that the revolution would stop at the bourgeois republic of the French type.

G.—In accordance with the picture which was given of the Russia of 1917 one had to be a very naive person to believe all this. . .

R.—They were and are such. Masons had learned nothing from that first lesson which, for them, had been the Great Revolution, in which they played a colossal revolutionary role; it consumed the majority of masons, beginning with the Grand Master of the Orleans Lodge, more correctly the freemason Louis XVI, in order then to continue to destroy the Girondistes, the Hebertistes, the Jacobins etc. . . . , and if some survived it was due to the month of Brumaire.

G.—Do you want to say that the freemasons have to die at the hands of the revolution which has been brought about with their co-operation?

R.—Exactly so. You have formulated a truth which is veiled by a great secret. I am a mason, you already knew about that. Is that not so? Well, I shall tell you this great secret, which they promise to disclose to a mason in one of the higher degrees, but which is not disclosed to him either in the 25th, nor the 33rd, nor the 93rd, nor any other high level of any ritual. It is clear that I know of this not as a freemason, but as one who belongs to "Them". . .

G.—And what is it?

R.—Every masonic organization tries to attain and to create all the required prerequisites for the triumph of the Communist revolution; this is the obvious aim of freemasonry; it is clear that all this is done under various pretexts; but they always conceal themselves behind their well-known treble slogan. (Liberty, Equality, Fraternity—Transl.) You understand? But since the Communist revolution has in mind the liquidation, as a class, of the whole bourgeoisie, the physical destruction of all bourgeois political rulers, it follows that the real secret of masonry —is the suicide of freemasonry as an organization, and the physical suicide of every more important mason. You can, of course, understand that such an end, which is being prepared for every mason, fully deserves the secrecy, decorativeness and the inclusion of yet another whole series of secrets, with a view to concealing the real one. If one day you were to be present at some future revolution then do not miss the opportunity of observing the gestures of surprise and the expression of stupidity on the face of some freemason at the moment when he realises that he must die at the hands of the revolutionaries. How he screams and wants that one should value his services to the revolution! It is a sight at which one can die . . . but of laughter.

G.—And you still deny the inborn stupidity of the bourgeoisie?

R.—I deny it in the bourgeoisie as a class, but not in certain sectors. The existence of madhouses does not prove universal madness. Freemasonry is also a madhouse, but at liberty. But I continue further: the revolution has been victorious; the seizure of power has been achieved. There arises the first problem: peace, and with it the first differences within the party, in which there participate the forces of the coalition, which takes advantage of power. I shall not explain to you that which is well known about the struggle which developed in Moscow between the adherents and opponents of the peace of Brest-Litovsk. I shall only point out to you that which had already become evident then and was later called the Trotzkyist opposition, i.e. these are the people, a part of whom have already been liquidated and the other part is to be liquidated; they were all against the signing of the peace treaty. That peace was a mistake and an unconscious betrayal by Lenin of the

International Revolution. Imagine to yourself the Bolsheviks in Versailles at the Peace Conference, and then in the League of Nations, finding themselves inside Germany with the Red Army, which had been armed and increased by the Allies. The Soviet State should have participated with arms in the German revolution. . . Quite another map of Europe would then have emerged. But Lenin, intoxicated with power, with the help of Stalin, who had also tasted the fruits of power, supported by the national Russian wing of the party, having at their disposal the material recources, enforced their will. Then was born "Socialism in one country," i.e. National-Communism, which has to-day reached its apogee under Stalin. It is obvious that there was a struggle, but only in such a form and extent that the Communist State should not be destroyed; this condition was binding on the opposition during the whole time of its further struggle right up to the present day. This was the reason for our first failure and all those which followed. But the fight was severe, cruel, although concealed in order not to compromise our participation in power. Trotzky organized, with the help of his friends, the attempt on Lenin's life by Kaplan. On his orders Blumkin killed the ambassador Mirbach. The *coup d'etat* which was prepared by Spiridonova with her social-revolutionaries had been co-ordinated with Trotzky. His man for all these affairs, who was immune from all suspicions, was that Rosenblum, a Lithuanian Jew, who used the name of O'Reilly, and was known as the best spy of the British Intelligence. In fact he was a man from "Them." The reason why this famous Rosenblum was chosen, who was known only as a British spy, was that in case of failure the responsibility for assassinations and conspiracies would fall not on Trotzky, and not on us, but on England. So it happened. Thanks to the Civil War we rejected conspiratorial and terrorist methods as we were given the chance of having in our hands the real forces of the State, insofar as Trotzky became the organizer and chief of the Soviet Army; before that the army had continuously retreated before the Whites and the territory of the USSR was reduced to the size of the former Moscow Principality. But here, as if by magic, it begins to win. What do you think, why? As the result of magic or chance? I shall tell you: when Trotzky took over the top command of the Red Army then he had by this in his hands the forces necessary to seize power. A series of victories was to increase his prestige and forces: it was already possible to defeat the Whites. Do you think that that official history was true which ascribes to the unarmed and ill-disciplined Red Army the fact that with its help there was achieved a series of victories?

G.—But to whom then?

R.—To the extent of ninety per cent they were indebted to "Them." You must not forget that the Whites were, in their way, democratic. The Mensheviks were with them and the remnants of all the old Liberal parties. Inside these forces "They" always had in their service many people, consciously and unconsciously. When Trotzky began to command then these people were ordered systematically to betray the Whites and at the same time they were promised participation, in a more or less short time, in the Soviet Government. Maisky was one of those people, one of the few in the case of which this promise was carried out, but he was able to achieve this only after Stalin had become convinced of his loyalty. This sabotage, linked with a progressive diminution of the help of the Allies to the White generals, who apart from all that were luckless idiots, forced them to experience defeat after defeat. Finally Wilson introduced in his famous 14 Points Point 6,* the existence of which was enough in order to bring to an end once and for all the attempts of the Whites to fight against the USSR. The Civil War strengthens the position of Trotzky as the heir of Lenin. So it was, without any doubt. The old revolutionary could now die, having acquired fame. If he remained alive after the bullet of Kaplan, he did not emerge alive after the secret process of the forcible ending of his life, to which he was subjected.

G.—Trotzky shortened his life? This is a big favourable point for our trial! Was it not Levin who was Lenin's doctor?

R.—Trotzky? . . . It is probable that he participated, but it is quite certain that he knew about it. But as far as the technical realization is concerned . . . , that is unimportant; who knows this? "They" have a sufficient number of channels in order to penetrate to wherever they want.

G.—In any event the murder of Lenin is a matter of the greatest importance and it would be worth while to transfer it for examination to the next trial. . . What do you think, Rakovsky, if you were by chance to be the author of this affair? It is clear that if you fail to achieve success in this conversation . . . The technical execution suits you well as a doctor. . .

R.—I do not recommend this to you. Leave this matter alone; it is sufficiently dangerous for Stalin himself. You will be able to spread your propaganda as you wish; but "They" have their propaganda which is more powerful and the question as to *qui podest*—who gains, will force one to see in Stalin the murderer of Lenin, and that argument will be stronger than any confessions extracted from Levin, me or anyone else.

G.—What do you want to say by this?

R.—That it is the classical and infallible rule in the determination of who the murderer is to check who gained . . . , and as far as the assassination of Lenin is concerned, in this case the beneficiary was his chief—Stalin. Think about this and I very much ask you not to make these remarks, as they distract me and do not make it possible for me to finish.

G.—Very well, continue, but you already know. . .

R.—It is well known that if Trotzky did not inherit from Lenin then it was not because by human calculations there was something missing in the plan. During Lenin's illness Trotzky held in his hands all the threads of power, which were more than sufficient to enable him to succeed Lenin. And measures had been taken to declare a sentence of

* Wilson's Point 6 read: "The evacuation of all Russian territory, and such a settlement of all questions affecting Russia as will secure the best and freest co-operation of the other nations of the world in obtaining for her an unhampered and unembarrassed opportunity for the independent determination of her own political development and national policy, and assure her of a sincere welcome into the society of free nations under institutions of her own choosing, and more than a welcome, assistance also of every kind that she may need and may herself desire. The treatment accorded Russia by her sister nations in the months to come will be the acid test of their good will, of their comprehension of her needs as distinguished from their own interests, and of their intelligent and unselfish sympathy."—Transl.

death on Stalin. For Trotzky the dictator it was enough to have in his hands the letter of Lenin against his then chief—Stalin, which had been torn from her husband by Krupskaya, to liquidate Stalin.* But a stupid mischance, as you know, ruined all our chances. Trotzky became ill unexpectedly and at the decisive moment, when Lenin dies, he becomes incapable of any action during a period of several months. Despite his possession of enormous advantages, the obstacle was our organization of the affair, i.e. its personal centralization. It is obvious that such a person as Trotzky, prepared in advance for his mission, which he was to realise, cannot be created at once, by improvisation. None among us, not even Zinoviev, had the requisite training and qualities for this undertaking; on the other hand Trotzky, being afraid of being displaced, did not himself want to help anybody. Thus, after the death of Lenin, when we had to be face to face with Stalin, who commenced a feverish activity, we foresaw then already our defeat in the Central Committee. We had to improvise a decision: and it was to ally ourselves with Stalin, to become Stalinists more than he himself, to exaggerate in everything and, therefore, to sabotage. The rest you know already: that was our uninterrupted subterranean struggle and our continuous failure to Stalin's advantage, while he displays police talents of genius, having absolutely no equals in the past. And even more: Stalin, possessing national atavism, which had not been uprooted in him by his early Marxism, apparently for that reason underlines his pan-Russianism, and in this connexion resurrects a class which we had to destroy, that is the class of National-Communists, as opposed to the Internationalist-Communists, which we are. He places the International at the service of the USSR and it already accepts his mastery. If we want to find an historical parallel, then we must point to bonapartism, and if we want to find a person of Stalin's type, then we shall not find an historical parallel for him. But perhaps I shall be able to find it in its basic characteristics by combining two people: Fouché and Napoleon. Let us try to deprive the latter of his second half, his accessories, uniforms, military rank, crown and such like things, which, it seems, do not tempt Stalin, and then together they will give us a type identical with Stalin in the most important respects: he is the killer of the revolution, he does not serve it, but makes use of its services; he represents the most ancient Russian Imperialism, just as Napoleon identified himself with the Gauls; he created an aristocracy, even if not a military one, one, since there are no victories, then a bureacratically-police one.

G.—That is enough, Rakovsky. You are not here to make Trotzkyist propaganda. Will you at last get to something concrete?

R.—It is clear that I shall, but not before I had reached the point at which you will have formulated for yourself an at least superficial conception concerning "Them," with whom you will have to reckon in practice and in concrete actuality. Not sooner. For me it is far more important than for you not to fail, which you must, naturally, understand.

G.—Well, try to shorten the story as far as possible.

R.—Our failures, which get worse every year, prevent the immediate carrying out of that which "They" have prepared in the after-war period for the further leap of the revolution forward. The Versailles Treaty,

* It will be observed that twice Rakovsky states that Stalin had been Lenin's chief; this may be a misunderstanding—Transl.

quite inexplicable for the politicians and economists of all nations, insofar as nobody could guess its projection, was the most decisive precondition for the revolution.

G.—This is a very curious theory. How do you explain it?

R.—The Versailles reparations and economic limitations were not determined by the advantages of individual nations. Their arithmetical absurdity was so obvious that even the most outstanding economists of the victorious countries soon exposed this. France alone demanded as reparations a great deal more than the cost of all her national possessions, more than one would have had to pay if the whole of France had been converted into a Sahara; even worse was the decision to impose on Germany payment obligations which were many times greater that it could pay, even if it had sold itself fully and given over the whole of its national production. In the end the true result was that in practice Germany was forced to carry out a phantastic dumping so that it could pay something on account of reparations. And of what did the dumping consist? An insufficiency of consumer goods, hunger in Germany and in corresponding measure unemployment in the importing countries. And since they could not import there was also unemployment in Germany. Hunger and unemployment on both sides; all this were the first results of Versailles. . . Was this treaty revolutionary or not? Even more was done: one undertook an equal control in the international plane. Do you know what that undertaking represents in the revolutionary plane? It means to impose an anarchical absurdity to force every national economy to produce in sufficient volume all that it needs, while assuming that to attain that one does not have to take account of climate, natural riches and also the technical education of directors and workers. The means for compensation for inborn inequalities of soil, climate, availability of minerals, oil, etc., etc. in various national economies, were always the circumstance that poor countries had to work more. This means that they had to exploit more deeply the capacities of the working force in order to lessen the difference which arises from the poverty of the soil; and to this are added a number of other inequalities which had to be compensated by similar measures; let us take the example of industrial equipment. I shall not expand the problem further, but the control of the working day carried through by the League of Nations on the basis of an abstract principle of the equality of the working day, was a reality in the context of an unchanged International Capitalist system of production and exchange and established economic inequality, since here we had to deal with an indifference to the aim of work, which is a sufficient production. The immediate result of this was an insufficiency of production, compensated by imports from countries with a sufficient natural economy and an industrial self-sufficiency; insofar as Europe had gold, that import was paid by gold. Then came the apparent boom in America which exchanged its immense production for gold and gold certificates, of which there was plenty. On the model of any anarchy of production there appeared at that period an unheard—of financial anarchy. "They" took advantage of it on the pretext of helping it with the aid of another and still greater anarchy: the inflation of the official money (cash) and the a hundred times greater inflation of their own money, credit money, i.e. false money. Remember how systematically there came devaluation in many countries; the destruction of the value of money in Germany, the American crisis and its phenomental consequences. . . , a record unemployment; more than thirty million unemployed in Europe and USA alone. Well, did not the Versailles Peace Treaty and its League of Nations serve as a revolutionary pre-condition?

G.—This could have happened even if not intended. Could you not prove to me why the revolution and Communism retreat before logical deductions; and more than that: they oppose fascism which has conquered in Spain and Germany. . . What can you tell me?

R.—I shall tell you that only in the case of the non-recognition of "Them" and their aims you would be right . . . , but you must not forget about their existence and aims, and also the fact that in the USSR power is in the hands of Stalin.

G.—I do not see the connexion here. . . .

R.—Because you do not want to: you have more than sufficient deductive talents and capabilities of reasoning. I repeat again: for us Stalin is not a Communist, but a bonapartist.

G.—So what?

R.—We do not wish that the great preconditions which we had created at Versailles for the triumph of the Communist revolution in the world, which, as you see, have become a gigantic reality, would serve the purpose of bringing victory to Stalin's bonapartism. . . Is that sufficiently clear for you? Everything would have been different if in this case Trotzky had been the dictator of the USSR; that would have meant that "They" would have been the chiefs of International Communism.

G.—But surely fascism is totally anti-Communist, as in relation to the Trotzkyist and the Stalinist Communism . . . and if the power which you ascribe to "Them" is so great, how is it that they were unable to avoid this?

R.—Because it were precisely "They" who gave Hitler the possibility of triumphing.

G.—You exceed all the boundaries of absurdity.

R.—The absurd and the miraculous become mixed as the result of a lack of culture. Listen to me. I have already admitted the defeat of the opposition. "They" saw in the end that Stalin cannot be overthrown by a *coup d'état,* and their historical experience suggested to them the decision of a repetition (repris) with Stalin of that which had been done with the Tsar. There was here one difficulty, which seemed to us insuperable. In the whole of Europe there was not a single aggressor-State. Not one of them was geographically well placed and had an army sufficient for an attack on Russia. If there was no such country, then "They" had to create it. Only Germany had the corresponding population and positions suitable for an attack on the USSR, and it was capable of defeating Stalin; you can understand that the Weimar republic had not been invented as an aggressor either politically or economically; on the contrary, it was suited to an invasion. On the horizon of a hungry Germany there sparkled the meteor of Hitler. A pair of penetrating eyes fixed their attention on it. The world was the witness to his lightning rise. I shall not say that all of it was the work of our hands, no. His rise, uninterruptedly increasing in extent, took place as the result of the Revolutionary-Communist economy of Versailles. Versailles had had in mind not the creation of preconditions for the triumph of

Hitler, but for the proletarization of Germany, for unemployment and hunger, as the result of which there should have triumphed the Communist revolution. But insofar as, thanks to the existence of Stalin at the head of the USSR and the International, the latter did not succeed, and as a result of an unwillingness to give up Germany to bonapartism, these preconditions were somewhat abated in the Davis and Young Plans, in expectation that meanwhile the opposition would come to power in Russia . . . ; but that, too, did not happen; but the existence of revolutionary preconditions had to produce its results. The economic predetermination of Germany would have forced the proletariat into revolutionary actions. Through the fault of Stalin the Social-International revolution had to be held up and the German proletariat sought inclusion in the National-Socialist revolution. This was dialectical, but given all the preconditions and according to common sense the National-Socialist revolution could never have triumphed there. That was not yet all. It was necessary that the Trotzkyists and Socialists should divide the masses with an already awakened and whole class consciousness—in accordance with instructions. With this business we concerned ourselves. But even more was needed: In 1929, when the National-Socialist Party began to experience a crisis of growth and it had insufficient financial recources, "They" sent their ambassador there. I even know his name: it was one of the Warburgs. In direct negotiations with Hitler they agreed as to the financing of the National-Socialist Party, and the latter received in a couple of years millions of Dollars, sent to it from Wall Street, and millions of Marks from German financiers through Schacht; the upkeep of the S.A. and S.S. and also the financing of the elections which took place, which gave Hitler power, are done on the Dollars and Marks sent by "Them."

G.—Those who, according to you, want to achieve full Communism, arm Hitler, who swears that he will uproot the first Communist nation. This, if one is to believe you, is something very logical for the financiers.

R.—You again forget the Stalinist bonapartism. Remember that against Napoleon, the strangler of the French revolution, who stole its strength, there stood the objective revolutionaries—Louis XVIII, Wellington, Metternich and right up to the Tsar-Autocrat. . . This is 22 carat, according to the strict Stalinist doctrine. You must know by heart his theses about colonies with regard to imperialistic countries. Yes, according to him the Kings of Afghanistan and Egypt are objectively Communists owing to their struggle against His Britannic Majesty; why cannot Hitler be objectively Communist since he is fighting against the autocratic "Tsar Koba I"? (Meaning Stalin—Transl.) After all there is Hitler with his growing military power, and he already extends the boundaries of the Third Reich, and in future will do more . . . to such an extent as to have enough strength and possibilities to attack and fully destroy Stalin. . . Do you not observe the general sympathy of the Versailles wolves, who limit themselves only to a weak growl? Is this yet another chance, accident? Hitler will invade the USSR and as in 1917, when defeat suffered by the Tsar then gave us the opportunity of overthrowing him, so the defeat of Stalin will help us to remove him. . . Again the hour of the world revolution will strike. Since the democratic States, at present put to sleep, will help to bring about the general change at that moment, when Trotzky will take power into his hands, as during the Civil War. Hitler will attack from the West, his generals will rise and liquidate him. . . Now tell me, was not Hitler objectively a Communist? Yes or no?

G.—I do not believe in fairy tales or miracles. . .

R.—Well if you do not want to believe that "They" are able to achieve that which they had already achieved, then prepare to observe an invasion of the USSR and the liquidation of Stalin within a year. You think this is a miracle or an accident, well then prepare to see and experience that. . . But are you really able to refuse to believe that of which I have spoken, though this is still only a hypothesis? You will begin to act in this direction only at that moment when you will begin to see the proofs in the light of my talk.

G.—All right, let us talk in the form of a supposition. What will you say?

R.—You yourself had drawn attention to the coincidence of opinions, which took place between us. We are not at the moment interested in the attack on the USSR, since the fall of Stalin would presuppose the destruction of Communism, the existence of which interests us despite the circumstance that it is formal, as that gives us the certainty that we shall succeed in taking it over and then converting it into real Communism. I think that I have given you the position at the moment quite accurately.

G.—Splendid, the solution. . .

R.—First of all we must make sure that there would be no potential possibility of an attack by Hitler.

G.—If, as you confirm, it were "They" who made him Führer, then they have power over him and he must obey them.

R.—Owing to the fact that I was in a hurry I did not express myself quite correctly and you did not understand me well. If it is true that "They" financed Hitler, then that does not mean that they disclosed to him their existence and their aims. The ambassador Warburg presented himself under a false name and Hitler did not even guess his race; he also lied regarding whose representative he was. He told him that he had been sent by the financial circles of Wall Street who were interested in financing the National-Socialist movement with the aim of creating a threat to France, whose governments pursue a financial policy which provokes a crisis in the USA.

G.—And Hitler believed it?

R.—We do not know. That was not so important, whether he did or did not believe our explanations; our aim was to provoke a war . . . , and Hitler was war. Do you now understand?

G.—I understand. Consequently I do not see any other way of stopping him as the creation of a coalition of the USSR with the democratic nations, which would be capable of frightening Hitler. I think he will not be able to attack simultaneously all the countries of the world. The most would be—each in turn.

R.—Does not a simpler solution come to your mind . . . , I would say—a counter-revolutionary one?

G.—To avoid war against the USSR?

R.—Shorten the phrase by half . . . and repeat with me "avoid war" . . . is that not an absolutely counter-revolutionary thing? Every sincere Communist imitating his idol Lenin and the greatest revolutionary strategists must always wish for war. Nothing is so effective in bringing nearer the victory of revolution as war. This is a Marxist-Leninist dogma, which you must preach. Now further: Stalin's National-Communism, this type of bonapartism, is capable of blinding the intellect of the most pure-blooded Communists, right up to the point at which it prevents their seeing that the transformation into which Stalin has fallen, i.e., that he subjects the revolution to the State, and not the State to the revolution, it would be correct. . .

G.—Your hate of Stalin blinds you and you contradict yourself. Have we not agreed that an attack on the USSR would not be welcome?

R.—But why should war be necessarily against the Soviet Union?

G.—But on what other country could Hitler make war? It is sufficiently clear that he would direct his attack on the USSR, of this he speaks in his speeches. What further proofs do you need?

R.—If you, the people from the Kremlin, consider it to be quite definite and not debatable, then why did you provoke the Civil War in Spain. Do not tell me that it was done for purely revolutionary reasons. Stalin is incapable of carrying out in practice a single Marxist theory. If there were revolutionary considerations here, then it would not be right to sacrifice in Spain so many excellent international revolutionary forces. This is the country which is furthest from the USSR, and the most elementary strategical education would not have allowed the loss of these forces. . . How would Stalin be able in case of conflict to supply and render military help to a Spanish Soviet republic? But this was correct. There we have an important strategic point, a crossing of opposing influences of the Capitalist States . . . , it might have been possible to provoke a war between them. I admit that theoretically this may have been right, but in practice—no. You already see how the war between the democratic Capitalist and fascist States did not begin. And now I shall tell you: if Stalin thought that he was capable of himself creating an excuse sufficient in order to provoke a war, in which the Capitalist States would have had to fight among themselves, then why does he not at least admit, if only theoretically, that others, too, can achieve the same thing, which did not seem impossible to him? . . .

G.—If one is to agree with your assumptions then one can admit this hypothesis.

R.—That means that there is yet a second point of agreement between us: the first—that there must be no war against the USSR; the second—that it would be well to provoke it between the bourgeois States.

G.—Yes, I agree. Is that your personal opinion, or "Theirs"?

R.—I express it as my opinion. I have no power and no contact with "Them," but I can confirm that in these two points it coincides with the view of the Kremlin.

G.—That is the most important thing and for that reason it is important to establish this beforehand. By the way, I would also like to know on what you base yourself in your confidence that "They" approve this.

R.—If I had the time in order to explain their full scheme, then you would already know about the reasons for their approval. At the present moment I shall condense them to three:

G.—Just which?

R.—One is that which I had already mentioned. Hitler, this uneducated and elementary man, has restored thanks to his natural intuition and even against the technical opinion of Schacht, an economic system of a very dangerous kind. Being illiterate in all economic theories and being guided only by necessity he removed, as we had done it in the USSR, the private and international capital. That means that he took over for himself the privilege of manufacturing money, and not only physical moneys, but also financial ones; he took over the untouched machinery of falsification and put it to work for the benefit of the State. He exceeded us, as we, having abolished it in Russia, replaced it merely by this crude apparatus called State Capitalism; this was a very expensive triumph in view of the necessities of pre-revolutionary demagogy. . . Here I give you two real facts for comparison. I shall even say that Hitler had been lucky; he had almost no gold and for that reason he was not tempted to create a gold reserve. Insofar as he only possessed a full monetary guarantee of technical equipment and colossal working capacity of the Germans, his "gold reserve" was technical capacity and work . . . , something so completely counter-revolutionary that, as you already see, he has by means of magic, as it were, radically eliminated unemployment among more than seven million technicians and workers.

G.—Thanks to increased re-armament.

R.—What does your re-armament give? If Hitler reached this despite all the bourgeois economists who surround him, then he was quite capable, in the absence of the danger of war, of applying his system also to peaceful production. . . Are you capable of imagining what would have come of this system if it had infected a number of other States and brought about the creation of a period of autarky. . . For example the Commonwealth. If you can, then imagine its counter-revolutionary functions. . . The danger is not yet inevitable, as we have had luck in that Hitler restored his system not according to some previous theory, but empirically, and he did not make any formulations of a scientific kind.* This means that insofar as he did not think in the light of a deductive process based on intelligence, he has no scientific terms or a formulated doctrine; yet there is a hidden danger as at any moment there can appear, as the consequence of deduction, a formula. This is very serious. Much more so that all the external and cruel factors in National-Socialism. We do not attack it in our propaganda as it could happen that through theoretical polemics we would ourselves provoke a formulation and systematization of this so decisive economic doctrine.** There is only one solution—war.

* Rakovsky is wrong; as he mentions in "Mein Kampf" Hitler had read the works of Gottfried Feder—Transl.

**The problem of a scientific formulation of this question and the propounding of a corresponding programme has engaged the active attention of the publishers of this book and their associates for some years. Their conclusions have been published.

In the translator's book "The Struggle for World Power," second edition 1963, p. 79 a full solution of the monetary problem is set out, and on p. 237 there is a full economic, political and social programme.

These conclusions can be obtained on application.

G.—And the second motive?

R.—If the Termidor triumphed in the Soviet revolution then this happened as the result of the existence of the former Russian nationalism. Without such a nationalism bonapartism would have been impossible. And if that happened in Russia, where nationalism was only embryonic in the person of the Tsar, then what obstacles must Marxism meet in the fully developed nationalism of Western Europe? Marx was wrong with respect to the advantages for the success of the revolution. Marxism won not in the most industrialized country, but in Russia, where the proletariat was small. Apart from other reasons our victory here is explained by the fact that in Russia there was no real nationalism, and in other countries it was in its full apogee. You see how it is reborn under this extraordinary power of fascism, and how infectious it is. You can understand that apart from that it can benefit Stalin, the need for the destruction of nationalism is alone worth a war in Europe.

G.—In sum you have set out, Rakovsky, one economic and one political reason. Which is the third?

R.—That is easy to guess. We have yet another reason, a religious one. Communism cannot be the victor if it will not have suppressed the still living Christianity. History speaks very clearly about this: the permanent revolution required seventeen centuries in order to achieve its first partial victory—by means of the creation of the first split in Christendom. In reality Christianity is our only real enemy, since all the political and economic phenomena in the bourgeois States are only its consequences. Christianity, controlling the individual, is capable of annulling the revolutionary projection of the neutral Soviet or atheistic State by choking it and, as we see it in Russia, things have reached the point of the creation of that spiritual nihilism which is dominant in the ruling masses, which have, nevertheless, remained Christian: this obstacle has not yet been removed during twenty years of Marxism. Let us admit in relation to Stalin that towards religion he was not bonapartistic. We would not have done more than he and would have acted in the same way. And if Stalin had dared, like Napoleon, to cross the Rubikon of Christianity, then his nationalism and counter-revolutionary power would have been increased a thousandfold. In addition, if this had happened then so radical a difference would have made quite impossible any collaboration in anything between us and him, even if this were to be only temporary and objective . . . like the one you can see becoming apparent to us.

G.—And so I personally consider that you have given a definition of three fundamental points, on the basis of which a plan can be made. That is what I am in agreement about with you for the present. But I confirm to you my mental reservations, i.e. my suspicion in relation to all that which you have said concerning people, organizations and facts. Now continue to follow the general lines of your plan.

R.—Yes, now this moment has arrived. But only a preliminary qualification: I shall speak on my own responsibility. I am responsible for the interpretation of those preceding points in the sense in which "They" understand them, but I admit that "They" may consider another plan to be more effective for the attainment of the three aims, and one quite unlike that which I shall now set out. Bear that in mind.

G.—Very well, we shall bear it in mind. Please speak.

R.—We shall simplify. Insofar as the object is missing for which the German military might had been created—to give us power in the USSR—the aim now is to bring about an advance on the fronts and to direct the Hitlerist advance not towards the East, but the West.

G.—Exactly. Have you thought of the practical plan of realization?

R.—I had had more than enough time for that at the Lubianka. I considered. So look: if there were difficulties in finding mutually shared points between us and all else took its normal course, then the problems comes down to again trying to establish that in which there is similarity between Hitler and Stalin.

G.—Yes, but admit that all this is problematical.

R.—But not insoluble, as you think. In reality problems are insoluble only when they include dialectical subjective contradictions; and even in that case we always consider possible and essential a synthesis, overcoming the "morally-impossible" of Christian metaphysicians.

G.—Again you begin to theorize.

R.—As the result of my intellecutal discipline—this is essential for me. People of a big culture prefer to approach the concrete through a generalization, and not the other way round. With Hitler and with Stalin one can find common ground, as, being very different people, they have the same roots; if Hitler is sentimental to a pathological degree, but Stalin is normal, yet both of them are egoists: neither one of them is an idealist, and for that reason both of them are bonapartists, i.e. classical Imperialists. And if just that is the position, then it is already not difficult to find common ground between them. Why not, if it proved possible between one Tsarina and one Prussian King. . .

G.—Rakovsky, you are incorrigible. . .

R.—You do not guess? If Poland was the point of union between Catherine and Frederick—the Tsarina of Russia and the King of Germany at that time, then why cannot Poland serve as a reason for the finding of common ground between Hitler and Stalin? In Poland the persons of Hitler and Stalin can coincide, and also the historical Tsarist-Bolshevik and Nazi lines. Our line, "Their" line—also, as Poland is a Christian State and, what makes the matter even more complex, a Catholic one.

G.—And what follows from the fact of such a treble coincidence?

R.—If there is common ground then there is a possibility of agreement.

G.—Between Hitler and Stalin? . . . Absurd! Impossible.

R.—In politics there are neither absurdities, nor the impossible.

G.—Let us imagine, as an hypothesis: Hitler and Stalin advance on Poland.

R.—Permit me to interrupt you; an attack can be called forth only by the following alternative: war or peace. You must admit it.

G.—Well, and so what?

R.—Do you consider that England and France, with their worse armies and aviation, in comparison with Hitler's, can attack the united Hitler and Stalin?

G.—Yes, that seems to me to be very difficult . . . unless America. . .

R.—Let us leave the United States aside for the moment. Will you agree with me that as the result of the attack of Hitler and Stalin on Poland there can be no European war?

G.—You argue logically; it would seem impossible.

R.—In that case an attack or war would be useless. It would not call forth the mutual destruction of the bourgeois States: the Hitlerist threat to the USSR would continue in being after the division of Poland since theoretically both Germany and the USSR would have been strengthened to the same extent. In practice Hitler to a greater extent, since the USSR does not need more land and raw materials for its strengthening, but Hitler does need them.

G.—This is a correct view . . . , but I can see no other solution.

R.—No, there is a solution.

G.—Which?

R.—That the democracies should attack and not attack the aggressor.

G.—What are you saying, what hallucination! Simultaneously to attack and not to attack. . . That is something absolutely impossible.

R.—You think so? Calm down. . . Are there not two aggressors? Did we not agree that there will be no advance just because there are two? Well. . . What prevents the attack on one of them?

G.—What do you want to say by that?

R.—Simply that the democracies will declare war only on one aggressor, and that will be Hitler.

G.—Yes, but that is an unfounded hypothesis.

R.—An hypothesis, but having a foundation. Consider: each State which will have to fight with a coalition of enemy States has as its main strategical objective to destroy them separately one after another. This rule is so well known that proofs are superfluous. So, agree with me that there are no obstacles to the creation of such conditions. I think that the question that Stalin will not consider himself aggrieved in case of an attack on Hitler is already settled. Is that not so? In addition geography imposes this attitude, and for that reason strategy also. However stupid France and England may be in preparing to fight simultaneously against two countries, one of which wants to preserve its neutrality, while the other, even being alone, represents for them a serious opponent, from where and from which side could they carry out an attack on the USSR? They have not got a common border; unless they were to advance over the Himalayas. . . Yes, there remains the air front, but with what forces and from where could they invade Russia? In comparison with Hitler they are weaker in the air. All the arguments I have mentioned are no secret and are well known. As you see, all is simplified to a considerable extent.

G.—Yes, your arguments seem to be logical in the case if the conflict will be limited to four countries; but there are not four, but more, and neutrality is not a simple matter in a war on the given scale.

R.—Undoubtedly, but the possible participation of many countries does not change the power relationships. Weigh this in your mind and you will see how the balance will continue, even if others or even all European States come in. In addition, and this is very important, not one of those States, which will enter the war at the side of England and France will be able to deprive them of leadership; as a result the reasons which will prevent their attack on the USSR will retain their significance.

G.—You forget about the United States.

R.—In a moment you will see that I have not forgotten. I shall limit myself to the investigation of their function in the preliminary programme, which occupies us at present, and I shall say that America will not be able to force France and England to attack Hitler and Stalin simultaneously. In order to attain that the United States would have to enter the war from the very first day. But that is impossible. In the first place because America did not enter a war formerly and never will do so if it is not attacked. Its rulers can arrange that they will be attacked, if that will suit them. Of that I can assure you. In those cases when provocation was not successful and the enemy did not react to it, aggression was invented. In their first international war, the war against Spain, of the defeat of which they were sure, they invented an aggression, or, more correctly, "They" invented it. In 1914 provocation was successful. True, one can dispute technically if there was one, but the rule without exceptions is that he who makes a sudden attack without warning, does it with the help of a provocation. Now it is like this: this splendid American technique which I welcome at any moment, is subject to one condition: that aggression should take place at a suitable moment, i.e. the moment required by the United States who are being attacked; that means then, when they will have the arms. Does this condition exist now? It is clear that it does not. In America there are at present a little less than one hundred thousand men under arms and a middling aviation: it has only an imposing fleet. But you can understand that, having it, it can not persuade its allies to decide on an attack on the USSR, since England and France have preponderance only at sea. I have also proved to you that from that side there can be no change in the comparative strengths of the forces.

G.—Having agreed with this, I ask you again to explain once more the technical realization.

R.—As you have seen, given the coincidence of the interests of Stalin and Hitler with regard to an attack on Poland, all comes down to the formalization of this full similarity of aims and to make a pact about a double attack.

G.—And you think this is easy?

R.—Frankly, no. Here we need a diplomacy which is more experienced than that of Stalin. There ought to have been available the one which Stalin had decapitated, or the one which now decays in the Lubianka. In former times Litvinov would have been capable, with some difficulties, although his race would have been a great obstacle for negotiations with Hitler; but now this is a finished man and he is destroyed by a terrible panic; he is experiencing an animal fear of Molotov, even more than of Stalin. His whole talent is directed towards making sure that they should not think that he is a Trotzkyist. If he were to hear of the necessity of arranging closer relations with Hitler, then that would be enough for him to manufacture for himself the proof of his Trotzkyism. I do not see a man who is capable of this job; in any event he would have to be a pure-blooded Russian. I could offer my services for guidance. At the present moment I would suggest to the one who begins the talks, that they should be strictly confidential, but with great open sincerity. Given a whole wall of various prejudices only truthfulness can deceive Hitler.

G.—I again do not understand your paradoxial expressions.

R.—Forgive me, but this only appears to be so; I am forced by the synthesis to do so. I wanted to say that with Hitler one must play a clean game concerning the concrete and most immediate questions. It is necessary to shew him that the game is not played in order to provoke him into war on two fronts. For example, it is possible to promise him and to prove at the most suitable moment that our mobilization will be limited to a small number of forces, required for the invasion of Poland, and that these forces will not be great. According to our real plan we shall have to place our main forces to meet the possible Anglo-French attack. Stalin will have to be generous with the preliminary supplies which Hitler will demand, chiefly oil. That is what has come to my mind for the moment. Thousands of further questions will arise, of a similar character, which will have to be solved so that Hitler, seeing in practice that we only want to occupy our part of Poland, would be quite certain of that. And insofar as in practice it should be just like that, he will be deceived by the truth.

G.—But in what, in this case, is there a deception?

R.—I shall give you a few minutes of time so that you yourself can discover just in what there is a deception of Hitler. But first I want to stress, and you should take note, that the plan which I have indicated here, is logical and normal and I think that one can achieve that the Capitalistic States will destroy each other, if one brings about a clash of their two wings: the fascist and the bourgeois. I repeat that the plan is logical and normal. As you have already been able to see, there is no intervention here of mysterious or unusual factors. In short, in order that one should be able to realize the plan, "Their" intervention is not required. Now I should like to guess your thoughts; are you not now thinking that it would be stupid to waste time on proving the unprovable existence and power held by "Them." Is that not so?

G.—You are right.

R.—Be frank with me. Do you really not observe their intervention? I informed you, wanting to help you, that their intervention exists and is decisive, and for that reason the logic and naturalness of the plan are only appearances. . . Is it really true that you do not see "Them"?

G.—Speaking sincerely, no.

R.—The logic and naturalness of my plan is only an appearance. It would be natural and logical that Hitler and Stalin would inflict defeat on each other. For the democracies that would be a simple and easy thing, if they would have to put forward such an aim; for them it would be enough that Hitler should be permitted, make note "permitted" to attack Stalin. Do not tell me that Germany could be defeated. If the Russian distances and the dreadful fear of Stalin and his henchmen of the Hitlerite axe and the revenge of their victims will not be enough in order to attain the military exhaustion of Germany, then there will be no obstacles to the democracies, seeing that Stalin is losing strength, beginning to help him wisely and methodically, continuing to give that help until the complete exhaustion of both armies. In reality that would be easy, natural and logical, if those motives and aims which are put forward by the democracies and which most of their followers believe to be the true ones, and not what they are in reality—pretexts. There is only one aim, one single aim: the triumph of Communism; it is not Moscow which will impose its will on the democracies, but New York, not the "Comintern," but the "Capintern" on Wall Street. Who other that he could have been able to impose on Europe such an obvious and absolute contradiction? What force can lead it towards complete suicide? Only one force is able to do this: money. Money is power and the sole power.

G.—I shall be frank with you, Rakovsky. I admit in you an exceptional gift of talent. You possess brilliant dialectic, persuasive and subtle: when this is not enough for you, then your imagination has command of means in order to extend your colourful canvas, while you invent brilliant and clear perspectives; but all this, although it provokes my enthusiasm, is not enough for me. I shall go over to putting questions to you, assuming that I believe all that you have said.

R.—And I shall give you replies, but with one single condition, that you should not add anything to what I shall say, nor deduct.

G.—I promise. You assert that "They" hinder or will hinder a German-Soviet war, which is logical from the point of view of the Capitalists. Have I explained it correctly?

R.—Yes, precisely so.

G.—But the reality of the present moment is such that Germany has been permitted to re-arm and expand. This is a fact. I already know that in accordance with your explanation this was called forth by the Trotzkyist plan, which fell through thanks to the "cleanings-out" now taking place; thus the aim has been lost. In the face of a new situation you only advise that Hitler and Stalin should sign a pact and divide Poland. I ask you: how can we obtain a guarantee that, having the pact, or not having it, carrying out, or not carrying out the partition, Hitler will not attack the USSR?

R.—This cannot be guaranteed.

G.—Then why go on talking?

R.—Do not hurry. The magnificent threat to the USSR is real and exists. This is not an hypothesis and not a verbal threat. It is a fact. and a fact which obliges. "They" already have superiority over Stalin; a superiority which cannot be denied. Stalin is offered only one alternative, the right to choose, but not full freedom. The attack of Hitler will come in any case of its own accord; "They" need not do anything to make it happen but only leave him the chance of acting. This is the basic and determining reality, which has been forgotten by you owing to your excessively Kremlin-like way of thinking. . . Egocentrism, Sir, egocentrism.

G.—The right to choose?

R.—I shall define it exactly once more, but shortly: either there will be an attack on Stalin, or there will come the realization of the plan I have indicated, according to which the European Capitalistic

States will destroy each other. I drew attention to this alternative, but as you see it was only a theoretical one. If Stalin wants to survive then he will be forced to realize the plan which has been proposed by me and ratified by "Them."

G.—But if he refuses?

R.—That will be impossible for him. The expansion and re-armament of Germany will continue. When Stalin will be faced by this gigantic threat . . . , then what will he do? This will be dictated to him by his own instinct of self-preservation.

G.—It seems that events must develop only according to the orders indicated by "Them."

R.—And it is so. Of course, in the USSR to-day things still stand like this; but sooner or later it will happen like that all the same. It is not difficult to foretell and to suggest for carrying out something, if it is profitable for the person who must realize the matter; in the given case Stalin, who is hardly thinking of suicide. It is much more difficult to give a prognosis and to force to act as needed someone for whom that is not profitable, but who must act nevertheless; in the given case the democracies. I have kept the explanation for this moment to give a concrete picture of the true position. Reject the wrong thought that you are the arbiters in the given situation, since "They" are the arbiters.

G.—"They" both in the first and the second case. . . Therefore we must deal with shadows?

R.—But are facts shadows? The international situation will be extraordinary, but not shadowy; it is real and very real. This is not a miracle; here is predetermined the future policy. . . Do you think this is the work of shadows?

G.—But let us see; let us assume that your plan is accepted. . . But we must have something tangible, personal, in order to be able to carry out negotiations.

R.—For example?

G.—Some person with powers of attorney and representation.

R.—But for what? Just for the pleasure of becoming acquainted with him? For the pleasure of a talk? Bear in mind that the assumed person, in case of his appearance, will not present you with credentials with seals and crests and will not wear a diplomatic uniform, at least a man from "Them"; if he were to say something or promise, then it will have no juridical force or meaning as a pact. . . Understand that "They" are not a State; "They" are that which the International was before 1917, that which it still is: nothing and at the same time every-thing. Imagine to yourself if it is possible that the USSR would have negotiations with freemasonry, with an espionage organization, with the Macedonian Komitadgi or the Croatian Ustashi. Would not some juridical agreement be written? . . . Such pacts as the pact of Lenin with the German General Staff, as the pact of Trotzky with "Them"—are realized without written documents and without signatures. The only guarantee of their execution is rooted in the circumstance that the carrying out of that which has been agreed is profitable for the parties to the pact, this guarantee is the sole reality in the pact, however great may be its importance.

G.—From what would you begin in the present case?

R.—Simple; I should begin already from to-morrow to sound out Berlin. . .

G.—In order to agree about the attack on Poland?

R.—I would not begin with that . . . I would display my willingness to yield and would hint about certain disappointments among the democracies, I would soft-pedal in Spain. . . This would be an act of encouragement; then I would drop a hint about Poland. As you see—nothing compromising, but enough so that a part of the OKW (German High Command—Transl.), the Bismarckists, as they are called, would have some arguments to put before Hitler.

G.—And nothing more?

R.—For the beginning, nothing more; this is already a big diplomatic task.

G.—Speaking frankly, having in mind the aims which have been dominant in the Kremlin until now, I do not think that anyone would at present dare to advise such a radical change in international policy. I propose to you, Rakovsky, to transform yourself in imagination into that person at the Kremlin which will have to take the decision. . . On the basis only of your disclosures, arguments, your hypotheses and persuasion, as I see it, it would be impossible to convince anyone. I personally, after having listened to you and at the same time, I shall not deny it, having experienced a strong influence from your explanations, of your personality, have not for a single moment experienced the temptation to consider the German-Soviet pact to be something realizable.

R.—International events will force with irresistible strength. . .

G.—But that would be a loss of valuable time. Consider something concrete, something which I could put forward as a proof of your veracity and credibility. . . In the contrary case I should not dare to transmit your information about our conversation; I should edit it with all accuracy, but it would reach the Kremlin archives and stay there.

R.—Would it not be enough to bring about that it is taken into consideration if someone, even in a most official manner, were to have a talk with some very important person?

G.—It seems to me that this would be something real.

R.—But with whom?

G.—This is only my personal opinion, Rakovsky. You had mentioned concrete persons, big financiers; if I remember correctly, you had spoken about a certain Schiff, for example; then you mentioned another who had been the go-between with Hitler for the purpose of financing him. There are also politicians or persons with a big position, who belong to "Them" or, if you like, serve "Them." Someone like that could be of use to us in order to start something practical. . . Do you know someone?

R.—I do not think it is necessary. . . Think: about what will you be negotiating? Probably about the plan which I have set out, is that not so? For what? At the present moment "They" need not do anything in this context; "Their" mission is "not to do." And for that reason you would not be able to agree about any positive action and could not demand it. . . Remember, consider well.

G.—Even if that is so, yet in view of our personal opinion there must be a reality, even if a useless one . . . , a man, a personality which would confirm the credibility of the power, which you ascribe to "Them."

R.—I shall satisfy you, although I am sure of the uselessness of this. I have already told you that I do not know who is a part of "Them," but have assurances from a person who must have known them."

G.—From whom?

R.—From Trotzky. From Trotzky I know only that one of "Them" was Walter Rathenau, who was well known from Rapallo. You see the last of "Them" who occupied a political and social position, since it was he who broke the economic blockade of the USSR. Despite the fact that he was one of the biggest millionaires; of course, such also was Lionel Rothschild. I can with confidence mention only these names. Naturally I can name still more people, the work and personality of whom I determine as being fully "Theirs," but I cannot confirm what these people command or whom they obey.

G.—Mention some of them.

R.—As an institutions—the Bank of Kuhn, Loeb & Co., of Wall Street; to this bank belong the families of Schiff, Warburg, Loeb and Kuhn; I say families in order to point out several names, since they are all connected among themselves by marriages; then Baruch, Frankfurter, Altschul, Cohen, Benjamin, Strauss, Steinhardt, Blom, Rosenman, Lippmann, Lehman, Dreifus, Lamont, Rothschild, Lord, Mandel, Morgenthau, Ezekiel, Lasky. I think that that will be enough names; if I were to strain my memory, then perhaps I would remember some more, but I repeat, that I do not know who among them can be one of "Them" and I cannot even assert, that any one of them is definitely of their number; I want to avoid any responsibility. But I certainly think that any one of the persons I have enumerated, even of those not belonging to "Them," could always lead to "Them" with any proposition of an important type. Of course, independently of whether this or that person does or does not belong to "Them," one cannot expect a direct reply. The answer will be given by facts. That is the unchangeable tactic which they prefer and with which they force one to reckon. For example, if you would risk beginning diplomatic initiatives, then you would not need to make use of the method of a personal approach to "Them"; one must limit oneself to the expression of thoughts, the exposition of some rational hypothesis, which depends on unknown definite factors. Then it only remains to wait.

G.—You understand that I have not got a card-index at my disposal at the moment, in order to establish all the men you have mentioned; I assume that they are probably somewhere far away. Where?

R.—Most of them in the United States.

G.—Please understand that if we were to decide to act, then we would have to devote much time to it. But the matter is urgent, and urgent not for us, but for you, Rakovsky.

R.—For me?

G.—Yes, for you. Remember that your trial will take place very soon. I do not know, but I think it will not be risky to assume that if all that had been discussed here were to interest the Kremlin, then it must interest them before you appear before the tribunal: that would be for you a decisive matter. I think it is in your personal interests that you should propose something quicker to us. The most important thing is to get proofs that you spoke the truth, and to do this not during a period of several weeks, but during several days. I think that if you were to succeed in this, then I could nearly give you fairly solid assurances concerning the possibility of saving your life. . . In the contrary case I answer for nothing.

R.—In the end I shall take the risk. Do you know if Davis is at present in Moscow? Yes, the Ambassador of the United States.

G.—I think he is; he should have returned.

R.—Only an exceptional situation gives me the right, as I see it, against the rules, to make use of an official intermediary.

G.—Therefore we can think that the American Government is behind all this. . .

R.—Behind—no under all this. . .

G.—Roosevelt?

R.—What do I know? I can only come to conclusions. You are all the time obsessed with the mania of political espionage. I could manufacture, in order to please you, a whole history; I have more than sufficient imagination, dates and true facts in order to give it veracity in appearance, which would be close to looking obvious. But are not the generally known facts more obvious? And you can supplement them with your own imagination, if you wish. Look yourself. Remember the morning of the 24th October 1929. The time will come when this day will be for the history of the revolution more important than October, 1917. On the day of the 24th October there took place the crash of the New York Stock Exchange, the beginning of the so-called "depression," a real revolution. The four years of the Government of Hoover—are years of revolutionary progress: 12 and 15 millions on strike. In February, 1933 there takes place the last stroke of the crisis with the closing of the banks. It is difficult to do more than capital did in order to break the "classical American," who was still on his industrial bases and in the economic respect enslaved by Wall Street. It is well known that any impoverishment in economics, be it in relation to societies or animals, gives a flourishing of parasitism, and capital is a large parasite. But this American revolution pursued not only the one aim of increasing the power of money for those who had the right to use it; it pretended to even more. Although the power of money is political power, but before that it had only been used indirectly, but now the power of money was to be transformed into direct power. The man through whom they made use of such power was Franklin Roosevelt. Have you understood? Take note of the following: In that year 1929, the first year of the American revolution, in February Trotzky leaves Russia; the crash takes place in October. . . The financing of Hitler is agreed in July, 1929. You think that all this was by chance? The four years of the rule of Hoover were used for the preparation of the seizure of power in the United States and the USSR; there by means of a financial revolution, and here with the help of war and the defeat which was to follow. Could some good novel with great imagination be more obvious to you? You can understand that the execution of the plan on such a scale requires a special man, who can direct the executive power in the United States, who has been predetermined to be the organizing and deciding force. That man was Franklin and Eleanor Roosevelt. And permit me to say that this two-sexed being is not simply irony. He had to avoid any possible Delilah.

G.—Is Roosevelt one of "Them"?

R.—I do not know if he is one of "Them," or is only subject to "Them." What more do you want? I think that he was conscious of his mission, but cannot assert whether he obeyed under duress of blackmail or he was one of those who rule; it is true that he carried out his mission, realized all the actions which had been assigned to him accurately. Do not ask me more, as I do not know any more.

G.—In case it should be decided to approach Davis, in which form would you do it?

R.—First of all you must select a person of such a type as "the baron"; he could be useful. . . Is he still alive?

G.—I do not know.

R.—All right, the choice of persons is left to you. Your delegate must present himself as being confidential or not modest, but best of all as a secret oppositionist. The conversation must be cleverly conducted concerning that contradictory position into which the USSR has been put by the so-called European democracies, by their union against National-Socialism. This is the conclusion of an alliance with the British and French Imperialism, the contemporary real Imperialism, for the destruction of the potential Imperialism. The aim of the verbal expressions must be to conjoin the false Soviet position with an equally false one of American democracy. . . It also sees itself forced to support Colonial Imperialism for the defence of democracy within England and France. As you see, the question can be put onto a very strong logical foundation. After that it is already very easy to formulate an hypothesis about actions. The first: that neither the USSR, nor the United States are interested in European Imperialism and thus the dispute is brought down to the question of personal hegemony; that ideologically and economically Russia and America want the destruction of European Colonial Imperialism, be it direct or oblique. The United States want it even more. If Europe were to lose all its power in a new war, then England, not having its own forces, with the disappearance of Europe as a force, as power, would from the first day lean, with all its weight and with the whole of its Empire, speaking the English language, on the United States, which would be inevitable both in the political and economic sense. . . Analyze what you have heard in the light of the Left conspiracy, as one might say, without shocking any American bourgeois. Having got to this point, one could have an interval for a few days. Then, having noted the reaction, it will be necessary to move further. Now Hitler comes forward. Here one can point to any aggression: he is fully an aggressor and of this there can be no doubt. And then one can go over to asking a question: What common action should be undertaken by the United States and the Soviet Union in view of the war between the Imperialists, who want it? The answer could be—neutrality. One must argue again: yes, neutrality, but it does not depend on the wish of one side, but also of the aggressor. There can be a guarantee of neutrality only when the aggressor cannot attack or it does not suit him. For this purpose the infallible answer is the attack of the aggressor on another Imperialist State. From this it is very easy to go over to the expression of the necessity and morality, with a view to guaranteeing safety, for provoking a clash between the Imperialists, if that clash were not to take place of its own accord. And if that were to be accepted in theory, and it will be accepted, then one can regulate the question of actions in practice, which would be only a matter of technique. Here is a scheme: (1) A pact with Hitler for the division between us of Czechoslovakia and Poland (better the latter). (2) Hitler will accept. If he is capable of backing a bluff for the conquest, i.e. the seizure of something in alliance with the USSR, then for him there will be full guarantee in that the democracies will yield. He will be unable to believe their verbal threats as he knows that those who try to intimidate by war threats are at the same time partisans of disarmament and that their disarmament is real. (3) The democracies will attack Hitler and not Stalin; they will tell the people that although both are guilty of aggression and partition, but strategical and logical reasons force them to defeat them one by one: first Hitler and then Stalin.

G.—But will they not deceive us with truth?

R.—But how? Does not Stalin dispose of freedom of action in order to help Hitler in sufficient measure? Do we not put in his hands the possibility of continuing the war between the Capitalists until the last man and the last pound? With what can they attack him? The exhausted States of the West will already have enough on their hands with internal Communist revolution, which in the other case may triumph.

G.—But if Hitler achieves a quick victory and if he, like Napoleon, mobilizes the whole of Europe against the USSR?

R.—This is quite improbable! You forget about the existence of the United States. You reject the power factor, a greater one. Is it not natural that America, imitating Stalin, would on its part help the democratic States? If one were to co-ordinate "against the hands of the clock" the help to both groups of fighters, then thus there will be assured without failure a permanent extension of the war.

G.—And Japan?

R.—Is not China enough for them? Let Stalin guarantee them his non-intervention. The Japanese are very fond of suicide, but after all not to such an extent as to be capable of simultaneously attacking China and the USSR. Any more objections?

G.—No, if it were to depend on me, then I would try. . . But do you believe that the delegate. . . ?

R.—Yes, I believe. I was not given the chance of speaking with him, but note one detail: the appointment of Davis became known in November, 1936; we must assume that Roosevelt thought of sending him much sooner and with that in mind began preliminary steps; we all know that the consideration of the matter and the official explanations of the appointment take more than two months. Apparently his appointment was agreed in August. . . And what happened in August? In August Zinoviev and Kamenev were shot. I am willing to swear that his appointment was made for the purpose of a new involvement of "Them" in the politics of Stalin. Yes, I certainly think so. With what an inner excitement must he have travelled, seeing how one after another there fall the chiefs of the opposition in the "purges" which follow one on another. Do you know if he was present at trial of Radeck?

G.—Yes.

R.—You will see him. Have a talk with him. He expects it already for many months.

G.—This night we must finish; but before we part I want to know something more. Let us assume that all this is true and all will be carried out with full success. "They" will put forward definite conditions. Guess what they might be?

R.—This is not difficult to assume. The first condition will be the ending of the executions of the Communists, that means the Trotzkyists, as you call them. Then, of course, they will demand the establishment of several zones of influence, as I had mentioned. The boundaries which will have to divide the formal Communism from the real one. That is the most important condition. There will be mutual concessions for mutual help for a time, while the plan lasts, being carried out. You will see for example the paradoxial phenomenon that a whole crowd of people, enemies of Stalin, will help him; no they will not necessarily be proletarians, nor will they be professional spies. There will appear influential persons at all levels of society, even very high ones, who will help the Stalinist formal Communism when it becomes if not real, then at least objective Communism. Have you understood me?

G.—A little; you wrap up such things in such impenetrable casuistry.

R.—If it is necessary to end, then I can only express myself in this way. Let us see if I shall not be able yet to help to understand. It is known that Marxism was called Hegelian. So this question was vulgarised. Hegelian idealism is a widespread adjustment to an uninformed understanding in the West of the natural mysticism of Baruch Spinosa. "They" are spinosists: perhaps the matter is the other way round, i.e. that spinosism is "Them," insofar as he is only a version adequate to the epoch of "Their" own philosophy, which is a much earlier one, standing on a much higher level. After all, a hegelian and for that reason also the follower of Spinosa, was devoted to his faith, but only temporarily, tactically. The matter does not stand as is claimed by Marxism, that as the result of the elimination of contradictions there arises the synthesis. It is as the result of the opposing mutual fusion, from the thesis and anti-thesis that there arises, as a synthesis, the reality, truth, as a final harmony between the subjective and objective. Do you not see that already? In Moscow there is Communism; in New York Capitalism. It is all the same as a thesis and anti-thesis. Analyze both. Moscow is subjective Communism, but Capitalism—objective—State Capitalism. New York: Capitalism subjective, but Communism objective. A personal synthesis, truth: the Financial International, the Capitalist-Communist one. "They."

* * *

The meeting had lasted about six hours. I once more gave some drug to Rakovsky. The drug it was obvious, worked well, although I was only able to observe this by certain symptoms of animation. But I think that Rakovsky would have spoken just the same in a normal condition. Undoubtedly the theme of the conversation concerned his speciality and he had the passionate will to expose that, about which he spoke. Since, if all this is true then an energetic attempt had been made to enforce the triumph of his idea and plan. If this was untrue, then there was an extraordinary phantasy and this was a wonderful manoeuvre for saving his already lost life.

My opinion of all that had been heard can not be of any importance. I have not got a sufficient erudition in order to understand its universality and horizons. When Rakovsky touched on the most important part of the theme I had the same feeling as at that moment when I saw myself for the first time on the X-ray screen. My surprised eyes saw something diffuse and dark, but real. Something like an apparition; I had to co-ordinate his figure and movements, corelations and actions to the degree to which it was possible to guess with the help of logical intuition.

I think that I had observed during several hours the "radiograph of revolution" on a world-wide scale. It is possible that in part it failed, was deformed, thanks to circumstances or personalities which reflected it; it is not for nothing that the lie and dissimulation are permitted in the revolutionary struggle and are accepted as moral. And Rakovsky, a passionate dialectician of great culture and a first-class orator, is first of all and above all a revolutionary fanatic.

I re-read the conversation many times, but each time I felt how there rose in me the feeling of my incompetence in this respect. That which until then had seemed to me, and to the whole world, to be the truth and obvious reality, like blocks of granite, where the social order stands as on a rock, immovable and permanent, all that became transformed into a thick fog. There appear colossal, unmeasurable, invisible forces with a categorical imperative, disobedient, sly and titanic at the same time; something like magnetism, electricity or the attraction of the earth. In the presence of this phenomenal disclosure I felt like the man from the stone age, whose head was still full of primitive superstitions concerning the phenomena of nature, and who had been suddenly transposed one night into the Paris of to-day. I am amazed even more than he would have been.

Many times I disagreed. At first I convinced myself that everything which Rakovsky was telling was the product of his extraordinary imagination. But even having convinced myself that I was a toy in the hands of the biggest of all the writers of novels, I tried in vain to find enough strength, logical reasons and even people with a sufficient personality, who would have been able to explain this gigantic progress of the revolution.

I must confess that if only those forces participated here, as also reasons and people, which are mentioned officially in written histories, then I must declare that the revolution is a miracle of our age. No, when I was listening to Rakovsky, I could not admit that a small group of Jews, who emigrated from London, had achieved that this "apparition of revolution," which had been called forth by Marx in the first lines of the Manifesto, had become to-day a gigantic reality and a universal threat.

Whether what Rakovsky told is true or not, whether the secret and real strength of Communism is International Capital, it is the obvious truth for me that Marx, Lenin, Trotzky and Stalin are an insufficient explanation for that which is happening.

Whether these people are real or phantastic, whom Rakovsky calls "Them" with an almost religious tremor in his voice, is the question. But if "They" do not exist then I shall have to say of them what Voltaire said of God: "He will have to be invented," since only in that case can we explain the existence, extent and force of this world-wide revolution.

After all, I have no hope of seeing it. My position does not allow me to view with great optimism the possibility that I shall survive until the near future. But this suicide of the bourgeois European States, of which Rakovsky spoke, and which he proves as being inevitable, would be for me, who has been initiated into the secret, the magisterial and definite proof.

* * *

When Rakovsky had been led away to his place of imprisonment Gabriel remained some time immersed in himself.

I looked at him, not seeing him; and in fact my own ideas and conceptions had lost the ground under their feet and were somehow suspended.

"How do you look on all this" asked Gabriel.

"I do not know, I do not know" I replied, and I spoke the truth; but I added "I think that this is an amazing man and if we are dealing with a falsification, then it is extraordinary; in any event it is a piece of genius."

"As a result, if we shall have the time, we must have an exchange of views. . . I am always interested in your opinion of the profane, a doctor. But now we must agree about our programme. I need you as a professional, but as a modest man. That which you have heard, as the result of your peculiar function, can be wind and smoke which is carried by the wind, but it can also be something, the importance of which cannot be exceeded by anything else. Here a moderate terminology is inappropriate. Given this last possibility, a strong feeling of precaution forces me to limit the number of people who know about it. For the moment only you and I know. The man who manipulated the recording machine does not know any French. The fact that we did not speak in Russian was not my caprice. In short: I shall be grateful to you if you will be the translator. Sleep for some hours. I shall now give the necessary instructions so that the technician would agree the time with you, and as soon as possible you must translate and write down the conversation, which he will reproduce for you to hear. It will be a hard job; you cannot use a typewriter and the recorder will have to move very slowly. When you will have done the French version, I shall read it. A few remarks and epigraphs will be necessary, and I shall add them. You can use a typewriter?"

"Very badly, very slowly, only with two fingers."

"Well arrange it somehow. Please make few mistakes."

Gabriel called the man. We arranged to begin work at eleven o'clock and it was already almost seven. We went to sleep a little.

I was called punctually. We sat down in my small study.

Gabriel had asked me to make two copies of the translation. I made three, in order to hide one for myself. I took the risk as he went to Moscow. I am not sorry that I had had the courage for this.

* * *

EPILOGUE

As is well known, Stalin followed the advice of Rakovsky. There was a pact with Hitler. Also the Second World War served solely the interests of the revolution.

The secret of these changes of policy can be understood from a further conversation between Gabriel and Doctor Landowsky, which is given in a later chapter of "The Red Symphony." Here are some extracts from it:

GABRIEL—Do you remember the conversation with Rakovsky. . . Do you know that he was not condemned to death? Well knowing all this you need not be surprised that Comrade Stalin had thought it to be wise to try that apparently so unlikely plan. . . Here nothing is risked and, on the contrary, one can gain a great deal. . . If you will strain your memory you will be able to understand several things.

DOCTOR—I remember everything rather well. Do not forget that I heard the conversation twice, then both times I wrote it, and in addition I translated it. . . May I find out if you know the people whom Rakovsky called "Them"?

G.—In order to shew you my confidence I shall tell you—no! We do not know for sure who "They" are, but at the last moment there was confirmed a great deal of what Rakovsky had told; for example it is true that Hitler was financed by the Wall Street bankers. Much else is also true. All these months during which I have not seen you, I devoted to an investigation, connected with Rakovsky's information. It is true that I was not able to establish just which people are such remarkable personages, but it is a fact, that there is a kind of entourage which consists of financiers, politicians, scientists and even ecclesiastical persons of high rank, wealth and power, who occupy high places; if one is to judge their position (mostly as intermediaries) by the results, then it seems strange and inexplicable, at least in the light of ordinary conceptions . . . since in fact they have a great similarity with the ideas of Communism. Of course with very special Communist ideas. But let us leave all these questions aside, concerning complexion, line and profile; objectively, as Rakovsky would have said, they, imitating Stalin blindly in actions and errors, are building Communism. They followed the advice of Rakovsky almost to the letter. There was nothing concrete, but there was no refusal and no tearing of mantles. On the contrary, they displayed great attention to everything. The Ambassador Davis carefully hinted at the past trials and even went so far as to hint that much would be gained in the public opinion in America, in case of an amnesty for Rakovsky in the near future. He was well watched during the trials in March, which is natural. He was himself present at all of them; we did not allow him to bring any technicians so as to prevent any "telegraphing" with the accused. He is not a professional diplomat and does not know the specific techniques. He was obliged to look on, trying with his eyes to say much, as I thought; we think that he raised the spirits of Rosenholz and of Rakovsky. The latter confirmed the interest which had been displayed at the trial by Davis and confessed that he made him a secret sign of masonic greeting.

There is yet another strange matter, which cannot be falsified. On the 2nd March at dawn there was received a radio message from some very powerful station: "Amnesty or the Nazi danger will increase" . . . The radiogramme was encyphered in the cypher of our own embassy in London. You can understand that that was something very important!

Dr.—But the threat was not real?

G.—How not? On the 12th March there ended the debates of the Supreme Tribunal and at 9 in the evening the tribunal began its considerations. And on that same day of the 12th March, at 5.30 o'clock a.m. Hitler ordered his armoured divisions to enter Austria. Of course this was a military promenade! Were there sufficient reasons for thinking about that? Or we had to be so stupid as to consider the greetings of Davis, the radiogramme, the cypher, the coincidence of the invasion with the verdict, and also the silence of Europe as being only accidental chances? No, in fact we did not see "Them," but we heard their voice and understood their language.

* * *

Translator's note: It would be quite superfluous to write a long commentary on this remarkable material. It should suffice to say the obvious—this is one of the most important political documents of the century.

Many of us have known the facts here brought out for decades, but for the first time we get a brilliant, detailed statement from an insider. Obviously Rakovsky was one of "Them."

Both the internal evidence of this document, as well as the circumstance that all subsequent events went exactly according to the formulae indicated, proves the truth of the story.

This book should be essential reading for all who wish to know what is happening and why, throughout the world, and also what alone can be done to stop the conquests of the revolution: the power of monetary emission must be returned to the States everywhere. If that is not done in time, Communism will win.

George Knupffer.

Index

Des Griffin's Books —
Fourth Reich of the Rich
and
Descent Into Slavery?

Give Copies To Your Friends:

Order either or both books at the following prices:

1-2 copies $16 each
3-5 copies $13.00
6-9 copies $10.40
10-19 copies $10.00
20-29 copies $9.00
30-49 copies $8.50
50 or more copies $8.00

Shipping: Orders up to $40 — $4.00
Orders over $40 — 10% of order total.

NAME______________________________

ADDRESS____________________________

CITY_______________________________

STATE__________ ZIP__________

Emissary Publications, 9205 SE Clackamas Rd., #1776
Clackamas OR 97015— Phone/Fax: (503-824-2050)
www.emissarypublications.com

DESCENT INTO SLAVERY?

by **Des Griffin** **$16.00**

In a book that has been described as "devastating," "magnificent" and "superbly documented" by readers on three continents, Des Griffin zeros in on the International Bankers and presents, in carefully documented detail, the story of their involvement in the Illuminati plot to create a totalitarian One-World government.

No punches are pulled by the author as he presents startling documentation and brings his readers face-to-face with the raw realities of power politics. Here, at last, is the full, true story of the power-crazed Internationalists and the methods they employ in steering all nations towards total social and financial ruin in preparation for their ultimate absorption into the planned worldwide dictatorship. The inside story behind World War II is truly eye-opening!

Des Griffin lays bare the hideous tragedy that lies ahead for the United States unless our people shake off the shackles of the conspirators and return to individual responsibility and fiscal sanity.

This is one book you can't afford to miss!

E-109 Biblical Insights Into 'GOD'S CHOSEN PEOPLE' $6.00

By Des Griffin — Who are God's Chosen People? The Jews? Born again Christians? Or some other group? This is an important question about which there is tremendous controversy. Who can authoritatively establish the true identity of God's Chosen people? Is the definitive answer found in your Bible?

Des Griffin, well-known author of five other blockbuster books, was challenged a few years ago to resolve this vital issue. Starting off with more questions than answers, he examined the matter from every conceivable angle. His finely-honed conclusions, anchored immovably in the pages of God's Word, are so clearly defined in scripture that many readers will "kick themselves" for not having previously understood the Creator's clear revelation on the matter.

As the reader is led systematically from *Genesis* to *Revelation*, previously overlooked scriptures will leap into life. Statements made by Jesus, Paul, Peter, and others will practically "jump off the page" as previously unrecognized truths come to light. The reader's mind will be flooded with the answers to former spiritual dilemmas. Previous misunderstandings and misconceptions will evaporate and vanish under the piercing light of God's Word.

Now enlarged to include two new sections: *What Do You Mean, Truth?* **and** *The Role of Religion In America.*

***God's Chosen People* is a powerful Bible study guide.**

E-104 ANTI-SEMITISM: AND THE BABYLONIAN CONNECTION $8.00

Des Griffin — ANTI-SEMITISM. That word strikes stark terror into the hearts and minds of many. Most will go to practically any length to avoid being smeared as "anti-Semitic."

Who is a Semite? Are all Jews Semites? What IS anti-Semitism? Is Judaism the God-centered religion of the Old Testament? What is Pharisaism? How important is the Babylonian Talmud to modern Jews?

How did the Talmud come into being? What does it teach regarding Jews — and non-Jews?

Are those people who ask ANY valid questions regarding the Jews and Judaism, wicked, nasty and evil — and worthy of being ostracized, socially?

Des Griffin believes that all these questions — and more — must be addressed honestly and freely in an open forum.

Delving into biblical and secular history, and a wide variety of Jewish sources stretching back more than 2400 years, Des Griffin has come up with a truly enthralling book — one that is exciting, explosive, revealing and educational! This book will CHALLENGE you. It will make you think about — and ponder — many factors you may previously have been unaware of.

ANTI-SEMITISM: And The Babylonian Connection is a book for TODAY. It addresses the issues of today head on. It is packed with thoroughly documented facts, with insights and understanding that will give you a totally new perspective on the world in which we live.

STORMING THE GATES OF HELL

E-104 $12.00

In this book, Des Griffin goes further than ever before in exposing the diabolical forces behind today's chaotic world scene. He also provides his readers with the wonderfully exhilarating answers to those conditions.

Storming the Gates of Hell is the culmi-nation of some 50 years of in-depth research. From its pages pour insights, commentary, and truths combined and put together with vivid clarity and depth of understanding.

Are you wondering how the jumbled and apparently unintelligible maze of world history could possibly make any sense and logic as we begin another millennium? As you read this book, all the pieces of the fascinating global jigsaw puzzle will fall into place in a thrilling manner; it will hold you in its grip from start to finish.

Are you turned off by religion? Are you sick and tired of the phony baloney that passes for Christianity on TV and radio — and in your own neighborhood church? If so, you need to read this book.

Condensed and focused, *Storming the Gates of Hell* is an easy-to-read, easy-to-understand book that puts history — politics, religion, secret societies, and Christianity — in proper perspective. There is real hope for the future following the **Big Showdown** between **good** and **evil.**